A Page in the Family Tree

Robert Page

authorHOUSE®

AuthorHouse™ UK Ltd.
500 Avebury Boulevard
Central Milton Keynes, MK9 2BE
www.authorhouse.co.uk
Phone: 08001974150

© *2009 Robert Page. All rights reserved.*

No part of this book may be reproduced, stored in a retrieval system, or transmitted by any means without the written permission of the author.

First published by AuthorHouse 3/25/2009

ISBN: 978-1-4389-4178-3 (sc)

Printed in the United States of America
Bloomington, Indiana

This book is printed on acid-free paper.

Contents

Illustrations	vi
Chapter 1 the Introduction	1
Chapter 2 Barbara	6
Chapter 3 the Loss	13
Chapter 4 –Setting the Scene	21
Chapter 5 -Why This?	31
Chapter 6 the Page Family	39
Chapter 7. Where they lived	59
Chapter 8 .The Hackman Family	76
Chapter 9 The first five years	107
Chapter 9 the days before School	121
Chapter 10 Sundays	130
Chapter 11 Leslie Page	134
Chapter 12 the First School(s)	145
Chapter 13 At least it wasn't the Pit	165
Chapter 14 Ripley Technical	167
Chapter 15 South Shields calls	183
Chapter 16 off to Sea	190
Chapter 17 the Rogers	222
Chapter 18 Barbara & I	233
Chapter 20 the Sealink years	243
Chapter 21 the Dairy	248
Chapter 22 Greece	252
Chapter 22 the New Millenium	259
Chapter 24 the Genealogy	263
Chapter 25 the future	266

Illustrations

Barbara Page 1973

Thomas Page 1920

Alice Lambert 1920

Cephus & Leslie Page 1930

Sawmill's Village School 1957

Alice Othen 1925

William Othen

John Josiah Hackman

Leslie & Mabel Page

Grandma Hackman & sons

Chapter 1 the Introduction

This story starts in the closing months of the first half of the last Century. Fifty years later inquisitiveness about those early years and the preceding centuries started thoughts of generations past; this in turn led to wondering about heritage. Look at the life errors and the form we all take, those links that tie us together become obvious. The height and build, the tendencies of our nature, our sensitivity, and lack of tact all carry a thread of similarity to others in the family's .Along the path of life, temperament, stubbornness, and principles are not determined by nurture, but nature.

In starting to trace family lineage, it became obvious that there was only a slim snapshot sample of the family tree, although it went back over five hundred years. Mainly just names and dates on a chart. The power of the numbers became obvious when trying to explain about the Crich family and my known Great, great , great , great great , great great , great great , great great , great great , great grandfather , burying ones head firmly into the tree there had not been a realisation that at that level there was thirty thousand of them . There had been time to talk the story over with father and mother, but the opportunity, spurred on by a belief in immortality never taken. So little knowledge of forebears and soon so little knowledge of this generation was a jolt of reality. Looking back to the early part of the Century, having scant chances to talk with any grandparents, so much of the true social history of their life is lost forever. The rich and famous, the heroes, and the villains have autobiographies galore, but records of the workers that formed the backbone of this country, so rare. Thoughts started wondering as to what questions one would ask of those ancestors now, not only who they were, but also what they did, how they felt, where they lived and who they loved. Looking at those forebears, their roots in the last twenty years of the Victorian age would have meant the answers would not be available to fulfil the curiosity of today. The Victorians and their children seemed to have a strong respect for privacy.

Leslie Page youngest son of Thomas started the original thought about family ancestry. A grain of memory caused an itch. In his later years, he related a strange story of how his elder brother Cyril had seen a letter addressed to "Thomas Blanton," and had taken it to their father Thomas Page. Thomas had dismissed any enquiry, but then proceeded to open it. Unusual, but what made this intriguing was the letters it bore instead of a stamp. "On His Majesty's Service," .Why did Granddad have two different surnames? The first reaction, somewhere between Uncle Cyril and Dad there had been an error, a lapse of memory; it seemed so unlikely, they were so sure of the facts. It must have caused a doubt in their own minds to remember a letter and its addressee for over forty years.

Obviously hiding a story, a mystery, niggling away, the trail to seek the truth to tread

A quick look at the eighteen eighty-one census provided the instant answer. The infant Thomas Blanton , living at his grandfather's house with his father George Blanton, his mother Mary Jane Blanton née Page and Thomas's maternal

Grandparents Benjamin and Clara Page. By the eighteen ninety one census, Thomas was renamed Thomas Page, Mary Jane and George Blanton were nowhere to be seen and the elderly Benjamin and Clara were bringing young Thomas up . Mystery solved but the Genealogy bug had bitten. Why does the family name change? Why to a lot more questions? .The research rolls on, albeit slowly. Stopping the studies though to write this, "the story so far," primarily so the grandchildren, and great-grandchildren, can know where we came from,

The whole story is a long way to completion, and the facts are getting harder to verify as research digs deeper into the past, so at this convenient point, words become laid into print for posterity. To our three children and their descendents, this is probably a load of boring old facts. These stories have been related so many times , and forgotten so many times why bother to record them , you may ask , the reason , is to give generations to come an insight into who we are and where we came from .

The genealogy itself has been difficult, vast chunks of the history missing. A few things appeared, leading me to believe that some were never too be found and certainly , never made public .There is no hidden scandal , nor dark secret ,no serious criminal past ,not even minor offences that appear , yet! .A Victorian principle appears that some things are private, not matters for public discussion.

Mum and Dad were proud of their roots even though they actually knew so little of them. The trail of their families leads back over five hundred years. Even now leads in a book on its way from Canada, by Lawrence Crich , takes the Crich family back to the eleventh century. To go beyond that, is believe not possible and that detail of record required unknown. Therefore, time in future will be usefully spent filling and padding the skeletal family tree, hopefully to create a picture of the past. The actual tree is too widespread to include here, it links us to over two thousand five hundred souls of past and present. However, this tree is as far as the contemporary generation; to go forward is for others.

The Blanton's have been hard to track .It seems to have been a family following the grey smoky path of the Industrial Revolution from its birthplace in the Shropshire vales , via the mines of South Staffordshire to the middle of Derbyshire . Apparently, the family originated on grandfather Thomas Page's side from Albrighton in Shropshire. The strange thing is, when once, after working for a whole summer in the late nineteen eighties without a single day off, needing to thank Barbara for her patience and understanding, opportunity took us for a romantic weekend at the Albrighton Hall Hotel, in the tiny rural Albrighton village. Little did we know that weekend had taken us back to the root of the Blanton's as then the "Blanton " family was still a mystery .The location is a rural idyll, this makes a believe that prior to tearing coal from the earth the forbears were probably agricultural labourers.

Included here, Barbara's family too, so our descendants have a path to follow to see their roots, and from what stock we had our beginnings in. The main families have moved very little in the last half millennium, but have branches spread over the entire world. The best-researched section is undoubtedly mother's maternal side, as the Leam's and the Crich family spread into Australia and Canada , the Blanton's appear in vast numbers in the United States. Barbara's family have similarities in this, although the Rogers have been hard to follow Barbara's maternal side, the Othen's and the Hatch families, both well documented making a long branch reaching from the North Western edges of the New Forest to bring us here. .The Othens originating from the Hedge End area and the Hatch family from descending from the Hampshire / Wiltshire border, in the New Forest, keep Barbara's forebears loosely in the Hampshire county boundary. Most of the records relating to Barbara's maternal side are from the South Stoneham registry.

The search along the descending line has proved fascinating. This is a road aiming this toward publication for self-satisfaction and amusement as much as to leave it all in the old-fashioned medium of the printed word. As this reflects, views and memories, accuracy can be opinionated, trusting the historical facts as told. Inaccuracies of fact are accidental so as an act of contrition to anyone offended, serious and profound apologies. All written here is to the best of personal knowledge from what I know, and what stories told to me. I have no desire to offend, and have avoided conjecture and assumption.

There is no guarantee of the memories being right. I have tried to avoid confrontation, and searched my memories to reflect what I know. Attempting to tell this without prejudice, especially the life of my parents with as much detail as possible, to paint the picture of what made us all, what we are today.

The families are the Page and Hackman's, and Barbara's lineage of the Rogers and the Othen's. Now to tell the story of those families, as far as can, today. This story will never be able to finished so this, the foundation for our children's children to build on. We languish here in the south of England miles from the roots that gave us our spirit, and the solid sense of fair play, working ethic, and sheer stubbornness, pondering the future.

1

Chapter 2 Barbara

Barbara was truly "love at first sight". Falling for the long legs and the Titian hair before we even spoke, She was dancing at the Royal Pier, over 21's night with her friend Eileen. I was out on my birthday for a beer; I was with Andy Braidwood, another Union Castle Junior Engineer. We had left the "digs," a pub on Shirley Road called "The Rising Sun "and walked into the City Centre. The town centre was not the busy hub that a major city such as Southampton suggested, and this Tuesday night was very quiet. Each hostelry quieter than the last, after a pint of what the South of England regarded as "Best Bitter "one drink led to moving on to another pub with a better brewer in situ. The popular beer and brewery Watney's offered "Red Barrel, "an insipid Keg beer that owed more to the Chemist than to the Brewer . This lived alongside Ind-Coope "Double Diamond, "Mitchell, and Butler "Brew XI," Bass "Blue label". The nineteen sixties leading a keg revolution, away from the thirty-five gallon barrels that needed daily attention, The spiels that tapped the barrel needing to be changed at each barrel , The beer needing to settle , the Ullage to be agreed with the area manager, change into the aluminium kegs that were so manageable and easy to carry was a progression !. The "Real Ale " brigade were, a fledgling organisation, and real ales seemed to relate to lifeless warm dish water .The CAMRA organisation, not yet named as such, were promoting a love of what was invariably warm and flat ales, with hops and flavour. The one exception was the Burton Brewer Marston, Thomas, and Evershed, they produced light and dark mild beers, "Pedigree," and ordinary beer, and in winter, a draught barley wine called "Owd Roger." The beer was strong, bitter and a favourite of Barbara's father, as I found out later. Our search that night was for a decent pint, and it was not easy. After the fourth pint of insipid weak brew we gave up, turned to the chemical taste of lager, not the range that pours forth today, but Whitbread Breweries version of the excellent Dutch Heineken or a British brewed attempt at its Danish companion Carlsberg accompanied by a vile set of British alternatives Skol, Carling Black Label, Harp (Guinness) . Despair had set in so desperate for distraction and the company of others, we headed to the "Dance at the Royal Pier" just after ten o'clock, and towards that venue we walked briskly as the cold November air cut harshly on our faces . Searching out the attraction we had a lengthy walk, due in part to our lack of knowledge of a town that had been our new base for less than half a day, but approaching the waterfront the wind was

frosting as it whirled along the high street. Crossing the familiar road that led to Dock Gate five , the mail boats laying alongside the one hundred and one and one hundred and three berths , the white pier gatehouse stood before us like a huge wedding cake surmounted by six heraldic lions bearing Hampshire's crests on their shields . We scrambled across the road tripping through that pavilion into Mecca's Ballroom .Our entrance paid , beer ordered , sipped and deposited on a passing empty table , dancing became an attractive idea .

   We stood at the edge of the floor looking vacantly   at the crowded floor. Most couples were girls dancing with other girls, some with their handbags as a central cairn to orbit. Men drifted across the floor in a sticky trail of spilt beer and gathered in groups around the floor edge. We had had one dance, but Andy had wisely chosen the most attractive of the pair, and Quasimodo, the alternative option, not only lacked stature but also personality. No more was such an important decision to be left in the hands of the Scots the next opportunity was to be at my behest. I scanned the floor looking for my choice and across the smoky haze; I saw her standing there, all my visions and fantasies fulfilled. I cut into their dance leaving Eileen to interpret Andy's broad Glaswegian accent , that was a total loss to Barbara who did not understand one word of whatever he uttered, not that any non-Scot fared much better. There Barbara stood she was all the birthday presents I had ever wished for.

   She was a tall slender girl with a very short white lacy mini dress in reality a trouser top, which accentuated her very elegant legs. Those legs covered in the trademark American Tan tights and slotted into strappy black shoes with the heels that Barbara always preferred. Her hair just below her shoulders in a vibrant auburn cascade. Eileen shorter and darker still had emotional ties to her ex partner John , who still stayed with her on occasions , as Barbara and I found out late one evening when he turned up very drunk at her flat . After several dances, it was time to settle into a drink, I stuck to Best Bitter and Barbara drank bitter and Lime in half pints. We sat and chatted, then danced some more. As the evening progressed, the girls realised that the last Southampton City Transport bus had departed for Thornhill, Andy and I offered a Taxi to return them home. Barbara collected her Black woollen coat with a golden maple leaf broach from the Cloakroom, and we started the climb along Bugle Street to the Bus Station where the most popular Taxi rank stood .Barbara accepted the offer of a piggyback and I carried her all the way to the bus stand. We climbed into a white bonneted "Streamline Taxi's "Austin Maxi Taxi, Its Black livery contrasting with the creamy white bonnet. The whole bonnet designated the car as a "Hackney Carriage "whilst a single white stripe showed a Streamline car to be a "private hire. ". When we reached, Thornhill Barbara made coffee and we sat and embraced until the early hours. Her warmth and smile took my heart that night, what a smile! Barbara as always, was concerned about Eileen walking home, so Andy and I were despatched to escort her to her Hightown first floor flat.

I should have known about Barbara's caring side, as throughout her life, she would in a instantaneous transformation become , " Saint Barbara" patron saint of lost causes .To do this she didn't even need the telephone box that Clark Kent walked into to re-emerge as Superman , she just stood there and transformed . This sainthood was a dangerous habit, whilst illustrating a fantastic love of the fair and true, it manifested itself oft at the wrong time and oft in the wrong place.

Quick to usher her away years later as she comforted a colleague who had borrowed a married man on a Friday afternoon , to be confronted by his return to his wife at the annual dance on a Saturday evening . Barbara comforted her as the rest of WASP's staff told her she was an idiot for having the affair in the first place. Barbara, who had no liking for the adulterous, had compassion for this silly girl who had believed a drunken Friday afternoon had meant a lifetime of happiness. "Oh! Poor Jane, she really believed that he loved her ", my Barbara hankie to hand. How she must have regretted that when she rebelled against the same group over their "clocking in "anomalies , and their quick absences that led them out to shopping and banking . Soon they turned on her and we used to arrive at the WASP factory to strains of Tina Turner belting out "Simply the Best "as I told Barbara, she was better than all the rest! The stress of working with this dishonest bunch led to her leaving one tearful afternoon. Be kind and nice to people and they do their best to kick you, especially if you are honest.

A ferry crossing from Killini to Zakynthos challenged her too, as the Tourist Astronomikos handcuffed a refugee. Whilst the man was pinioned, the police officer began kicking at his legs to destabilise him and put his arms planed backwards causing indescribable agony, the young man stumbling down an adjacent staircase, the police officer holding his arms at a high level. , St. Barbara tried to become involved in the man's defence against an armed officer , it was simpler to opt for her disapproval rather than argue an Albanian's defence to a Greek Policeman , cowardice came into play , and acceptance was easier than attack , It did not please Barbara though .But enough of this distraction and on with the story !.

This enforced march to Eileen's was not before we arranged to meet on Thursday, under the Guildhall Clock. Barbara had omitted to tell me that the four clock faces covered several hundred yards of pavement. Waiting by the Southampton Guildhall side of this quadrangle, I saw her skipping towards me, the reddish hue of her hair reflecting the sodium streetlights, causing a twinkling halo around her face. Hand in hand, we strode together south towards the "Bargate." We ate that Thursday night at the Angus Steak House, in Below Bar after a few pints of "Lowenbrau" German Lager in Southampton's then trendy basement Beer Keller .It was looking into those dark brown eyes that night that the realisation came, that here is the girl with whom I wanted to share life and eternity.

Our next date nearly ruined the dream, I, falling asleep at the digs, and running late, ruined a trip to the cinema. On a particularly wet night, missing the rendezvous and with no idea of addresses, a taxi, working by memory found her abode. It had been a disaster , Barbara's umbrella had turned inside out and she had broke a heel , I was forgiven , but wisely she insisted that in future I collected her and removed the chance of missing the encounter .

The punishment for poor timing was a laborious task scraping wallpaper, as Barbara prepared the lounge for redecoration. Barbara despite a shortage of funds fed us with luxurious smoked ham sandwiches, and full milky coffee served in clear glass cups popularised in the coffee bars of the day. I felt at home for the first time since my sojourner existence had began some five years before.

I joined my ship the R.M.S. Pendennis Castle, and sailed for the five and a half week round trip taking the Royal Mail, the Passengers and freight, to Durban and back with copper, gold, diamond, and oranges in the holds. Christmas at sea lay ahead, but my mind was in Thornhill with the ideal woman. The voyage was distracted by my thoughts and dreams in which that woman starred.

We corresponded almost daily ,the thin blue air-letters getting posted at each port , and the slender light blue replies from Barbara , who unbeknown to me was assisted by her friend Margaret Mould , in penning the early responses . Margaret was a good friend, but very highly strung, and nervous. As time progresses the letters became Barbara's sole domain. My new acquaintance became my pen friend, then my life then my eternal hope.

As the Beach Boys sang

Well I walked up to her and I asked her if she wanted to dance She looked awful nice and so I hoped she might take a chance
When we danced I held her tight Then I walked her home that night And all the stars were shining bright
And then I kissed her Each time I saw her I couldn't wait to see her again I wanted to let her know that I was more than a friend
I didn't know just what to do And so I whispered I love you And she said that she loved me too
And then I kissed her
I kissed her in a way that I'd never kissed a girl before I kissed her in a way that I hope she liked for evermore
I knew that she was mine so I gave her all the love that I had Then one day she'll take me home to meet her mom and her dad
Then I asked her to be my bride And always be right by my side I felt so happy that I almost cried
And then I kissed her And then I kissed her And then I kissed her
It is all in that song! By Phil Spector

Chapter 3 the Loss

After Barbara's death, I spent a lot of wasted time being concerned looking for ways to explain and justify "why"! Losing Barbara to a particularly active form of Breast Cancer was not "fair," we had been robbed! Reading books about bereavement did not help , in condescending tones , the pages dictated how I was to feel , what I was to feel , yes, I am distraught at my loss, our loss, for the family fell into the matriarchal love of Barbara. Barbara was always quiet, as she engagingly reminded, but the raising of one eyebrow in her distinguished manner had more words of chastisement than any thesaurus holds. Her love was absolute, without question. There is a Barbara shaped hole in my life that only she can fill. I didn't know which way to turn , our children are filled with their own sense of loss ,their own anger , their own denials , so I try hard to keep my personal deep severance from them , as I would only heap more misery on to the funeral pyre .

When I close my door at night and realise that tinnitus is the only relief from the drone of reality television's constant outpourings, of," I am a forgotten, short term personality, who will perform any depravity, or eat any disgusting larvae, worm, or body part to regain my lost popularity ", then my heart screams to hear the warm caramel of her voice. I loved that rolling tone as she purred, in contrast though, she would shout and a screech would emit from her. I suspect that she was not born to shout.

Reading of the "Five Stages of Grieving "a somewhat complicated emotion helped very little. Yet, grief is something that, unfortunately, we all inevitably experience. Not believing the books and pamphlets given out with sympathetic abandon, a decision made not to follow the prescribed pattern. Like everyone else I Did! The psychologists tell us that If we are stuck in one stage or the other, the process of grieving is not complete, and cannot be completed. I dismissed this as Psycho Blah Blah! , you go one step forward then take two steps backward, all part of the process, and individual . I have learned all of this the hard way.

The five stages are:
1. Denial-"this cannot be happening to me," looking for the Barbara in familiar places, or acting as if she is still in living here. No crying. Not accepting or even acknowledging the loss.
2. Anger-"why me?" feelings of wanting to fight back, anger at the Barbara, blaming her for leaving.
3. Bargaining-. Attempting to make deals with God to stop or change the inevitable outcome. Begging, wishing, and praying for her survival.
4. Depression-overwhelming feelings of hopelessness, frustration, bitterness, self-pity. Mourning, as well as the loss of hopes, dreams, and plans for the future...
5. Acceptance-there is a difference between resignation and acceptance. You have to accept the loss, Realization that Barbara is gone that it is not her fault; she did not leave on purpose.

I started to try to explain why the old saying "Only the good die young "was true. I spent some time at Easter in Greece (2008) celebrating Pascha, that Greek reverential week preceding Black (Good) Friday, with our good friend Sakis (Dionysus Fournougerakis) and his family. They were spending time showing me how the Greeks spend a time of mourning followed by the celebration of the resurrection , interspaced with a small wedding with about three hundred guests , the pre-ceding engagement and the general Easter parties that spit roasts whole lambs , head intact , all over Greece .. Easter had always been a special time for us , we had always caravanned , relaxed and enjoyed Easter as a wonderful festival, I didn't want to face Easter at home , it reminded so much of how Barbara picked Easter Eggs with such a deliberate precision an home .. The opening of eggs on Easter Sunday was important to her. The plot failed as Greek Orthodox Easter fell a whole month after the Roman Christian one. I just wanted to be somewhere else for both Easters. I had celebrated our Easter and as at all family gatherings of significance went to my empty house, and faced the emptiness .The Greeks, do not have early empty hours, and it was rare in that fortnight if I left the Fournougerakis house before three AM. When I reached the Lithakia Beach Hotel some fifteen-minute drive away, my sleep was synonymous with pillow contact.

The complete Greek nation comes out at night to sit pouring over coffee and liqueur to philosophise, at street cafes, or backyard verandas. If the world took note , it's return to righteousness is resolved each night as the stars illuminate the Hellenes , by the whole populous debating the ills and tribulations of the cosmos .They all seem to believe that Aristotle reigns as the debates roll out . The world and the environment , life , love , all subjected to night time discussion .The degree that fate is accepted was well illustrated one morning around two AM when sitting outside a café in Zakynthos Saint Marco's square , a friend of Sakis was bemoaning how his father had left his land divided between , his brother, his two sisters and himself. His father had divided the rich pasture, Strema by Strema between the brothers, and likewise the costal swamplands between the two sisters. Why didn't, his father realise that farming was hard work, and the sisters had sold off the costal swamp, un-farmable as it was to developers, and hotels stood on the useless land. The sisters, lived in Athens, enjoyed financial security, and the brothers scratched a living from the bare earth of mountain pasture. Philosophy, coffee and pure night air, a recipe for relaxation of the mind.

It was in the early hours of one morning , sat in Sakis' living room, dining room, office, print shop and factory that some of my thoughts ripened . I was attempting to explain the loss of fifty per cent of my persona to Tanya, Saki's Greek-Australian wife ,when she related that losing her mother in her late twenties caused her anger to spill over , and ask a cousin, why Tanya's mother had died rather than her cousin's mother who was in no way as nice a person ?. That is exactly how I felt as I looked at our loss .Some self-centred people, the greedy, the dishonest, and the deceptive, why could evil people approach a century on this earth and beautiful people fail before their retiring age. I thought my internal hatreds were a unique experience, apparently not.

I moved to the acceptance stage as the Island Hopper ATR-42 turboprop carried me back to Athens and the Olympic Airbus flight to Heathrow , to beg forgiveness of the Lord for my poor negativity spattered with a jealous hatred of the living whether they were deserving of the life wasted or not. I felt that anger lift as the little plane struggled along the bumpy runway with more than the forty two passengers that it was built for on board, as the plane lifted so did my ill feelings, a transition stage in the bereavement steps reached .

My mind was diverted from leaving Zakynthos some fourteen hours late , as Olympic took May Day as a strike day , by these thoughts , and considering that my Athens departure was to be some twenty four hours late, I was content that I had moved from the Anger stage into an air of acceptance. The Olympic ground staff busied themselves hastily arranging my overnight stop at Gylfada, having been harassed by the tour operator to take care of my comforts. Returning to work the following week my determination to reduce my hours and relax strengthened. I had taken a step in Grief and in Life.

I talk incessantly to Barbara in our empty house, and I base our decisions on a joint approach that I have followed for two thirds of my life. I console myself in the belief that our love will bring us back together one day, if the Lord God gives us that grace. I had considered these monologues to an empty room were a sign of madness, induced by distress, but as I speak, I see lights flicker and feel that it is the party trick, Barbara promised as a sign of her overshadowing presence. Having told Kerry that only she would understand Barbara's humour as she decimated the house lights from a world beyond, mine have flickered at some unexplained times. I know that humour only so well! Barbara had a very slapstick sense of fun, with a dark undertone. She would look at cyclists as we sped past them in the car, and pronounce her desires to roll down the window and forcibly dismount them with a sideways blow, and watch as they fell into the gutter. The thought of cyclists in an abandon of free falling was not without a concern for their health, but was a satisfying, clowning view on the world of the tumbling victim.

The conclusion as to the cancer that took her from us was that she probably had HRT for too long. I remember the confusion that she had pre the HRT, the route in hindsight, still be the right one to follow, and HRT benefits outlined to us were a resistance to that bone destroying disease osteoporosis. The cancer risk known, but the probability outlined as small. We were told that there was less than a one per cent increase in the risk factor, minimal, was the word. We then did not realise the expanse and looming presence of the raft of disease called cancer. One in three of British people will succumb to its attack; some will survive, with the shadow of the disease lurking forever in their lives. The statisticians wax lyrical about thirty percent improvement in survival rates but only when you purify the mathematics that the percent is not allied to thirty in a hundred, or thirty more of the seventy five people in a hundred expected to survive breast cancer, it means thirty percent less of the twenty five doomed, will transcend this world as a victim of the disease. We thought breast cancer a single illness, but had little realised that there are at least twenty varieties and mutations of the core. Some slow, some hormonal, some ductal or lobal, some genetic some random. Of those, some are aggressive, lobal, resistant to the genetic pool, and hard to find as well as cure, that is Barbara!, get the worst one in the range. We gave it our best fight and lost!

The irritable fact in this was our avoidance of Chicken imports, because the hormones added to increase the breast meat, the antibiotic pumped into the bird to resist disease laying a path to cause the cell mutation that belies cancer. We deliberately rejected imported vegetables, because of the fungicides, and insecticides liberally sprayed on them, each with their associated cancer links. The organophosphates were high on our list, of things not included in our diet. Barbara had reduced her intake of red meats and saturated fats linked with them. We also circled around the transfats, hydrogenated liquids, chemically solidified. Barbara kept fit, used her Gym membership regularly , after her day at work , and lived healthily, she worked hard , we played well, and enjoyed ourselves, even then Barbara, had kept, as always her alcohol consumption on the lower side of moderate. She lived and ate to avoid the cancer that took her so prematurely from us. The missing link could only be the HRT that we saw her take so willingly.

I have heard the words "sell by date " so many times in

recent months , related to God's plan for us as individuals , that I firmly believe whatever we do our life has a pre-planned schedule that has the decisions we take mapped , and our fate preordained .

I started to write a journal on holiday in two thousand and seven as I meandered through the Peloponnese, in two thousand and eight I finalised it. I despair at the lonely singletons staring into empty sunsets. To avoid this, a journal to share vacation thoughts with Barbara was the solution . I still talk to her as I criss-cross the Ethnikki Odos , the Greek national network of motorway style roads , with just two and a half lanes , each seeming to lead me through the tunnel and toll booth on the outskirts of Tripoli . The insane toll is set at €2.90 , so nobody ever has the correct money , necessitating all to stop and exchange a "Kale Meres Sas " and patiently await ticket and change . I added another few chapters, and sit finalising the editing at the enchanting Kalamitsi Hotel, at Kardamili, in the Mani section of Messina.

Wandering the house talking to my late wife is a little barking insanity, but then reading an article in the Rowan's Hospice magazine written by Lance Blake TSSF. (The Chaplin there) Referring to his Grandma being in constant conversation with her deceased husband, this worrying him, he challenged her sanity, rebuffed with the statement that she had talked to him every day for fifty years so why should she change now. Ah! Ah! I am not mad, just carrying on living life talking to the woman of my dreams.

The life ahead lay open to review so many times; the answer always is love for Barbara and the desire to reunite with her one day. We had always been Christian in belief, though the practice and principle was not as strong as it should be, and our love of Christ grew in our later years together. There was no substance to the belief in reunification, just a hope that as love grows it is indestructible, and the trust that as Heaven is a perfect place, perfection in life would involve a continuation of that relationship started on that cool winter night so long ago.

I know Barbara has a deep belief that the Lord Jesus Christ had died to save us sinners from eternal hell, and she confessed her sins daily and asked forgiveness. The thought that she is in an eternal world keeps me so happy, and keeps my thoughts a little purer.

Chapter 4 –Setting the Scene

We had in previous eras, truly been "Great Britain." In the potted history of our formative years, we hear of the great inventors and explorers, warriors, and scientists, when you look closely they were not all of noble birth, but many were humble men who became great. The history tells that although wealth had advantages, unaccountable to the working person, the engineers who built the empire were scholars with less prominent beginnings. History could show that the supreme naval command of the seas was only available to Britain, because of the Chronometer developed by John Harrison a simple carpenter and clockmaker. That single development gave our country the mastery of longitude. That single device gave us the Seas. James Watt the instrument maker, son of a Greenock shipwright gave us the lead in Steam engineering. Michael Faraday from a poor family was an apprentice book-binder , self taught , he gave us electric power From these leading innovations Britain kick started the industrial revolution .These huge leaps came not from the ruling elite , the landed gentry , the academics , but from men who beat their way against the odds from the trades . If there is a vein of richness that runs within the spirit of Britain, it is the engineers and scientists, who from this small isle, have given the world a wealth, unsurpassed by modern man.

When I started as an apprentice the college class was a mixed bunch , a public schoolboy or two , a surgeons son , an architect's offspring an ex policeman , sons of welders , ship repairmen , Gift shopkeepers , the whole spectrum of the country as well as a Kenyan Tribal Chief's son .

I struggled from a broad Derbyshire accent too devoid of all grace notes a sharp, flinty twang, vowels that flatten words like "right" to "rat", words like " art all rate" to inquire as to someone's health " Hey up " for hello , T' for "the" , "They" for " you", "snap" for lunch , so many things that were so hard to be understood . My upbringing then left me with feelings of inferiority. As I have looked historically, I have become so proud of the men who looked upwards as they laboured in dark, odorous coal seams to raise their chances and choices. Far from shame of a hard working class background, I stand on those stepping-stones with immense pride.

Those chances born on hard graft were our inheritance, dad bore the title Councillor for many years like a gleaming medal, bright, for all to see   in the days when there were no fixed expenses, and you did it for civic pride. His Brothers all had senior jobs in the pit, as Derbyshire referred to its mines .Promotion is only won by labour and shear hard work to corrupt another, amongst the workers of the world, there is no cash for bribery. We had little cash, but much grit. We were never outwardly emotional, no kissing or embracing, but love was present in the home and in the family.

I cannot envisage the six-foot tall man bent over in a seam of coal that forces his posture permanently bent. It is abhorrent to think of the water running around their feet, as their backs compressed and buckled .The foul dust laden air eating away at the fabric of their lungs the taste of sulphur in the air, the constant heat, digging deeper it must have felt like a tunnel to Hell to those men. The ignominy of starting your day's pay at the face having clocked in at the surface , descended the dark shaft in an open cage at a phenomenal speed, then setting off on a treck to the face which could easily be several miles away , all in your time until the face was reached . Look to all the sons who followed Thomas Page into the deep mines , each rose to a level higher that the miner they started as , following in the footsteps of their own father who was the "Ganger " responsible for his men at his coal face .

Coal mining throughout Derbyshire known since the fourteenth century, at first quarried in open workings situated on the outcrop of the seams. As the workings carried forward, the overlying rock became a very thick over-hang and collapses were common with the accompanying deaths. The rainwater ran down into the quarries, making it more difficult and expensive to get the coal. The miners then found it better to "mine" rather than quarry the coal, and so sank shallow pit shafts to the coal seams. The coal extracted from between roof and floor and the mine kept open with wood props. Because the seams sloped, further into the earth they gradually sunk more deeply. At first, these mines were a hundred metres deep, but they grew in depth to well over five hundred metres .Sinking of a shaft is very expensive, fewer mines put down but a greater area worked underground from one shaft. The working places underground, 2, or even three miles distant from the shafts. The miners walking this roadway in their own time, pay starting at the face. From the bottom of the shaft, several spacious passages called "gates" radiated. Branching and re-branching until they reached the "working face." At the "face" the seam several feet thick overlain and underlain with rocks. As the collier removes the coal, he places it in "tubs." .The waste builds up in the space behind the working face. The loaded tubs pushed on rails laid close to the face until they reach a gate. Horses drew them to the "haulage-planes" where they are attached to wire-rope cables and are transported by steam power to the bottom of the shafts. From here, trucks rise to the surface by steam engines at a speed of Thirty miles per hour. Large volumes of air are required for the men to breathe as well as to remove the dangerous fire-damp that escapes from the coal seams. There are two shafts to each mine; the air goes down one and up the other, drawn by a revolving fan that may circulate a current of hundreds of thousands of cubic feet of air per minute throughout the mine. At the turn of the Century Derbyshire mines produced fifteen million tonnes of coal per year, the accident rate though was phenomenal,

At the time of Granddad leaving school, around eighteen ninety two, boys and girls started in the mines at twelve years old . Boys became men so quickly . A study by Seebohm Rowntree, a pioneer sociologist, concluded that between up to thirty per cent of the population of Derbyshire lived either below the level of what was necessary for actually staying alive, or in a state of poverty. A skilled worker earned only some one pound fifty pence per week to keep an average of four children. The Derby & District Housing Reform Association instigated a major study of the life of the poor in the town but found great difficulty in obtaining the information they sought, for the poor do not care to disclose their poverty. There was an average of five and a half persons per house. Total weekly income was an average of eighty pence, appallingly low, the mother or the children earned three pence. Rents varied between twelve and thirty pence a week. Estimated expenditure on boots and clothing was twenty-eight pence per week for each family. Spending on coal would be five pence each week for fifty kilogram's. Insurance, sick, and burial clubs took another five pence. Household requirements costed at six pence a week and lighting at one penny a night this left only forty-five pence for food a week for the entire family, two pence for an adult, and one penny for a child each day. A sparse diet indeed from such an Income took no account of the need for tobacco or beer or any innocent gaiety, despite the obvious need for some diversion. All these figures were only applicable when trade is good, short time, unemployment, or "Lock outs" in time of dispute, obviously devastated family life. We have no idea of how thankful we should be for our lot.

Conditions in coalmines improved enormously as the new century (Twentieth) approached. Progressively, various "Mines Acts" had lowered the minimum wage of underground child labour, although the reality dragged behind the legislation. In eighteen forty two Children younger than ten could no longer be employed in the mines, in eighteen eighty-seven it was twelve and by nineteen hundred, thirteen. What seemed like improvements were not always so; the introduction of flame safety lamps gave off poor light, thus straining the eyes and causing painful eye conditions. Unless there was a lot of dangerous gas, miners tended to maintain use of lighted candles for this reason. Working conditions for the miner were as primitive as ever. There were no canteens or showers. Miners resisted the introduction of pithead baths; it was not so much for the oft-quoted reason of a fear that water would weaken their backs, more that they would have to pay for it themselves - to the tune of a penny per week. Most miners in any case bathed at home on completion of their shift. As for the coal miners, more serious matters arose .In 1893, as the young Thomas would be readying himself for work a great, national lock out took place, arising out of a refusal by the men to accept a wage cut of 25%. From July 28th, some 300,000 miners, suffered, locked out across the country and the dispute was to drag on for four months .Four months of no wages. Derbyshire miners adopted a hard line over the lock- out, stubbornly refusing any notions of submitting .Soup kitchens were set up everywhere in the mining areas. Many local tradesmen gave help and massive public donations and collections of food assisted to allay the cruel bite of hunger. In the mining villages in particular, small shopkeepers depended on the trade of the colliers in the good times and thus found themselves obliged, not only by community feeling, but also by sound business sense to give credit during strikes and lockouts. Many tradesmen ensured that miner's families did not actually starve. Often the shopkeeper went bankrupt. How did Granddad feel, that is what is missing from this story. There was an undercurrent of dislike through Derbyshire for the great wartime leader Winston Churchill , who at the time of one of these reoccurring disputes , replied to a question on Derbyshire Miners starving , with a suggestion that they could return to work or go and eat grass . Did Churchill remember Marie Antoinette's fate after offering the French Peasant's cake, grass was at the least provocative? It is stupid inane remarks like those, that fester's revolution. Did Sir Winston remember those comments as the country chose socialism to take the land for ward as the nineteen fifties dawned?

Meanwhile more police and army reinforcements arrived from throughout the country, to the displeasure not only of the miners and their families but to the community at large. Bullets were easier to get than bread for the Derbyshire miner. Contemporary newspaper accounts fudge the issue of police harassment and provocation, but this side of the story must have been disturbing enough for the Liberal MP for Mid-Derbyshire, to condemn the presence of a great many blue-coated soldiers and their red-coated companions. A force of some 800 red-jacketed Royal Irish Fusiliers was already at Alfreton, soon joined by a trainload of Second Dragoon Guards. The police from Derbyshire itself no longer rusted to maintain a vigorous stance had reinforcements, thousands of police, imported from far-away counties. The police and army naturally well fed and well dressed, the very sight of them aroused great indignation. No wonder, when the disputes arose under the government of Margaret Thatcher, that this seemed Déjà Vue, to those Derbyshire miners.

The fare enjoyed by the forces contrasted sharply with that enjoyed by the miners and their families. A soup kitchen organiser wrote to the Derbyshire Times "we have a great deal of dripping given and I am sure that if it were known that broken bread and dripping would be accepted, many people would give it gladly. These pieces of bread dipped in water and put in a very cool oven to crisp through, and then put away in flour kept fresh for weeks. The little bits thrown into the soup and boiled with the vegetables, (meat has no mention here), to make an excellent thickening".

Already existing bad living conditions, made unbearably worse by the sharpness of the experience. A contemporary described the "dens" in which the colliers and their families lived , as long, narrow, stone runs, consisting of a couple of wretched rooms on the ground floor and a loft on the second floor. The average rent being ten pence a week. There is no bedding. In many the beds - if such they can be called - consist of a number of rags on the boards. When considering these dark candlelit dwellings, the smell of the damp, the dust and the insanitary is beyond imagination.

New techniques and approaches to coal getting would be the source of many difficulties. In 1895, the men at one pit were told to use forks instead of shovels when filling their tubs, in order to reduce the amount of small coal sent to the surface .These were known as screens and one of these wide forks lay for many years in our coal house . This practice spread over the years until detailed arguments about the kind of fork and the space between the prongs became commonplace. There were conflicts in the courts and at the collieries about the non payment of hewn coal as a form of fining workers , recompense being proportional to the tonnage cut , and cutting the prices of coal, containing what the owners thought as too much dirt. This payment per tonne also caused much conflict when during World War II, miners took to the forces to escape their lot, Anuran Bevin arranged an alternative to fighting as a conscript soldier, and you could be a conscript miner, one of the Bevan Boys, the "Boys "were paid a weekly wage regardless of output.

Miners were reluctant to support the liberal anti-brewing temperance leagues. A typical mining village, Clay Cross, possessed twenty-three pubs in its centre alone. Action soon taken against the number of public houses saw vast reductions in numbers. Licences confiscated and the licensee compensated. Miners viewed the issue of temperance quite differently than did the press, the liberal middle class, religion and the establishment at large. After finishing twelve hours a day in a dark, dusty mine, carrying out backbreaking work, the sweaty collier must have thought kindly of the beer that would cleanse his dry, dusty throat.

At the turn of the Century the NSPCC described the children of a Ripley miner, typical of so many, as wretchedly clothed scarcely an ounce of bread in the house. There was practically no furniture in the house, an apology for a bed, dirty and unhealthy - with a single sheet - served the entire family of five children and parents.

The infant mortality rate was startlingly high in these years. Simply to compare the mining villages of Derbyshire with the general position nationally, reveals the full scale of the tragedy. Two hundred newborn infants died for every thousand born with such dreadful poverty and suffering, desperation! I always thought that miners were a quarrelsome dissatisfied bunch , ever bemoaning their plight , when you read the history , those were hard , struggling men just trying to feed a family and keep the mine owners in the lap of luxury , they felt they so richly deserved .

The coal from Denby transported in Mule drawn tubs along the gangway lay down as an extension to the canal from Little Eaton to the Denby pits and the Denby ironworks by

Benjamin Outram around 1810. The tubs were on a wheeled chassis these ran on Outram's edge railway (forerunner to the flanged rail) and at the end of the track simply ran on the highway. When the carts arrived at the wharf at Little Eaton, they were lifted by an arm crane straight into the barges this ran up until the first decade of the twentieth century.

A pity , that the socialists representing the working classes have so little knowledge of that class. Throughout history, the proletarian has always relied on the bourgeoisie to lead them. How Marks was so right in his definition of Capitalism, its sole root being in the exploitation of the proletariat by the bourgeois. Why do we never see the Slave owner helping his charges, as we are absorbed in the thought that the poor can win, we fall for the propaganda each time. I look in today's climate, where the socialists rebranded as "New Labour "consists of a Scottish mafia of privately educated Oxbridge graduates, the Conservatives an Etonian Mafia of Oxbridge graduates. How those faux socialists have trodden down their charges, those that voted them in. Father remembered and recanted so often, how it was a Labour government that closed the mines and the railways.

The Drury Lowe family grew richer and those miners grubbing the coal from the face worked harder and fought for every penny they could get for the untold work they did, getting poorer at each wage cut, at each tonne rejected for "dirt." When anyone tells of the fight of the transported African, condemned to slavery, by his brothers' greed, it makes one think of those miners condemned to slavery by a need to survive. The slave ship-owners and the mine owners enjoying the same comforts built on the bones of their captives.

The miner's houses in Rykneld Hill built and owned by the Drury-Lowes, in the same tied cottage system that agricultural workers endured. In some areas unscrupulous, mine owners would evict widows of the men who died in the pits, so a replacement could take the house. No house no money, condemned those widows to the Parish, to the workhouse so well described by Charles Dickens. Families split up never to mingle. Men and women separated into dormitories, couples married for a lifetime forced apart as their circumstances dictated the parish as their guardians. Menial hard works to earn a meagre crust as the daily thought .Those harsh regimes were still in the memories of my parents. My mother dreaded Babington hospital, where she was recuperating from her illness. Her attitude made her feel that she had ended up in the former Belper Workhouse.

The building completed in September eighteen forty, constructed from local stone at a cost of fewer than ten thousand pounds. This Workhouse was to accommodate three hundred inmates. Inmates were the Poor, Imbeciles, Blind, deaf, all those pitiful beings that society wanted locked out of sight. Those inmates provided much of the labour to run the establishment and minimise costs. The weekly food bill was sixteen pounds for one hundred and sixty inmates. That equates to ten pence per person to provide over twenty meals a week. A half of one penny per meal per inmate bought no luxuries. This alternative to employment designed to discourage idleness, and unemployment. This was no real alternative, so the ethic was to work hard and enjoy a sparse few pleasures .Boy inmates taught shoemaking and tailoring... After nineteen thirty, control of the site passed to Derbyshire County Council and became" Babington House Public Assistance Institution." I had never realised the workhouse existed to the times of World War II

Chapter 5 -Why This?

On a previous touring holiday a journal kept to hold my thoughts , led me to consider my past , and my future , and my regrets ,so it lead to my first attempts to write this tome . I once bothered that we were simple folk, of solid mining stock, the working class that built this country and, from a time when the empire lay resplendent in "pink "on all the globes taking up greater land mass than China. One Fifth of the world and a quarter of the population were The Empress Queen's lands and subjects. What made us this great? I decided that it is time to tell a version of how our own families' ideals and thoughts left the melting pot of the genetic and social mixes. Our own prejudices, our way of life that must began, within that our genetic history .My own father destined as the youngest not to take the underground route, went his own way to his proud moments. If the face had collapsed all the men family would have been lost , in one fall , sense ruled and some had other work to keep the women left behind in financial safety . Leslie was to go to the pipe-works, Slater's of Kilburn. He though nevertheless worked just as hard, for probably less reward than the rest, and put effort into Public service well beyond his own portion of responsibilities.

When about four years old, there is a vague memory of Granddad as a frail shadow of a man with a huge white walrus moustache lying in a large bed in the front downstairs room of the family home at Rykneld Hill in Denby. I felt quiet scarred as the imposing figure laid quiet in a huge bed , in the semi darkened room , the shadow was grandfather ,Thomas Page in his last weeks of life , A mere impression of his formidable former self , laying still, waiting for the angel of death to collect him ,. Listening to the stories from my own father my picture leaves a thought of a very tough wirey man, with a larger than life appearance and, little fear. Now there is so much to ask the former Thomas Blanton, things not crossing my four-year old mind, standing in awe quivering at the ghostly man in his dotage.

As the past opened, it was obvious what a secretive bunch our predecessors were. Things not talked about, locked away, what were those things? No one knows. Freedom of information was never a Victorian consideration and coming across the slight embarrassments of the past, there is growing plethora of unanswered questions. I do not believe that they were "secrets "just none of anyone else's business. Apologies for prying are due though this is a story that needs telling. When I ever asked my dad for help , whether , homework , gardening or world politics , he gave me a neutral answer telling me to find out for myself as he had done in his youth . Thomas, from many people, left me with the impression of an austere parsimonious man, with a limited amount of personal attraction. I now see deeper into that unpolished world that formed him, and cry for the pains of his seventy-three years. The chances that are wasted by us all were just never available to Thomas.

Considering what questions to ask of me in fifty years time when no longer here to answer them, the first words appeared. The history of the last half of the last century may one day be of interest to descendants ', so this is my record "the autobiography of Robert Page." The post war generation born in the first half of the twentieth century are starting to become a scare commodity, and although much is in print about wars and inventions, I try to include here what we feel and did.

There will be prejudices here, we all have them, my father had many, and he was a total xenophobe. The prejudice he had, lumped Black, Asian, Frenchman, and Belgian together as inferior to Great Britain's own sons. Those feelings could demand apologies, as he suggested to an Italian waitress in a Port Solent restaurant, when she failed to understand his Derbyshire accent that she should "bugger off back to where she came from, and learn English." This embarrassingly left us spluttering an apology, and trusting that she did not spit on *our* steak.

Dad did a similar prejudiced act of stupidity when the general practitioner refused to give out a free prescription for Paracetamol, angering dad to a point where the doctor was openly invited to "return to the jungle, as he was a bloody witch doctor " dad growling as he departed the surgery. There was no consideration that the man was possibly from Birmingham not Botswana. It was here, at that man's knees that I learned of that British superiority , that made the white Anglo-Saxon protestant " The Master Race" , little did my father and his peers realise that was exactly what they had spent those heady days of their youth , so proudly fighting against . The master plan to eradicate all non-white, non-protestant non-Aryans, was after all Hitler's plan.

It has taken most of my life to fight off those ideals taught at my father's side. He was the irate taxpayer, who avoided any tax he could preferring cash to anything with the slightest hint of V.A.T. attached to it .This man had spent his life funding all of these " foreign buggers," with his taxes and contributions , and none of them was exuding the required gratitude.

These prejudices were very offensive and deeply ingrained in the spirit; they did affect those delicate formative years of late teenage, when for a brief period of my life I thought that he might have been right, but misunderstood. Those in built hatreds took many years to shed. Loathing any hatred now, based on colour, creed, ancestry, or dimension. Learning hatred of the Non-British has cost dearly as the years have drifted past. If tolerance and understanding are learned early in life, then the world is better for our thoughts and deeds, not ashamed of them.

The family roots struck in the mire of poor England, the labourers, navigators, and miners. Hard work for hard won pay was the order of the day, and in the fire of life, we have forged our own paths. The migrants, who run to our shores now for political or just economic stability, are following that path of survival that drove our own ancestors to do the backbreaking, death-defying labour in the mines of yesteryear. How can we show them prejudice or deny their attempts to climb the economic ladder from that primeval swamp of misery that they aspire to. How can we be prejudiced against them, it defies our own roots?

Here is as much of the family history as I know, but live forever in hope of sparing the time, one day, to add flesh and further bone to those pencilled names that adorn the family tree. The history takes us back to the dawn of the sixteenth century, when mother's forebears were the landed gentry with titles. The Crich Baronetcy, if she had known that, her pride would have puffed her out with glee. The thought of where we all came from led back there to the Crich dynasty that lost their fortunes four hundred years ago when Cornelius Crich led that branch into poverty. The history would have glazed her with smugness, like the winner in a lottery. We should all be proud of our roots whatever they are, whoever they were, for it was those genetic strands and the way we lived that makes us who we are now. All its contributors, rich, poor, healthy, or wealthy, enrich the genetic pool that is who we are today.

I look at the twenty first century and the teenagers who will build the future, and I despair. There seems to be a culture change at large. We have a deep moulded work ethic that demanded our labours to get reward. There was a love of employment, get a job was an unwritten motto ,and in the thirty five years of my parents working life in my memory , I don't believe that either ever signed on the "dole" . Even facing unemployment when redundancy fell on the mines, Dad set forth and joined Securicor within days. To sign on was a shameful occupation in both parental minds. There was a rule, unwritten that said it is easier to get a job from a state of employment than from the Dole queue. Despite paying National Insurance for their combined ninety-five working years, claiming was not ever a consideration. When Mum was severely ill it was with a deep reluctance that Dad attempted to claim for mobility and carers allowance if, mum had known about the claim, she would have been furious. The claim was rejected. We have always been good at contributing to the state's coffers; we have been poor at collecting from them. I realised that when facing my second redundancy asked about job seekers allowance, the new name for the "Dole "and was summarily rejected on the grounds of having too much money , and therefore not needing the state support that I had contributed towards all my working life .

The principles that came from our families gave us both a respect for others and hopefully the good manners that were always encouraged, despite my own inability to resist putting my elbows on the dining table. I feel that stems from flimsy tables, and an inclination of the pressure of several elbows to dislodge the top. Barbara always had strong feelings on politeness and gratitude, she believed firmly in respect shown, this seems to be lost. The simple "thank you " was so important , the slightest show of gratitude was a requirement , that we placed on our children , and too this day , that learned at their mothers knee ,is still applied . If these principles are lost, our children will lose .It makes us responsible for not passing on those basic building blocks of life. None of us truly wants a society of rude, or arrogance. It is lack of respect breeding the gun culture of our inner cities. I hope that the earned respect that we showed to our elders will remain at the heart of this family as the generations move onwards

I think of those commandments that my grandmother Hackman inscribed. I remember today Grandma Hackman's words to me as a young child, when pulling a particularly odd expression one day , using her living room window as a makeshift mirror , she chided, "get that look of your face" in her dulcet voice , "if the wind changes it will set , and you will never look right again". Did I believe it? I think I did, after all, my Grandma would not lie, would she? Do you take a chance, your face setting into a new expression with a change of the wind? I thought if I relayed that to a child today they would question the ability of a face to take up a permanent change and assure me that if that were the case, a second wind change would enable a reversal. Within moments the Internet would furnish, an answer, and possibly the answer   .That I would see as an advancement of knowledge, aided by the resources of international data collection and the World Wide Web. Children now have resources that we could not even dream of, making a huge difference to the ease with which research reaches fruition. Would this plethora of information have made a difference if it had been around fifty years ago , I'll never know , but the reason I drone on about work hard at school and maximise your opportunity is because I sailed through , drifting , doing just enough , and had to spend time catching up , time which could have been "our" time with Barbara .

When I was at School I spent my last summer working for Bowmer and Kirkland for the seven weeks of the holiday as a crane driver's mate, and machinery mover, I was paid about twelve pounds a week and the digs money when working away. I was with the Lorraine Thew one hundred and ten ton lift crane as it was recalled from Didcot power station, after a collapse of the three hundred foot of jib squashed a workman, breaking virtually every bone that was breakable.

I spent time around the quarries and sites in Derbyshire and Leicestershire with a thirty-five tonne mobile crane as banks man. These jobs started a fascination for the other mans point of view. There is so much to be learned from the experience of others. In those far away days, I saw firsthand prejudices, and hypocrisy that helped forms my own character. Early in my working life , there was a Lorry driver at Butterly Brick Works , at Ambergate called Herbert (Herman) Daff , His lorry was constantly tampered with and he suffered abuse , for his "criminal" Nazi past . Sitting with Herbert at lunchtime he related here, that as a prisoner of war he had met, and against much opposition, married a local English Girl, near the Swanwick prisoner of war camp. He put up with the jibes and taunts so he and his wife could be near her loving family, who had been so supportive of them at this time. He was no Nazi, never would be, and never could be. He had chosen to fight in the Luftwaffe, because the alternative, although not defined, known to be Hell, a living death. That lunchtime bought realisation of the age-old saying, you never know how a man feels until walking in his shoes for the day. That day walking through lunch hour with Herman , bought realisation , that we can be small minded village folk , full of small village ways , when we all need to grasp life and face the world , the truth and the future . If we do not, another dictator with excellent publicity control, and a good spin-doctor, will have us believing in him and not his politics, then we will believe in one man's invincibility, and doom will have arrived.

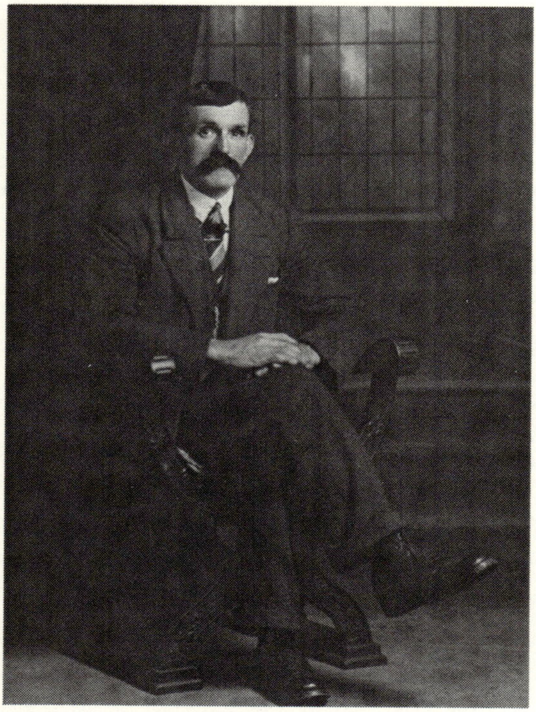

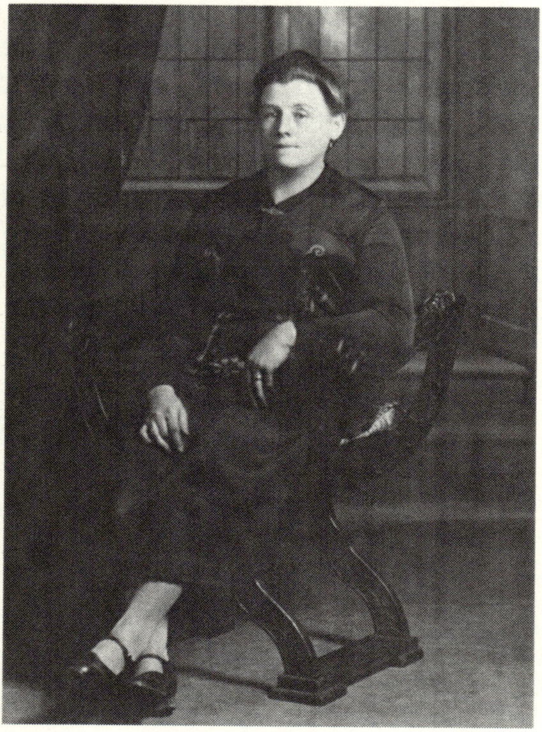

Chapter 6 the Page Family

Dad was one of one of the seven Children of Thomas Page (formally Blanton) and his wife Alice Lambert. The Lambert's originated in Wolverhampton, Benjamin, Alice's father being a furnace watchman, he married the twenty four year old Elizabeth Jane Philip, and lived in Willenhall Staffordshire with the five children of that union. In eighteen sixty-eight he had left the area when his wife at the age of thirty-seven passed away. He travelled to Kilburn, met, and soon wed the local Kilburn girl Omenius Musson, (also known as Hannah), in the next ten years, they added three more children to their growing family . The youngest was Alice, Grandma. Omenius was the daughter of a Nottingham man Nathan Musson and a local Belper girl Elizabeth Beresford. It is the only time I have ever come across this first name, "predictor of evil "seems to define this. Why would a daughter have such a name? She was one of a large family of eight. The Musson's were in the Eastwood Area in the mid seventeenth century .At the turn of the twentieth century Omenius and Edward lived in 142 New Row at Kilburn.

New Row seems to have been long demolished without trace possibly though situated at Smalley Common. The area populated with Coal Miners and labourers, gives an impression that the dwellings were small cottages in long terraces, or possibly arranged around a yard. The overcrowding must be un-thinkable in today's climate. Although married for the first years of their union, Grandma and Granddad were living in separate accommodations. Both though lived close by each other. In eighteen ninety one Thomas lived at 144 Allderads row between houses occupied by the Carlin family to one side and an Annable family to the other .Alice and their first child Maud born just before the twentieth century lived with Edward and Omenius, Alice's father and mother. Alice's sister Elizabeth and her Husband Joseph Allen with their three children lived here too , as did their twenty three year old brother Walter .The two up , two down arrangement of rooms was common in these houses . The two upper room's bedrooms, the downstairs a living room and parlour, these houses could easily be home to two or more families. Siblings sleeping in the same rooms well into adulthood. Sisters in one bed, brothers in another, sleeping head to tail, three one-way three or more the other, no one complained about the overcrowding .Younger children sharing the same bed regardless of gender. I assume the Allen family had one room and expect the parents slept in the parlour. Alice with the infant Maud possibly sharing the other room .Walter fits in somewhere No room at this house at this time for Thomas Page.

Edward was in nineteen hundred already seventy five ,this means that he was over fifty when he fathered the three children that he and Omenius produced between her fortieth and forty-eighth birthdays .Despite the age gap they both died in the year nineteen eleven .

There were a few of these Victorian terraces left in Derby, in the nineteen sixties , the lifeless soot stained brickwork edging the pavements , a cobbled courtyard at the rear , or

Staffordshire Blue Bricks laid on edge , as the washing lines threaded the sky over , dripping the remnants of the washday water onto the yard , making a skaters paradise below . The white washing soaking up the grey atmospheric dust from the coal fires around , belching their sulphurous , ash laden smoke to form the light industrial smog that enveloped all midland towns of those days .The one most vividly in memory, in Derby was near the canal, low ceilings and small doors, these places built for a smaller generation. The beams supporting the floor above struck any head brave enough to venture over five foot six inches tall. The windows were low sills and gave the impression of being set for the race of gnomes that dwelled a hundred years before. The Edwardian panes were tiny no more than four inches square for each pane. The frames of all the door and windows were crumbling as the softwood gave way to age and the damp that gave a distinct smell of must to the whole dwelling. The general air of neglect gave these tiny cottages certain meanness about them. They were the starter homes of the Victorian age and the two bedrooms sat over two downstairs rooms, a generous kitchen and a front room little used. The kitchens as had a dominant jet-black range providing the heat, the cooker, and the limited hot water. I saw many such places as I accompanied Dad each Saturday, to collect monies due to Albert Wheatley for the coal delivered previously Coal was less than one pence per kilogramme , as the fifty kilo sacks were delivered to the door , these houses had a sack a week consumption . Each four weeks in winter another load of four or five sacks was deposited in the coal house , in the grate covering the coal cellar , or in some areas the coal resided in the downstairs solitary bath , Summer they took less but still needed the coal to provide hot water and cooking facilities .

.Alice was a pottery ball maker. The men were coal miners, hewing the black rock from under their feet. The pottery ball makers pounded the raw clay into a workable ball shaped lump for the potters to turn into a usable salt glazed bottle that made the Derbyshire stoneware internationally known. In these days when kitchens sport an array of white goods that defies us to do any labour , it is easily forgotten , that not only did wives bear a dozen children , and labour to make their homes , but pre breeding days were a riot of intensive , and very hard labour , equivalent to many of the men . Equality was here , women and girls , mined , laboured , dug and farmed , they could work as hard as their men-folk , but for much less money .

In 1881 we find Thomas at two years old living in 144 Allderads Row at Horsley ,listed in the census return as a scholar , he was living with his 68 year old grandparents Benjamin and Clara Page, and Benjamin was even at that great age of seventy four in a later census listed as a Coal Miner . Their Daughter Mary Jane Page and her Husband George Blanton are nowhere in the records the conjecture then is as I surmise below.

The records show Mary Jane producing a second child a year after Thomas's Birth, This child named Isaac. From this, point in eighteen eighty one there is no record of Mary Jane as either Page or Blanton. I am assuming that Isaac died soon after birth joined by his young mother shortly afterwards. I can yet find no death record for either. George, I believe was unable to bring up the infant Thomas, so the nurture left to Clara, Thomas' Maternal grandmother. George appears later with another wife in the Ilkeston area, was he a serial widower? Is it the same George, more work to do?

In the Easter sojourn to Zakynthos, Sakis' daughter Maria, asked, why if Barbara has died do you not have another wife? After all her Granddad had a new wife, how the logic of a six year old can bring a large lump to the throat. I was not able to explain about eternal love or the idealistic woman that I had shared my life with , I explained weakly that unlike daddy and granddad , I could make coffee , cook . Silently in my own heart, I knew that there was no replacement, ever, that could meet the warm femininity, the enigmatic smile, and the love of Barbara. As an addendum to that thought, the sheer trauma of watching someone you love that much perish to a incurable disease is all that I would ever do in one lifetime. As I look back in history, Granddad, Great Granddad, and so many others re-married. I am so glad I can make coffee. If my children ever bother to read this, that is the proper version initiated by infusing beans, as opposed to the instant variety created by powder and hot water.

It seems that we descend from nearly two hundred years of coal miners. On this branch of the family tree, George and Mary Jane originated from Codshall in Staffordshire, and migrated with the rest of the family north to the mid Derbyshire coalfields. When you look closely at the records, we seem to have older generations delivering their families still into their middle ages. Was this a need to produce huge families as financial assurance , or just poor contraception , The rates for infant mortality were disgracefully high , as too was death in childbirth .

The pancreatic cancer that took Granddad at Christmas time in 1953 allowed him to see the letter from Buckingham Palace that showed Granddad was to receive a British Empire Medal for services to mining in the young Queens New Year's Honours list. This medal is for living recipients and not awarded posthumously, it, like granddad died as Elizabeth II took the throne. It gave dad several years of dissatisfaction of the honours system and the lack of a medal for the sixty years his father had tore away at coal seams.

Thomas and Alice had two daughters and five sons. Harold, Alice, Cyril, Cephus, Hedley, and Leslie followed Maud. They were spaced at roughly forty month intervals , seemingly telling us that family planning revolved around , one weaned , next one started principles , I was once told that Breast feeding was a perfect contraceptive , as it hormonally prevented further pregnancies' but actually doubt the science of that theory . Hedley a sickly child did not reach his teenage years, but the rest left this world strictly in the order they entered it. Maud to Leslie all passed to memory.

Thomas was, interred in the church of St Mary the Virgin at Denby near the ancestral tomb of the Pack-Drury-Lowe family. Dad and uncle Ceph kept vigil at their father's bedside as he faded away. Dad had his father's watch chain and Uncle Ceph the silver watch that accompanied it .The watch and its chain now reunited, in a glass dome on my desk remind me of whom we really are. Those now, are the only memento of Thomas Page. It seems so hard that a lifetime of hard work is like the chalk on a school blackboard, wiped away and forgotten. On the morning of granddad's death, His widow, dad's stepmother, removed a roll of five-pound notes from the front room sideboard where the dying man had laid, dad and uncle Ceph exchanged glances at the large wad of currency that the cupboard had hid from them. The family fortune escaped their grasp; the roll of notes would have been partially available for rescue, if its whereabouts known during the long night at their fathers' bedside. We have never been lucky with inherited wealth, but we hold memories that are far more precious than any money. There is no memory of attending granddads funeral , suspiciously age was a factor , being too young , to attend Grandma Hackman's funeral some six years later .Some years later accompanying dad to concrete and tidy the grave . There is a strong memory of the lead markings showing Grandddads name and details were then (well over fifty years ago), parting from the stone that leans awkwardly at granddad's head.

Grandmother Alice (née Lambert) had died from septicaemia following an operation in Derbyshire Royal Infirmary during 1932 .Leaving young Leslie aged eleven and his closest surviving brother Cephus at seventeen. Thomas re-married a widow who had lost her husband to Tuberculosis.

Mrs. Amelia Pykett became the second Mrs. Thomas Page. This bought more complications to the Page household in the form of Amelia's children , Amelia ,Lois , Elizabeth , George , and Alf , they added to the busy household , but relieved Aunty Alice and Uncle Cyril's wife Aunty Janet of the contribution they had made to the running of Thomas's household as well as their own . Dad always seemed to get on well with his stepsiblings. Despite the outward appearance, he had felt a great loss on his mother's death, and had an underlying resentment of sharing his household with five newcomers. Dad claimed in later years that whilst his new siblings had trousers and shoes, he was condemned to bib and brace overalls and hob-nailed boots. I know that was his perception, although he individually got on well with each of them. Alf always known as Sonny, due to his father , relocated to the garden shed in his dying days, to help his breathing, singing to him the Al Jolson hit Sonny Boy. The perception of Tuberculosis, or consumption, was that fresh air helped the symptoms. In those days before Alexander Fleming accidentally discovered the fungus penicillin, little could stop TB consuming its victim. Moreover, the discovery in nineteen twenty eight did not come into general use until the late nineteen forties.

Alf came over to me at dad's funeral," Hello I'm your uncle Alf, "he said, Alf, Alf, I don't know any Alf's, ". Try Sonny ", he said, and the realisation of which one of dad's relatives he was fell into place .He regaled the stories of how, when called for school the teenage Leslie hammered his boots on the floor in pretence of getting out of bed and then rolled over and resumed his slumber. This causes Leslie to be late many a day for his school attendance. His stepbrother sent to get the late Leslie. Remembering Dad's recollection of Mr Dicks as the formidable Headmaster of Denby School he never expanded on why , then forgot to mention why he was more than a little concerned at his mentor's ferocity . The service over dad's body committed, and I have no chance to take up a discussion, on school timekeeping, with the man whose reassurance that he never missed, never was late, and never aggravated his teachers was rock solid. Oh, evidence, why you arrived posthumously. I shall take Alf's version of the story, as I know dad would be at odds with it, he always got upon time, and he assured me of that regularly.

Alf was injured during World War II , as a paratrooper he was in the famous landing at the " Bridge Too Far " at Arnhem and was shot and injured whilst descending from the plane . That resulted in his capture by the retreating Wermacht starting its long awaited return to the Fatherland. Dad with his legion contacts aided Alf in a claim for assistance from the military during the nineteen eighties, understanding was there was a long-term complication resulting from the lack of treatment and mistreatment he had suffered during time in German hands.

Maud, the eldest of the Page family, born at the turn of the last century was into her fifties when I first met her. She was married to Jack Upton who always seemed a harmless scoundrel of a man who enjoyed his life with the occasional drink and trip to the pubs in Horsley Woodhouse. They had five children (I think) and the eldest died young leaving her brood in her mother's safe hands, my aunty Maud. Their family weddings were pub affairs where beer flowed, in sharp contrast to the sober affairs of the Annable family. The family resided at Stanesby Crescent at Horsley. Their council house lay at the bottom of the crescent and was one of dad's stops on Christmas day when he would set out on a family tour, as Christmas lunch cooked away. Maud was one of his rarer visits .I believes that she was married and away before dad was a toddler. In her later years she lost a leg to gangrene , but on the regular Christmas outing , still undertaken, even when Barbara and I took the children to enjoy Christmas in the frozen north , she still exuded a cheery spirit , and always had a glass of it nearby to offer . Reflecting on those Christmas rounds, it was a good thing that the breathalyzer was rarer commodity than these days. In mitigation, roads were less crowded, cars slower, and drink, according to the parental chauffer had no effect on him. Does that defence stand in court, or was wishful thought the order of the day.

Harold, the eldest son, was married to Beatrice and they have two daughters Maureen and Hazel. I firstly remember Uncle Harold's house at Denby Bottles, where they lived until their move, to Street Lane at Denby in the nineteen sixties. Street lane had a few houses and a rail crossing that allowed coal trucks to pass into the yard at the Old Denby Colliery. The houses had much smaller rear gardens than the Rykneld hill houses, but were similar in layout. The front garden of each had a pair of trees pollard cut, as though they were temple entrance pillars .Uncle Harold the first son of Thomas and Alice. Uncle Harold and Aunty Beatie, always kept dogs, I remember well a Pekinese who was more than a little frightening. I believe this fearsome creature known as Mitzi. The dog's lack of stature compensated for by a furious Bravado, and no fear. Uncle Harold worked in the "family business" as a miner, becoming a deputy, (the title for the supervisors). One or two of the lamps that I have are the Re-lighters that those same deputies used. If miners lamp went out it returned for re-lighting at the surface in the lamp cabin, the Deputies had a flint wheel arrangement allowing theirs to re strike the flame. In those days, mining was a hard occupation, cuts and bruises were an occupational hazard .Injuries minor and serious were common and safety under such arduous conditions was not as prominent a feature as today's health and safety standards order. I am a great critic of the madness of the legislation binding industry with the red tape that chokes the wheels of progress , but as I look backwards , no-one would welcome a return to the careless way lives were disregarded in the effort to maintain production .

The Drury-Lowe family, who lived at nearby Locko Park, owned the mines. A land agent, Mark Fryar managed their estates, and controlled the mining interests of this powerful local family. He had claimed that the coal seam stretched as far as the edge of Derby and that there was enough recoverable coal to keep the Drury Lowe's in an accustomed style for several generations. The post war Labour Government took the dream away as they nationalised the mines and the countries mineral interests. The miners in gratitude went on strike against the government , who in their ultimate wisdom held the belief that they , as the miners friends , were giving the working man what he wanted .The repayment came years later as the Labour Government of Harold Wilson closed pits , turned new power stations to oil burning , and decimated the miners . I cry no tears for the loss of dangerous occupation that killed and maimed those human moles, who satisfied the need for cheap energy, before, the Oil Barons discovered the North Sea Bonanza.

Aunty Alice and Uncle Bert (Annable) lived also at Denby Bottles; they lived a little further up the hill, until they moved to 78 Chapel Street at Kilburn opposite the Kilburn Miners Welfare. Bert worked all his working life at Derby Cables, and spent his Sundays preaching in the Baptist ministry. They have two daughters also Audrey and Barbara. I can never remember visiting Audrey, and certainly she fell on to her mother's disapproval list when her marriage ended. Barbara married an Auto Electrician. They lived on the Outskirts of Derby, I remember only one visit there, and a large Edwardian house opposite a park, there was a corrugated Steel Sheet Mission at the bottom of the park, which was the local Salvation Army Citadel. Aunty Alice was a regular call on dad's visiting list When you called there my memories hold on to the smell of fresh baking , Bakewell Tart , Jam and curd tarts , cake , all manner of delicacies , all the sweet tasting food that I could think off . The houses fronted Chapel Street, but no one ever used front doors, we accessed the kitchen from a path off a side road. This was a communal path for all the residents. This led into the main living room via a single story kitchen. There was a doorway to the enclosed stairway off this room and on the same inner wall a doorway at the far end of the living room, this led to a front, or, best room. I never ventured into that inner sanctum and was only aware of its existence through a conversation many year s later. Aunty Alice in the early years of my life did all the wall papering and decoration for my mum and dad, she was always accompanied by her friend ,which gave rise to them reminding me of a famous comedy duo of the time , Gertrude and Daisy . As well as being the decorators, I still remember with fondness the trifles that she always produced. My mother's attempts at trifles originally started with on the dehydrated sponge cake and a large shot of Jelly. ,the tuition of Aunty Alice made them super desirable Aunty Alice's trifles involved a jam and cream sponge cake soaked in the juice of canned strawberries, mum varied the recipe by adding a schooner of Harvey's Bristol Cream Sherry to the marinating cake   . The wet sponge conglomeration liberally coated in vanilla custard, the yellow Birds custard that started life as a pink powder, when the custard set and the cake congealed the top finally spread with whipped double cream. There was, in the original a dusting of hundreds and thousands, but along with many other s, it was part of dad's dislike rule, and if he disliked it, we never had it. It was not that he actually disliked anything, but some things were bold enough to disagree with him, and this confined them to banned product status. I had believed that Aunt Alice had been a mainstay in dad's upbringing after his mother's death; I know Aunty Janet was also part of this, but bearing in mind that he was only at school until nineteen thirty six, when he went to Slater's Pipe Works. The stories related by Alf Pykett, must have mean the two families having combined around a year after my grandmothers death.

    The main times that we enjoyed family gatherings were at the many weddings that threaded through the late nineteen fifties and early nineteen sixties. The weddings started with Aunty Maud's children then Uncle Bert and Aunty Alice's daughters Audrey and Barbara both held the Baptist Church and afterwards the adjacent Chapel hall.

Aunty Alice in the early nineteen sixties suffered from a calcium encasement of her heart, slowing her down, it was then that she had new surgery at the Grobey Road Heart Hospital, (later "The Glenfield") in the districts specialist unit, on the edge of Leicester. Her blood group was a rare one, dad and Uncle Cyril were on standby if an urgent transfusion suddenly became required during the operation there was an awful lot of tension, and worry accompanying what was a very serious operation at the time. Dad was so pleased being on the short-list for transfusion duty, he was always at his best when someone needs him, for advice, his prolific letter writing skill, or even the odd pint of blood. My father delighted in recognition of any of his deeds and although unselfish in his giving added his importance in the plan to his many stories .The operation was a success despite its pioneering flag, and Aunty Alice was still baking cakes in the mid nineteen seventies, when Barbara and I visited.

Uncle Cyril was married to Aunty Janet (nee Palfryman) they had two children Cyril who died at birth and Desrene. On several occasions, Uncle Cyril and Aunty Janet chauffeured us out on a Saturday evening. He had an Austin, the pre Farina model with the black and chrome that befitted cars of the nineteen fifties. The styling was a timeless tribute to Austin's design team, fifties style and British construction. . I believe Uncle Cyril was the first in the family to own a car. On at least two of these occasions, we ended at Desrene and Brian's house, which I believe, was at Spondon. . When we got near to the huge cemetery at Chaddesden, Its impressive lodge and Entrance, designed in the mid eighteen hundreds by H I Stevens, Aunty Janet would have a nostalgic tear at the thought of her baby lying in a communal grave, unmarked. In those far off days, the internment arranged by the hospital for children who did not survive beyond their first days was a mere coincidence; the stiff British exterior barring the emotion of a grieving mother as her infant son was interred Aunty Janet was bound to the hospital . As one scoffs at the counselling and mollycoddling available in this age, despair that the overabundance available today belies the starvation of yesteryear. On one journey, with dad sat alongside his brother, Aunty Janet started to comment on the speed, Uncle Cyril turned off the instrument cluster lights to avoid further discussion. They, from my earliest days lived at a house three doors down the hill Granddad's in Rykneld Hill. The house had a huge lawn at the front, and the vast rear garden, with its orchard at the bottom home to a few chickens if memory is correct. The lawn neatly trimmed with a push along lawn mower that whirred loudly as it sailed down the slope, returning much more sedately up the steep gradient that formed the lawn. As part of what seemed a family tradition, they always seemed to have a dog too. The first in memory was a large Staffordshire bull terrier called Rex. The dog was a Brindle colour and was the last of a breeding line of Staffordshire Bull terriers that Granddad had nurtured and shown at the Cruft's Dog show some years before, were they were reputed to have been prizewinners. That is a task to add to the research list. When I have exhausted my patience checking the humans, start on the dogs. I always believed granddad's dogs to have been the more common white ones. Rex was not a friendly dog, well secured, on a long line of heavy chain outside the back door; it kept visitors without of the radius of Rex's limiting chain. If I had known how easily Rex could uproot the chain and troop off with fifty foot of heavy links in tow, I may have been even more scared of this canine ferocity. I for one despite, my dad's re-assurance remained always much scarred of Rex .This house similarly arranged as Granddad's has had an entrance in a kitchen opposite a small-enclosed yard. This main kitchen was a large room with a boiler, to provide water for the washing. There was centrally a large kitchen table. This room had a large window overlooking the small yard, with doors to the scullery and the lounge. I remember it despite the large sash window as being a dark room lit by a solitary central ceiling lamp. The kitchen opened out in to a large living room there centrally placed being a large side window with an aspect over the drive, and doors to the kitchen and the front hallway. Aunty Janet had a huge grey tiled fire place in this living room, totally covered in highly polished cast brass ornaments. When the adult conversation, became rapidly boring, and monotonous, I would sit and relieve my time counting those highly polished and a many brass ornaments. I am the count reached well over a hundred, the polishing and cleaning of these must have taken Aunty Janet a whole morning to complete. Fascinatingly too in a position of prominence a set of fire irons in the shape of a cloaked knight stood proudly on the hearth. From the front a cloaked armoured knight cast in iron, and coated in a vitreous glaze, this facade hiding the poker, brush and fire tongs that were essential to maintain the coal fires, burning away in the grate. The fire never seemed to be able to burn well without the poker adjusting the burning coal; those tongs lay ready to catch the spitting coal as not embers launched onto the heart rug. Aunty Janet had the traditional three pottery ducks in a hibernating flight soaring across the outer wall next to the window those ducks were a badge of chic in those days , strangely enough the flight always took three , never more , nor less .

This as the living room housed a dining table and a three-piece suit. The room in comparison to our own in Nether Heage was huge .Aunty Janet devoted a lot of time to dusting and polishing, anyone entering would see the shine and smell the polish of those labours instantly. As a child touring relatives is one of life's double edged challenges , on one hand a trip out , and no child ever wants to miss one of those , but , the other side is the boring hour as the adults talk, supping away at repeated mugs of tea ,. I made the same mistakes as a parent, you are engrossed in your own agenda you forget the child. The conversation is something that is , to the child is boring , and possibly scandalous , if you understood the content it would have been worth memorising as , you dutifully and silently sat waiting for the ordeal to end , and the interesting part , the trip in the car , to resume .

The front hall had a large stairway with a door shaped to fit the angle of the stairs, leading to an under stairs cupboard, and a doorway leading into a front room. The front room as in many houses was a preserve opened for only the most special of occasions. I remember one sojourn to this inner sanctum. We went there to await news when Desrene took ill on her wedding day. I vaguely remember being ushered into that room when as a family we visited around Christmas; there was to my memory an imposing leather three-piece lounge suite. Moreover, the room was a preserve of polish and gleam. A coal fire dominated this part of the house too. The huge front window overlooked the lawn and the hedge alongside Rykneld Hill. The coal fires seemed to be permanently alight in occupied rooms. They blazed all at the time. The cheeriness of the open blaze belied the dust that created vast work. The ash and debris created clouds of it; the dust settles finely everywhere causing so much polishing which Aunty Janet took in hand vigorously.

Uncle Cyril was, as many of the local families endowed with a coal concession from the mines that gave them coal for a meagre transportation cost. We on many a summer evening took the farm van from Sid Gadsby and shovelled coal into potato sacks filling the van from a large coal-pile in Uncle Cyril's huge driveway .I always thought the loan of the van a totally unselfish act , but there was always a payment in kind , or later in dads labour , to balance the account . The van was originally a Fordson Thames, this being a derivative of the Ford Popular car, soon after this van though the replacements were always Land Rovers. The farm needed a van , as milk transported by the farmer to his local dairy , which in Sid's case was the Ripley Co-op on Nottingham Road at Ripley avoided a surcharge off the monthly milk cheque if the haulier collected your ten gallon churns for you . All milk bought by the farmer owned co-operative the Milk Marketing Board, and paid for on weight and butterfat content. Dad though had to share his fortune with Sid as van rental, despite providing the effort and the coal. There are some people in life who always seem to draw the short straw in any lottery, and dad was firmly in this category, his collection tin, was always full of "Thank you notes ," never coin. His nature though to dispense advice and help, always free to all was part of what made him admired by many and disliked by others. When offered monies or compensation for his efforts or time dad always refused, his politeness had become his generosity. If you say, "no" enough people believe you actually mean it.

Uncle Cyril, rose to senior over man, he would deputise for the under manager too, this was manager who managed the underground workings. After the mines closed, many miners took pensions and alternate work. Uncle Cyril moved firstly to Openwoodgate and then to East Leake when he took on the security of the power Station that dominated the M1 adjacent to Kegworth, Radcliffe – on –Soar. The most modern power station of its day, coal fired. The huge boilers fed by a constant flow of rail trucks automatically discharging to a huge coal heap. If the miners striking against Margaret Thatcher had realised the vastness of that store, they may have never engineered their own destruction by defying "Maggie Thatcher ,The Iron Lady "

Uncle Cyril was always Dad's favourite elder brother, and we were regulars at Openwoodgate, East Leake and on Uncle Cyril's retirement, Littleover. Dad always felt a special bond to his brother Cyril, as the big brother he could rely on, whereas he thought a lot of Uncle Ceph, dad felt him to be headstrong and prone to jump in feet first. The visits were a double pleasure for dad as a trip to Littleover British Legion club was always a welcome. In the early nineteen seventies, I remember the warm welcome that Barbara I and the Children always received. Aunty Janet always whooped an excited call.

The children loved the visits and Barbara sat attentively as she listened to family stories of people that she did not know from times before we were born. The boisterousness of the stories of the pre war days always greeted, with a yawning indifference would be a rich anthology to thread into this story, bearing in mind the possibility that conjecture could be very wrong. Pre DNA testing, Aunty Janet could define paternity by which the child looks like, a risky but tested method in her book. Aunty Janet earned a special place in our hearts for her outgoing nature. . When visiting it was a nice afternoon diversion to enjoy the occasional pint of Guinness with Uncle Cyril at the Littleover British Legion too, whilst Barbara listened patiently to Aunty Janet, as the family history was unveiled. Whenever Barbara heard these stories, she was never able to have them committed to memory, as she never knew the characters, If only Barbara had written it all down.

As Aunty Janet aged, her eyesight failed her badly and unable to live independently she entered a retirement home at Makeney, near to the old "Peckwash "factory. We visited her at Derby City Hospital one afternoon and spent well over an hour listening, about, how devoted and wonderful her daughter Desrene was to her. We were so impressed with the praise heaped upon to praise. Desrene appeared, greeted, with a scowl, "about time, where have you been all day? You do not care! ," the onslaught was incredible from a woman who had been singlehandedly the most adored mother in the world just two minutes previously.

Uncle Cephus was originally married to his stepsister Lois, who died of Consumption (Tuberculosis) in the late nineteen thirties. Lois in her final days became a permanent patient in a specialist chest sanatorium in North Derbyshire near Chesterfield. Public transport in the far off pre war days resulted in visitation problems for Uncle Ceph. He borrowed a Tandem and enlisted his younger brother Leslie as a power pack to speed the journey and set off to visit his terminally ill wife. It seems a tradition that once someone passed away, his or her name instantly delisted from the conversation. Not once did dad discuss, his mother, Hedley or Lois. The impression given that Uncle Ceph's independent spirit was a little uncontrollable at times. Dad would relate that on a Saturday night a full Aitch Bone of Beef would be lying on the kitchen worktop in the Rykneld Hill home, ready for the Sunday Joint, It was a regular occurrence for Ceph to slice a steak from it and cook it for the two of them. The joint would feed the family from Sunday to Wednesday .It was the meat in the stew Monday, and would appear minced in a pie for the Tuesday and cold on Wednesday. The steak on Saturday night was additional to the planned meals from this joint.

Uncle Ceph had later remarried to May Hancock, the daughter the Landlady of the Fox and Hounds at Coxbench. They had one son David Ralph, known as Ralph. Ralph died in his thirties in nineteen eighty. He was working at British Rail at Derby and found too late in the toilets having suffered a massive heart attack. Ralph had married Pat a few years before and they had settled well together. Alison had stopped at Mum and dad's house over the summer holidays in her fifteenth year and was full of praise for Ralph. Uncle Ceph and Aunty May had moved from the bungalow that they had had built the top of Golden Valley in Horsley Woodhouse to be near May's cousin Arthur at Lincoln. The loss of Ralph pre-ceded their return to Derbyshire. They returned to live in Malthouse lane at Nether Heage. Uncle Ceph was also in the family mining team and was a shot fired. He also failed to retire from the underground existence becoming a victim of redundancy. After a short spell at British Rail in Derby, he retired fully. A few lost lunchtimes soon spent with uncle Ceph at the Jolly Colliers in Wainsgrove, showed that if he ever crossed paths with another ancient mole, vigorously dug coal, and pumped water from long closed workings.

The Jolly Colliers run by Alan Peacock and his wife Ivy. Ivy had been a close friend and workmate of my mother and their two Daughters Susan and Jeanette always were a firm favourite of my parents. We would go for a drink as families with Alan, Ivy. When we returned to their house behind Deggie's Garage in Swanwick, Ivy would take an unsliced loaf and fashion cheese sandwiches with the skill of a quarryman blasting stone. The slices were always a triangular section fitted together to provide a diagonal for the filling. Uncle Ceph had served in the Army in Italy in World War II, and I believe was in the landings at Anzio and Monte Cassini in Italy where a monastery lay under repeated attack. . Left in American hands, and then re-taken after the American forces lost it, before that, he was fighting in the North African desert. Uncle Ceph was renowned for having a fiery temper and on one occasion, at a relaxing Saturday evening discussion in the Fox and Hounds with his brothers took Uncle Cyril outside to finish off the argument that had started earlier in the week at work . Dad as peacemaker got in the middle and separated them. It seems so strange that such a profession was, after work taken so to heart. I have heard miners twenty years after the pits closed arguing over seams of coal, who did what, who did nothing. If mining was the hotbed of the revolutionary left , their leaders such as Arthur Scargill stood no chance in the war against the proletariat , the miners seemed to busy arguing amongst themselves .

Hedley was a mystery and I only knew of him when I was well past forty from Dad, who never expanded on the story that Headley was a sickly child. He is also the growing research list, Hedley Page born in nineteen eighteen. Died early in the nineteen thirties .All we know of Headley is his frailty, Always sick, not very strong. That was dad's contribution to the story of his long lost brother.

Leslie will have his own stories and chapter as he richly deserves. This introduced the family on father's side.

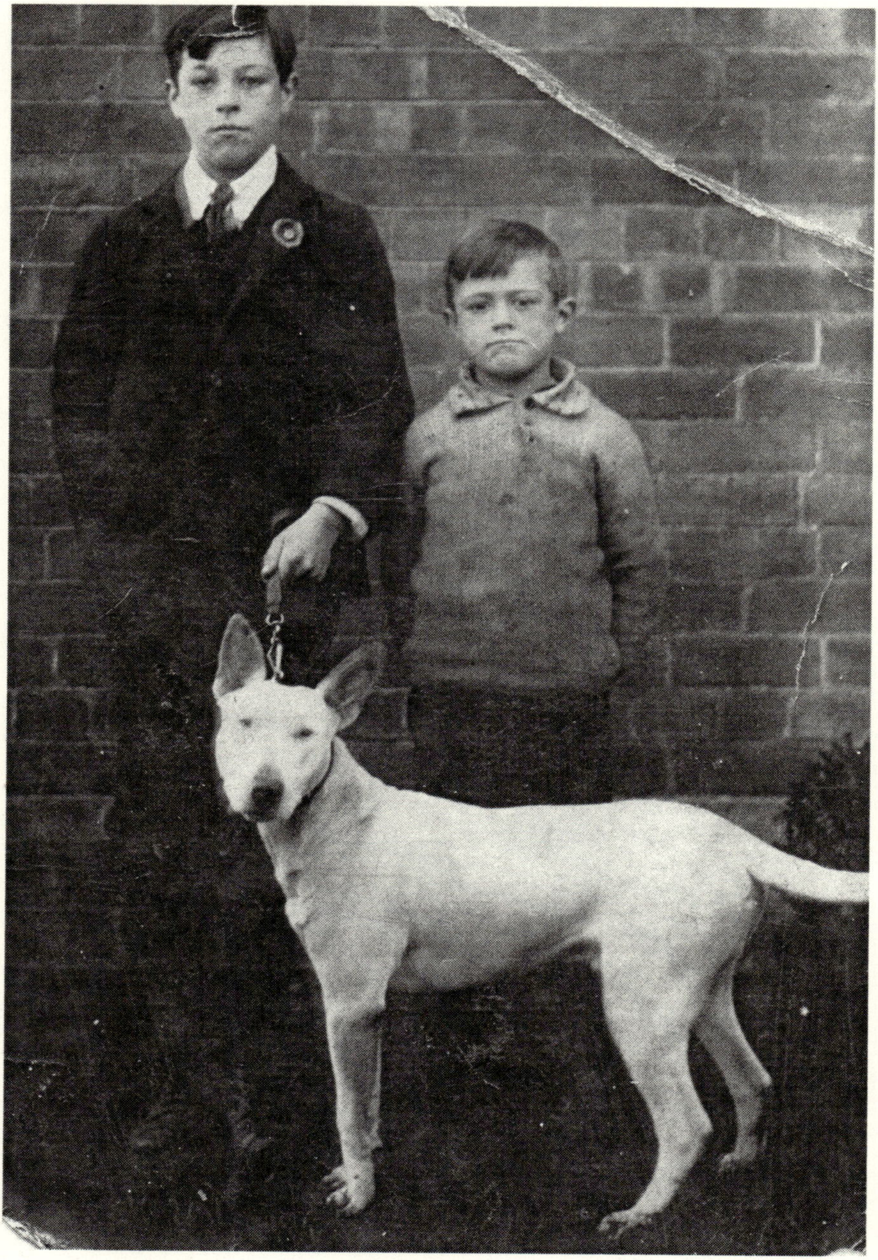

Chapter 7. Where they lived

The entry in Kelly's Directory for Denby 1891

DENBY *is an extensive parish and large scattered village, with a station on the Ripley branch of the Midland railway, miles southeast from Belper, 8 miles north from Derby, 4½ northeast from Duffield, and 134 from London. In the Ilkeston division of the county, hundreds of Morleston and Litchurch, Belper union, Belper and Ilkeston County court district, Smalley petty sessional division, rural deanery of Duffield, archdeaconry of Derby and diocese of Southwell .*

The church of St. Mary the Virgin consists of chancel, clerestoried nave, aisles, south porch and a Decorated western tower of three stages, with a parapet relieved by a wavy line of moulding, from within which rises a spire with two rows of dormer lights. The tower contains 4 bells, the 3rd and 4th of which are dated 1604: the chancel is of good Decorated character, and has a four-light east window with flamboyant tracery, filled with stained glass in 1889. In its south wall are two sedilia of equal height, with ogee crocketed canopies, and a piscine. The communion table is of 17th century date .In the north wall is a recess or almery, and in the projecting chancel pier at the east end of the north aisle a rather rudely cut piscina, with a credence shelf above it: the nave is separated from the south aisle by two rounded arches, springing from a circular central pier, and two semi-circular responds. The opposite arcade, believed to have been Saxon, was removed in 1838, when the wall of the north aisle was made level with that or the nave, and the north clerestory windows placed above those of the aisle . The east window of this aisle is Decorated, the remaining windows of the aisles being Perpendicular, c. 1450. The high-pitched and picturesque porch dates from about 1735. Against the north chancel wall is the large and costly monument or Patrick, son of Jasper Lowe, and Jane, his wife, daughter of Sir John Harpur kt. of Swarkeston, consisting of two canopies, with full-sized kneeling effigies, the former in plate armour, and the latter in French cap and ruff . In the background are the figures or four children; the inscriptions are missing: there is also a mural monument to John Lowe, 5th in descent from the Patrick above mentioned (1771), and another to Richard Lowe, of Locko Park, his brother (1785) : there are 320 sittings, 200 being free. The register dates from the year 1577, for all entries. The living is a vicarage, average tithe rent-charge £10, net yearly value £140, including 32 acres of glebe, in the gift of William Drury N. Drury-Lowe Esq. of Locko Park, and held since 1845 by the Rev, James Mockler M.A. of Trinity College, Dublin. Population in 1881 was 1,287. The tithes are impropriated to Sir Henry Wilmot Bart, and a portion devoted to repairing the chancel and maintenance of alms-houses in Derby. There is a Methodist chapel here, erected in 1841, and one at Bottles. A charity of £6 10s. Left in 1817 by the Rev. Francis Gisborne, formerly rector of Staveley, is distributed by the vicar in clothing to the poor of the parish at Christmas. Denby is noted for its extensive collieries, the property of William Drury N. Drury- Lowe Esq. ; here also are large blast furnaces for the production of pig iron, belonging to the Derby Iron and Coal Co. Limited. There is a large pottery and extensive brick and tile works. The locality produces also ironstone, cement, and brick earth. William Drury N. Drury-Lowe Esq. is lord of the manor; the principal landowners are William Drury N. Drury-Lowe Esq. and Mrs. Eckersley. The soil is clay subsoil, clay. The chief crops are wheat and oats, and about two-thirds pasture, The area in acres is 2,395 ; rateable value, £8,739;

The population in 1881 was 1,394.
POST OFFICE.-Henry Briscoe, receiver. Letters received through Derby, arrive at 5.30 a.m. dispatched at 7 p.m. The nearest money

order office is at Kilburne. Kilburne is the nearest telegraph office for delivery & Denby station for dispatch of telegrams
POST OFFICE, Smithy Houses.-: Mrs. Ellen Pym, receiver, Letters received through Derby, arrive at 5.45 a.m. ; dispatched at 9-45 a.m. & 7,30 p.m. The nearest money order & telegraph office is at Kilburne
Endowed School (mixed & infants) endowed with £30 yearly, arising from a sum of money left in 1739 by Mrs. Massey, & invested in land; the school was erected in 1867, enlarged in 1875, & again enlarged 1885 for 110 boys & girls & 60 infants ; average attendance, 113 boys & girls & 43 infants; John Northam, master; Miss Elizabeth Jane Weston, infants' mistress

Denby is, in the Doomsday book as Denebi, the village of Danes. Rykneld Hill a long straight road, From Bourdon in the Water deep in Gloucestershire to Templebrough, north in Yorkshire laid originally in Roman time cuts across the turnpike from Derby to Sheffield in the village centre. The road heads along Street Lane towards Alfreton via Hartsay and Pentrich this formed a section of roadways from Alexandria in Egypt to Perth in Scotland bringing the Roman army over the known world. When those legions of soldiers first landed, there was a huge army to defend these shores of over forty thousand chariots [1] defeated by the military precision and training of the centuries of Rome. This road was the thoroughfare trod by Emperor Hadrian on his way to the boarder of the Empire, Penda the King of Mercia on the way to slay King Edwin. This was the road Alfred the Greats daughter Aethelstan and her son Athelstan marched to attack sixty thousand Norse and Scots at Rotherham. Edward 1st and his army strode here to their defeat at Bannockburn; Oliver Cromwell sped on his way to Marston Moor. Sleepy Rykneld Road, the highway of the empire, it seems so quiet now. The Pottery dominates the area now but it was Old and New Denby (Denby Hall), pits that dominated the village previously. The pottery established in Denby when rich pottery clay in abundance found as the A38 drove out through the countryside as a turnpike in 1806. This is reputed to be the finest stoneware clay in Europe .The stoneware pots and jars were receptacles for ink and beer, ginger beer and lemonade and a myriad of other liquids. In 1832, this pottery of Joseph Bourne was the country's largest exporter of bottles and jars. The Wallow workers filled buckets with clay in pits ready this readily hauled to the pottery were the hand thrown pots continually produced ever since . The pottery throwers used clay balls as a starter for each jar. Women and children made these; one of those young girls was Alice Lambert, Grandmother. When the pots entered the kiln, during firing, handfuls of salt thrown into the kiln gives the classic salt glaze brown shiny coating.

Denby is still a tiny village , but lays claim to the birthplace of John Flamstead , (1646 – 1719) Astronomer Royal , who lends his name to the local school , and Benjamin Outram , also immortalised in scholastic names , a , famous railway engineer . Two miles nearer to Derby is Kilburn. There, was an Ironworks, Copper smelting and a clay pipe works of Slater's, which formed Leslie Page's post school education. The copper ore for this produced locally on the Estates of the Duke of Devonshire and Ecton, in Staffordshire. The ore was broken into small pieces and transported by Ass and Horse, across the ford at Milford, Formerly known as Muelford. The Drove of Horses named a Jag was led by an Ore-Jagger. The coal and Ironstone were mined locally. During Edward 1st reign there is evidence of coal mining and Edward 1st 's Grandfather was killed by a truck of coal and killed , in the area in twelve eighty nine . There was a coal mine spaced every few miles , Hartsay , Ripley , Salter wood , Winnings , Kilburn , Denby Hall , Denby , many of these later merged underground with the workings of Denby. In eighteen eighty three two new pits were dug into the Kilburn seam at Denby .They for all the sensible economic reasons soon joined at the pithead at New Denby. There was a modern Bath House where the coal dust thoroughly washed away before the pitmen boarded the bus home. With each mine was a huge spoil heap , Street lane and the A38 had several of these loose mounds of underground waste , blackened by shale and slack , some stood a dark red to show the results of their self ignition . The spoil heaps polluted the streams and were unsafe areas , as to climb on them easily resulted in landslides The rock and slag piled high was chemically suspect too , even defiant kids stayed away from those pit heaps . Their prominence came with the infamy of the Abervan tip in Wales, which engulfed a Primary School and its class of Children, wiping out a whole generation from that village. Miners boarded the Alfreton Bus in the clothes they had worn during their shift from the mine at Marehay. The great sanitary facilities at New Denby were a boon for not only the workers but for the travelling public too. The villages were mining villages with the majority of the population employed in the local mines. Trent motor traction ran early morning buses to take each shift in, these Pit Buses preceded the days where everyman aspired to car ownership and unlimited mobility.

The pottery also dominated the village as it still does today with its visitors centre and miniature shopping arcade the remnants of industry in the area now mining has totally disappeared. The clay was bought from the Drury Lowes by William Bourne of Belper in eighteen nine. Street lane bordered on both sides with fields, which hid coal seams close to the surface, this road divided an opencast mine. A large block making plant was opened there in the late nineteen sixties making aerated blocks for a Butterly company (now Hanson) Aglite .The pub, long demolished, at the side of the A38 was the "Drury Lowe Arms", showing the village's loyalty too its landowner in name

Nether Heage

The Village is in two main parts, separated by Dungely Hill, which cuts the Nether Heage section off very cleanly from its bigger brother Heage. Nether Heage (or formerly High Heage and Low Heage) form part of the Parish , the differences are few but Heage itself is bigger with more facilities .Neither village has a centre but consists of houses and cottages along the roads and lanes, with some small estates of modern housing. The name is from the Anglo-

Saxon 'Heegge' meaning high, lofty, or sublime .Situated in the Amber Valley area, the main occupations of the original inhabitants would have been farming. There are still family-owned farms today The, Spendlove and England and Gadsby families have carried on for what seems forever .There is sheep and dairy cattle, cereal and root crops.

Remembering the early morning exodus of miners, who set off around five AM to Denby Hall, Alfreton, Ripley, and all the other local collieries as clearly as they waited at set points for their lifts from colleagues? The car owners always seemed to share in a car pool, the bus fare handed over as a recompense for petrol money

The village changed little in all those years. A few new houses, a few new faces, but largely the same the never altering face of Nether Heage When I was younger there were mainly people at the Johnson's Wireworks , Stevenson's Dye works and the Pits . People commuted from Ambergate station to "Rolls Royce Aero Engine's " factory at Sinfin in Derby to the Railway works in there too .The fledgling Litchfield plastics factory built on a former World War two prisoner of war camp, constructed to house Italian Prisoners was the only industry in the two villages. Bowmer & Kirkland had a large yard covered in Lorries and cranes from their Heavy Haulage division, and a large builder's works and carpenters shop. The villages were self-sufficient and supported two Post Offices, Two large Co-operative shops. Two general stores, one newsagent, two butchers, one chip shop. A small tobacconist sweet shop by Heage Church and two smaller general stores once found in the upper part of Heage are now long closed. The Co-operative had a mobile butchers, and fishmongers vans. The baker delivered fresh bread three times a week , from Loaders bakery , the fresh loaves being left in a large white enamel tin , marked " Bread" and left by the front door .The delivery would be late on a Friday as the Baker collected the due monies from the week . Sketchley collected the laundry, sheets returned crisp and starched with a razor edge crease, shirts heavily starched so the sleeves had to be prized apart as your arm forced entry. There was a "Beer at Home "service from the Davenport brewery. Corona delivered "Pop" fizzy drinks to the door , Flavours not popular now were the Dandelion and Burdock , Cream Soda , Cloudy lemonade , Limeade , cherryade , flavours long replaced by the Americanisation of the drinks industry . Wherever we look now we see either the Cola or Pepsi brands, as the two majors slug it out for market share. Coca-Cola with its companion," Fanta" and "Sprite", the tasteless lemonade substitute aim for the vending and shops, whilst Pepsi and 7-up fight back for their share.

The two Villages supported six public houses. The White Hart at the top of the hill , The Black Boy on the Belper Road , The Green Man in upper Heage , The White Horse in upper Heage too , The new Inn , now called the Eagle Tavern and the Spanker in Nether Heage. Each pub was entirely different, different breweries, different atmosphere .The Green Man was owned by the Gibson Family and was a true spit and sawdust pub. The Eagle Tavern a traditional Pub, the white Hart, quieter with a large function room, and a bar full of Bowmer & Kirkland men on their way home, most evenings. Samson Stone ran the Black Boy as a sideline to his building company. Frank and Lilly Gibson ran the Spanker as an add on to their haulage firm. The ERF rigid fifteen tonne trucks standing outside the huge garage next to the pub itself .Each named , "Spanker Princess " , Spanker Pride " etc .

The village was a triangle of roads. Brook Street ran into a "Y" junction at the "Guide Post" and the road with all the shops to the right was "Shop Lane "the one with the Spanker Pub to the Left Spanker Lane. The third side was Malthouse Lane. The Malthouse Lane, shop lane junction had Ridgeway lane running from it, and the Malthouse Lane Spanker Lane led to Heage Firs. Guidepost house was residence to Doug and Elsie Cuttel, There was a large pump in that garden for drawing water. Elsie was Bill Hackman's Daughter, how the families intertwine. Josie was the village Hairdresser had the small shop situated in Litchfield's Garden; this had originally been Bill Hackman's House for his lifetime. Bill's Daughters are still living in the village today. That business started in the late fifties by Jan and Darrel. They had a shop in Heage next to "Parkin's News-agency "this had been Bookies from the days when bookmaker's shops were legalised. Before the gambling legislation, bets placed with Sam who delivered the morning papers and collected the bets. The local bookies runner provided the Papers, winners, and losers to the dual community. Nether Heage started mid hill at the house that was originally John Gadsby's in the centre of the Hill. there was a new bungalow built by Mr & Mrs Betterton , This was added to when their son David joined them with his own bungalow many years later .The bottom of the Hill was home to Kath and Bill Fox ,they had two daughters Carol and Lynn . There was a bungalow to the rear of this house. Opposite to the Fox's house was a small cottage, backing onto the Rolleston property. Mr. & Mrs... Ernie Rolleston and their Granddaughter Barbara . Their daughter in law having died when Barbara was an infant, and Ivan the Rolleston's son had deposited the infant with his parents, so she was bought up in grandma's house. The cluster at the Brook housed Mr & Mrs Percy Jackson. and the Hodgekinson', our semi-detached cottages adjoining the Coopers. the Hoult's were opposite , The Nichols farm above them and the two Gadsby's Farms , Bent Farm & Sewage Farm along the lane .Fred and Edie Gadsby lived at Bent farm , Percy and his family at sewage farm . Mrs Gadsby until her death cooked on the open fire, excelsior range in their living room. A large Grandfather clock stood in the room; this had been painted in the imperial purple gloss paint that decorated the kitchen walls. Fred kept a few chickens and used to sell tomatoes from a vast greenhouse in the huge rear garden. Aunty Lizzie and Uncle Mac were at 20 , grandma at 22 with Aunty Kit , Uncle Charlie , and Uncle Frank , Mum's cousins the Coopers at 24 , Harold and Nancy Mee at 26 , The Holtoms and their battery chicken farm at 28

, (which became my home from nineteen sixty two until our marriage . The Litchfield family filled the gap to the Guide Post; the first house was rented to relatives of the Litchfield's, Mr & Mrs Hooley, whilst the main family lived in the larger unit.

The Village always seems so sleepy that it exuded stability. It still gives me that feeling of permanence .The attachment has waned in the later years and even when travelling as far as Belper, the view over that sleepy vale has little attraction.

The Bentfield Road area was looked down on as a Council Road, and was thought to house a few rough families .Dad's biases always showed through. He preferred to rent privately rather than owe money to a bank or to live in "public housing." I do not remember any particularly different people there though. There were a couple of large families though. The day that Michael Edwards lost an eye to his brother Dennis's violence was a rarity .There was the Fagin family a large Irish family with loads of kids and not many assets , The rest were mainly miners . The rest of the thirty dwellings were mainly family homes with two or three children in each .Joe & Jim Hardy., the Spencer's, Lineker, Ottewell, Goadbys, featuring large amongst those houses .The Mines , Bowmer & Kirkland , Wireworks and Dye works occupied most of the men .

We had good recreation grounds, swings and a slide, and would play in the Spanker and Milner's fields at the upper apex of the village triangle . We played cricket with Milner's sheep as an audience. We played cowboys and Indians, but no one was ever the Indians, so we played cowboys, out on an imaginary vast range. We put the first and second finger together to create a revolver and banged away at each other like the legendary John Wayne film characters. We ran on imaginary horses, lassoed imaginary cattle rescued imaginary friends. The imagination of youth was boundless. We were knights of King Arthur's round table, Robin Hood's merry men. We could not play war games, no one would be German, and the atrocities of the recent war were so fresh with our parents. We knew that the Germans were bad; after all, they had tried to kill our parents, Mum always reminded us that we had a Jewish ancestry, and as $1/8^{th}$ Jewish we would have got the worse of any invasion. The subsequent genealogy does not show this at all. This is why I commit these stories to paper to give following generations a chance to follow and correct what I report here.

There was an annual fair in the Spanker fields too , There was a Chair'o'plane's , roundabouts , slot machines , swing boats , and the catch penny , pick a duck , darts in the board , and air rifles . Small but a huge event in the otherwise dull village .The-travelling fair was an annual summer event. The fair was small, and the family lived in a converted single Decker Leyland bus converted to be a mobile home. The large Foden truck that hauled the Chair'o'plane's trailer had a massive diesel generator on its bed. This had a cover over to protect it from the rain. the generator thumped away in the background as the fair ran, the music from a barrel organ pounding away to drown the thump out .There was the sweet smell of candyfloss, toffee apples, and cheap prizes. The air was filled with the per-clang of the air rifle pellets as they pinged off the steel back plane. The target was never scored high, We as kids always thought that the barrels were bent to save dishing out prizes. We did not consider that the prizes were less than the entry money and there was no need to fiddle the guns, the battering that they took at the hands of the public was enough to distort the aim. The "Wins" were in the form of tickets that you collected to improve the prize value, Key rings ran into cuddly toys. Such a small fair, but so exciting, it left Nether Heage, went to Heage, and vanished for a whole year, into thin air. Was it spirited away I wondered, or just over the next hill?

The village lacked Scouts, which dad insisted would have done me the world of good, I should cycle to Sawmills and join theirs, was his suggestion. No school runs then, cycle, or walk was the choice .The trip to the scout hut at the bottom of the brickworks quarry road was a good couple of miles and would have been in the dark. I also knew no one from sawmills or Bull Bridge. Scouts therefore never appealed to me. The roads were unlit and not well surfaced. I didn't get my first bike until I was eleven either .Dad unfortunately was busy so like many things I was self taught at cycling , this meant falling off that bike with its 26" wheels and full size frame more often than usual .

The youth clubs were there though as was church and chapel groups. The Ambergate church youth club was on a Tuesday, It cost a sixpence to enter, a whole two and a half pence in "new" money. That was a small fortune out of the half a crown a week pocket money that I got, That equated to twelve and a half pence per week. On those Tuesdays, we played billiards on a one third-size table. we listened to nineteen fifties records, The Stones were too racy for youth club records .We would waste a further three-pence on chips and always asked for bits, The bits were the batter "bits" scooped from the frying fish adding a hot crispy flavour to the potato. The richer days enabled us to get a sixpenny mix. The mix was chips and bits with a large scoop of very mushy marrowfat peas ladled over the top. The mix needed a wooded flat fork to shovel it into your mouth. Chips were formed from huge potatoes then fried in a clarified beef dripping imparting an additional flavour to the potato. Why do memories taste better than the present I wonder? The other youth club was at Heage School but was for over elevens only That had similar entertainment, Table Tennis, Billiards, and girls dancing together to the music from a Dansette record player. These Dansettes were a heavy auto-changer that took ten 45-rpm singles, seven-inch discs piled on the deck. The music was mono, stereo from a radiogram was a noise for music buffs, and The classical appreciation society needed the stereo to get a full Hi-fidelity definition.

To select a disc you would go into College's music shop in Oxford Street , or Ripley Co-op's Department store at the bottom of Grosvenor Road , select the record you wanted , go into the soundproof booth , pick up the headphones and listen to your choice .The booths were full of school kids on a Saturday afternoon . You could at a serious "squash, "get three of you intimately into a booth. The records were over five shillings each .making them a fortnightly experience rather than a weekly one.

The entertainment for the school holidays was to take a walk in the woods. I would fish for minnows under the wireworks dam , you scooped your hands into the water and quickly grabbed the fish hauling it from the water and tipping in into a fresh Jam Jar half full of river water .I went without approval and without dad's consent would splash and swim in the river there . We would swim in the river too at Buckland Hollow; we always avoided the canal as the thick mud on the bottom was regarded as capable of trapping unsuspecting swimmers. The Wireworks employees would wade in the downstream water from the Dam in their lunch hours. The sun always shown in the summers. We had old cut down wellingtons to protect our feet from the stony river bottom. I played there with Phillip Griffin. He was not on Dad's approved person list either. Many of my peer group were on that list. Dad was quick to judge , eyes to close together , lived in the wrong street all automatic pronouncements of one's guilt .That guilt was a yellow card to my association with them . The yellow quickly became carmine if I was spotted near those banished ones . dad was NEVER wrong at spotting a wrong-un , well that's what he told me !.

. We avoided the Dam race as the water flowed too fast and was too dangerous.
Ambergate had much more variety than Nether Heage. We had the Canal, Rivers, and Railway, lime Kilns, Quarries, and many "not boring" activities in places that would now be

fenced against ingress of teenage youth. We corral our young on the corners of streets, and hear them bemoan the lack of facilities . In summer evenings we went train spotting at the station, running around the three huge platforms with an "Ian Allen "book of train numbers, underlined when you spotted the number on a passing engine or railcar .The station staff turned a blind eye to our harmless presence . We would ask thee drivers of the huge steam engines if we could climb into the cab, and would smell steam oil and coal, feel the heat, Is that were my adoration of Steam engines began. The remaining train spotters today are labelled as anoraks and geeks, scoffed at as a legacy hobby enjoyed by old men in woollen sleeveless cardigans, these enthusiasts able to expound on the timetable to a degree of boredom un-imaginable to all.

The Fishing for newts in the quarry ponds, all trespassing , all non destructive and all what filled in our non gaming time , what today's youth would regard as Chilin' would fill in the rest of this

We fished the canal for the red finned roach and the large predator the Pike, a fish that would unashamedly attack as you extracted the hook from its mouth. The Rivers Amber and Derwent held beautifully striped Perch and the wily Grayling. For bait, we bought bluebottle maggots, and flung the left over bait to the water, as leftovers in the ambient of the shed allowed the maggots to pupate, and form a huge swarm of flies, big blue flies.

I arrived there in November 1949 and stayed there to September 1966. There is a tie to the heart from the place your youth was expended. The secret places where the feathers of your wings dried as you stretched them whilst learning to fly into adult hood. We all survived Nether Heage. no child was lost to anything in those balmy days .The fields were broad and the scrapes close , the roads paths and hedgerows all shared lumps of my flesh and the scars live on to prove it .

We had trips out , often by train or one of Trent Motor Tractions , long distance buses , later replaced by Mike Horton or Albert Wilde's luxury coaches .The trains were steam hauled often pulled by a Jubilee class engine . Those engines named after strange unheard of countries of the Empire. Ambergate station standing at the triangular junction of the London Manchester, and the London Sheffield line, and allowing a Sheffield to Manchester connection the waiting rooms had coal fires in winter and a huge staff, The Station Master lived in a massive five bedroom house beyond the car park, the staff in the terrace of Railway cottages. The station was in a maroon and cream livery, leading to the old LMS railway, superseded by British Railways after World War II, These railways well over a hundred years old at my birth The Station the only six line triangular station in the world.

Huge coal and stone freight trains pulled vast loads through the platforms. The rail coal and stone trucks designated to type, named after sea creatures, there were Shark Brake vans Sea-cow and Sea-lion trucks a veritable ocean of names the express trains to Sheffield or on the Sheffield Derby line flew through the Toadmoor tunnel. The carriages resplendent in red and cream livery ,The blue and white scheme emergent twice daily on the Midland Pullman from St Pancreas to Manchester ,South in the morning , North at night . As a train-spotter we leaned over the bridge at Toadmoor or stood on the platforms. The station is still there but sports a single line to Matlock. The beautiful line cut through the Peak district beyond Rowsley now lying deserted made this one of the most picturesque lines in the world. The tunnels cut through the mountain side joining the fleet e slowly creeping in to Dales at Monsall and Millers Dale together. As you emerged from each long tunnel railway viaducts spanned the valley floor, giving a view along the rivers and, streams running as a dividing line along the centre of the valley floor.

We walked the Cromford Canal, running from Butterly to Cromford through the long lost Hag tunnel where as children we ran and practiced our echoes. The hemispherical arch of the tunnel was dripping with water that had caused a green slime on the tunnel inside giving an eerie atmosphere, as the surface water dripped through the sodden brickwork, splashing, and rippling the silence of the still canal water. The straight tunnel always meant that an end was in sight, the echo was great, as we shouted and whooped through the tunnel. . The road to the canal passing the derelict lime kilns. The canal ran to the Cromford mills where the barges collected stone for the iron works at Ironville. The lime being made at the Ambergate or Bullbridge kilns. The canal was use by horse drawn barges, the horse treading the towpath; I think the Canal was only about four feet deep, deep enough to drown in. Mum always used to worry but not without reason .Her uncle had died in a drowning accident some years before her birth

Copied from Ripley and Heanor News

DROWNING FATALITY NEAR RIPLEY

INQUEST AND VERDICT

On Saturday a sad case of drowning occurred in the Cromford Canal at Lower Hartshay, the victim being a young man about 18 years of age, named Israel Nally. It appears that the unfortunate young fellow had gone to the water for the purpose of bathing along with two or three others, and so met his death. He had previously resided with his parents at Heage, and was very much respected in that village by all who knew him.

The inquest was held at the George Inn on Monday afternoon, by Mr. W. H. Whiston, coroner, when the following gentlemen were on the jury: Messrs. Barker (foreman), Elliot, Cresswell, Machin, Webster, Gwynne, Wood, West, Burch, Cutts, Charville, and Tipper.

Francis Nally, who said he was a banks-man and lived at Heage, identified the body as that of his son. He said he was 18 years of age on the 28th of March last, and up to the time of his death worked at Ford's pit. He last saw him alive at dinner-time on Saturday, between one and two o' clock. He went out of the house, but did not say where he was going to. Apparently he was in good health when he left home. Witness did not know whether he could swim, as he had never heard him say. He first heard of his death about three o' clock on Saturday afternoon. It was the first time he had been to bathe this year, but other years he had gone regularly. By a juryman: He believed there were others with him. .Albert Sparham, who is a miner living at Heage, said he knew the deceased and last saw him on Saturday, when he asked him if he (witness) was going for a walk, and he replied yes. They walked together down the Cromford Canal, with the intention of bathing. Nally was the first to suggest they should go. Geo. Henry key was with them, and when they reached the canal deceased undressed and plunged into the water, whilst they remained on the bank for a short time. He (deceased) appeared to be knocking about, as he always did when bathing and they thought he was playing. He could not swim and no one else was in the water besides deceased. At length they saw his head fall back, and he (witness) called to him, but he did not speak. Witness stood on the opposite side to where the deceased was, but he went into the water to try to rescue him from his perilous position, although he himself could not swim. He reached him and just laid hold of his fingers, but they slipped out of his hand again. They both went down together, but witness reached the other side. Deceased never came up again, and he and Key ran for assistance. The water was deep there, and none of them could bottom it. They had bathed there before, but since then the canal had been cleaned out, and they did not know of it. There were some weeds, but he was clear of them. Jos. Booth helped witness to get him out. They could not see the body in the water when they got back. They did not perceive him strike against anything, and the body was not bruised when they got it out. They tried to restore him as best they could by working his arms. Witness could not say how long they did this, as he went to fetch a constable. The body would be about three or four feet from the towpath.

George Henry Key said he lived at Heage, and knew Israel Nally, and corroborated to a very considerable extent the evidence given by the previous witness, and said the first person they asked would not come and render assistance, and the second when told that a man was drowning replied that it had nothing whatever to do with him.

Joseph Booth, miner, said he lived at Hartshay, and when coming out of the house on Saturday afternoon he heard somebody say that someone was drowning. On being told where, he ran to the wharf. Richard Hill said, "He is in the water yet." He was not long in finding him though he experienced difficulty at first. Someone handed him a pole and he dragged it on the bottom of the canal until he felt something, which he thought was the body of the deceased, and it proved to be so. He at once got him out. The depth of the water would be about 5ft. 3in. When the water was high it would be nearly 5ft.9in. The water was very cold and he (witness) was some time before he could speak after he got in. It seemed to take his breath. A lot of dredging had been done there very recently. The canal was very deep just where the warm water ran into it. The position of the body was lengthways of the canal and about in the middle. The jury returned a verdict of "Accidentally drowned."

At the conclusion of the inquest, the Coroner called the last three witnesses into the room, and addressing them, said the jury wished him to thank them for the brave manner in which they had risked their own lives in trying to save that of their comrade, and he hoped that nothing would ever occur to make them regret what they had done that day, and trusted that should their services ever be called into requisition on a similar occasion, they would act as promptly as they had done in that case.
. The funeral of the deceased took place on Tuesday afternoon, and a good number the villagers were present
Friday June 22 1894

Ripley & Heanor News

My Great Uncle Israel Nally.

Chapter 8 . The Hackman Family

Mabel Hackman was born in number one Spanker Row Nether Heage on February 16 nineteen twenty, to John and Ellen Hackman. Mum followed Lillian , Edith ,Ethel ,George, Jack , Lucy , Elizabeth and Agnes , she in turn was followed by Charlie and Mary . None of them knew about their eldest brother Israel who had died as an infant. Grandma had a full team of eleven players.

Grandma was born Ellen Nally. The family claimed Irish Ancestry but their grandfather was London born, and lived his early life in Derby. Great Grandfather Francis Nally was actually born in Leeds in eighteen fifty five, his father Francis shown as being born in London in eighteen thirty six. Mother always ascertained that her Grandfather was Irish born and had lost his land in the partition of Ireland, but as Partition was incorporated in nineteen twenty one if seems inconceivable that the family fortune of the Irish farm in Killarney was lost by a man who died in eighteen ninety-five.

The searches of the census shows them living in a community of Irish workers in the St Aulkmund's district of Derby .The ancestry story may have some truth in it and at some time the trail from London may lead to Killarney as told, but yet it is unproven. . They were railway labourers, the original Navigators, that crowd of Irish Navvies who cut the canals and laid the railways. Mum was certain that her grandfather was one of the workers who cut the tunnel at Duffield leading onwards to Belper on the busy London –Manchester line. They certainly may have the Irish connection but it was probably before Eighteen thirty.

Another family legend with little substances committed to the bin along with many of the old unproven legends. Great granddad Nally had died in nineteen hundred and eight, Twelve years before mother's birth .He was one of four children, Mary, Emma and John who shared a dwelling in Derby's St. Aulkmund's district with his father Francis, bon in London Middlesex, in 1833, and his Mother Mary who hailed from Nottinghamshire. When Francis moved to Heage, he married Mary Leam .The marital home of the Nalleys was 167 Bakers Hill Heage. The Leam Family are our longest list of forebears. Mary lived in the row of houses behind the Black Boy Public House, where her father Charles was a Framework Knitter; He had married Hannah Newton also of Heage. His father Thomas another Heage resident, married to Mary Moore, again from Heage. Thomas was though however the son of Abijah (1751-xxxx) of Fritchley , Abijah was the son of Abijah (1726 – 1810) married to Mary Shore of Fritchley , They had moved a little as his father William was from Crich , he was William ,son of William and Mary Flickson of Crich . Abijah (1751) had married Martha Crich .It is Martha's family who lead us back to the Doomsday book. Her family is the longest line, and she was from Pentrich.

The Irish connection though much lauded by mother had always a credible thread to it; in the nineteen seventies, a

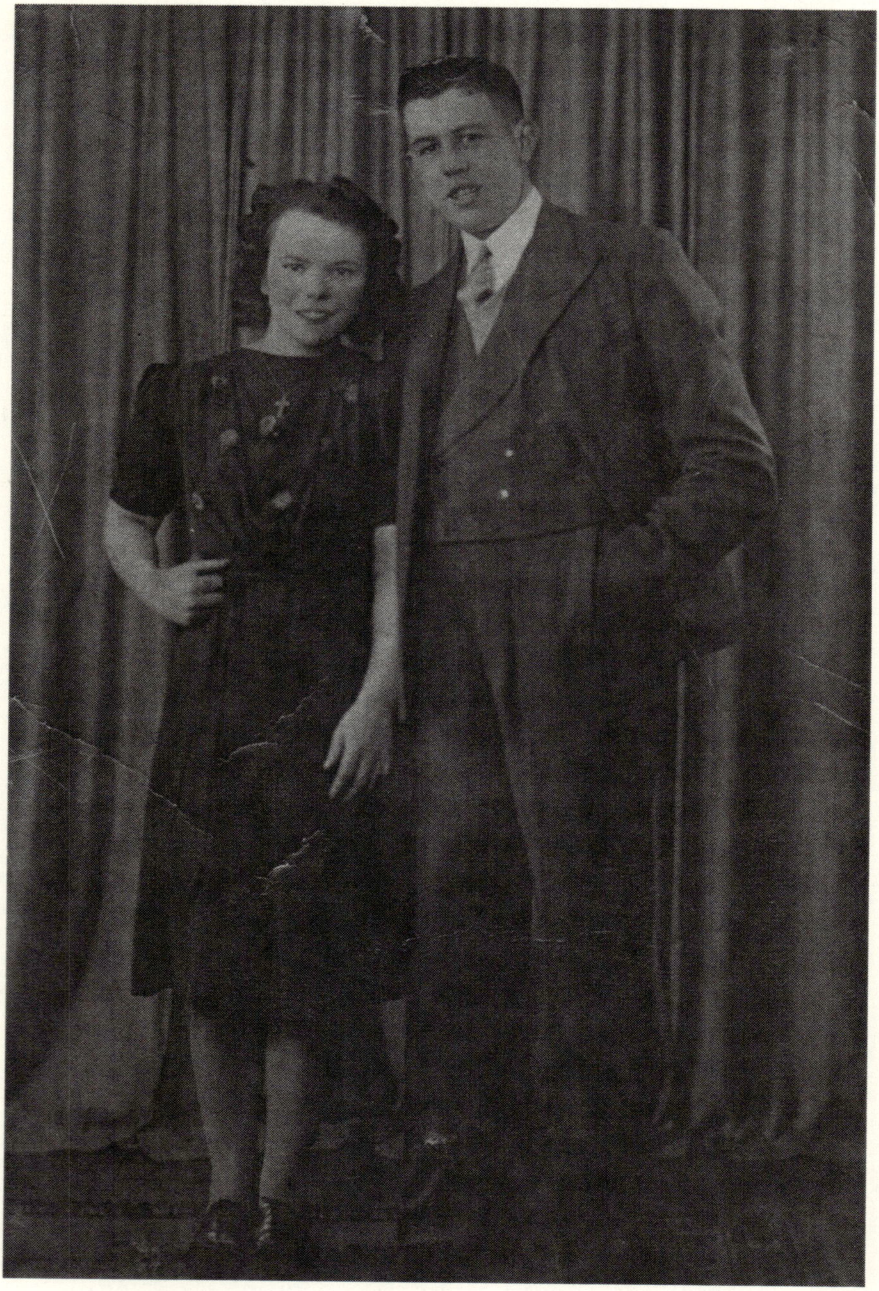

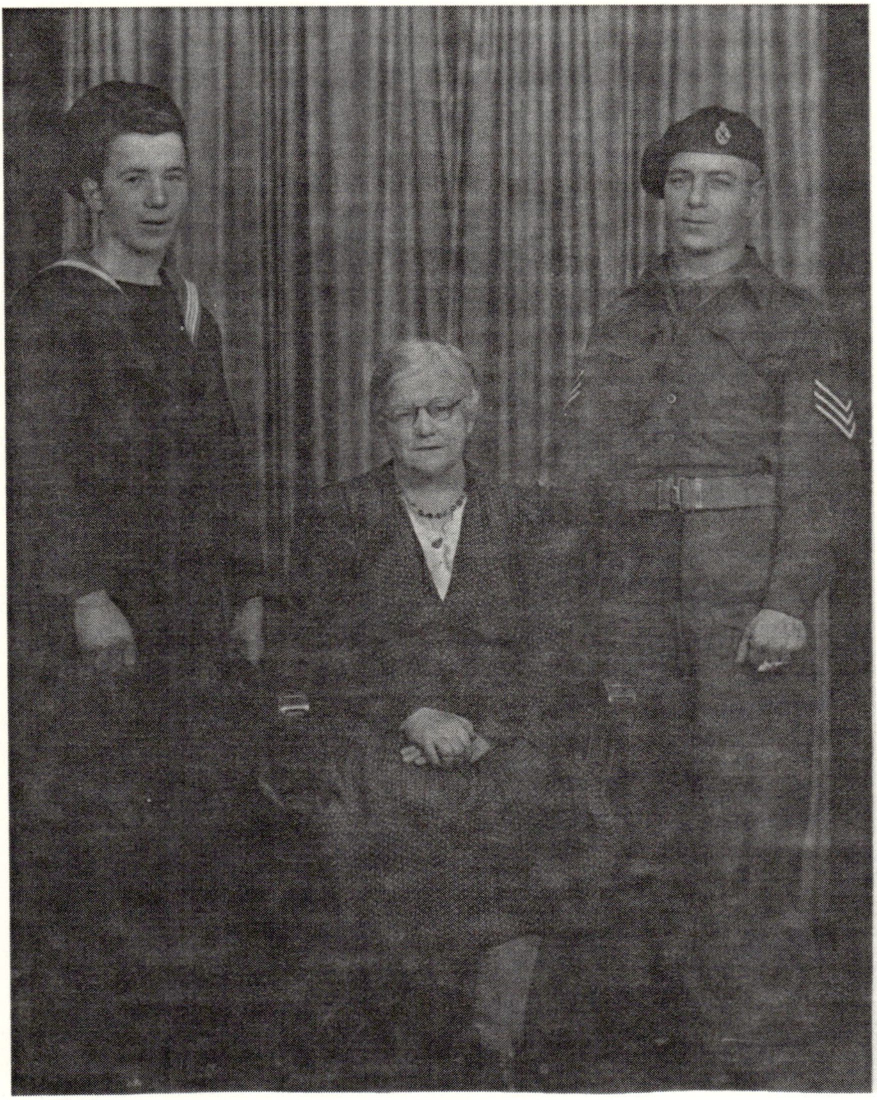

catholic priest who had been a favourite of Grandma Hackman visited the parents one Saturday, and enjoyed their Hospitality. He was called Fr O'Flaherty. He was lodging with a nunnery at Nottingham, and dad was to return him there by car. It was in the days of his Riley one point five , Hydrolastic , variant of the Austin eleven hundred , , so somewhere around nineteen sixty nine to nineteen seventy four . . Why a catholic priest had been so favoured, I can only speculate. The family were certainly Methodist rather than Catholic, of either Roman or English persuasion .Grandma also had a surprisingly good relationship with the eccentric Dr Ryan. The good doctor would stride in unannounced on a Sunday and cut himself a slice off the family joint. That was only something that a true friend would have got away with without a fight. This Irish connection is therefore going to niggle away until I eventually resolve it.

Martha's father Adam had moved there from his birthplace in Ashover where his father William (1678) was born the son of Adam (1642) the son of William (1600) of Clipstone , he was the son of Ralph of Ashover . Interestingly the son of Sir William Crich of Ashover was the son of Sir Ralph, who in turn was the son of Sir John who was born in fifteen sixteen. In five hundred years, my mother's family did not migrate more than twenty miles. I know that destroying the traditional tale of the Irish farmers , turned miners and navigators , the fortune robbed because they were unable to turn a sod of their Irish lands would have been a sour taste to her , there was a certain degree of romance about the Irish link . Having put a degree of doubt into the exactness of the Irish forebears , I have no doubt that beyond mothers own Grandfather , the Londoner , that the name Nally has Irish connotations and it may just be a generation further away that links us to the Emerald Isle . Still that is the story she had lived, but to find a sixteenth century baronetcy would have more than compensated. She would have strutted as her newly found aristocracy surged through her. Chest out head held back for all to see, Aristocracy, that is where we come from Les, not Staffordshire Miners .She would have relished those long gone lords of the manor , with as much pride as could be mustered . Probably Cornelius Crich has had a lot of explaining to do in his eternity as to how the family fortune was flittered away.

The Hackman family not Germany as told, Mother thought it was a corruption of Eichmann, wrong again! However, from Godlaming in Surrey was not as exotic as a refugee background, but facts never seem to match legends. The Hackman family mother believed were Jewish and had escaped some eastern European persecution. The name was early English a corruption of a hack man, a woodcutter.

Ellen Nally my grandmother married John Hackman, born in Derby, twelve years older than she was .He was the son of George, born in Godlaming in eighteen forty seven, and when the whole family came to Derby from their Farncombe home, George married a local Derby girl Harriet Merrin. Harriet was the Daughter of John, son of William (1790) son of George (1773) son of John (1736) son of William (1713) son of Francis (1683) Son of Francis (1658) all of Derby. For ten generations we have our history established in Derby town .It is only in recent memory that despite its Cathedral, Derby achieved its proud status as a City

George Hackman's father Josiah was born in Church Street Godlaming one of the eight children of George (1787) also of Godlaming. The tracing of the Hackman family all seems to return to this root set in rural Surrey .There appears to be a core of the family left in Farncombe, whilst George migrated to Derbyshire, from those roots a branch re-divided off and headed towards Cardiff.

Mabel was here from 1920 until 1994, the last few of her seventy-three years fraught with illness. The crippling Arthritis she had , had taken its toll of her and her hands twisted and deforming as the arthritic muscles pulled on them . We had been to visit shortly before and mum had a severe chest infection, she though unwisely, dispensed with the need for doctors. On our way home, I rang her GP a Dr. Taylor and explained that mum was not well. When I got home, the phone was ringing furiously with one angry woman who did not need a doctor and knew I had called him. Her grounds for the assumption was that my Father would not Dare! She had been given a strong anti-biotic to rid herself of the infection .A bronchial attack in this degree was weakening her and the persistent cough lingered as a permanent feature of her .Mother in her own indomitable way refused to stop smoking, which I believe was contributory to the chest infection and to weakening her. She went on to the heart attack and was rushed , blue lights flashing, sirens blaring in an emergency ambulance attended by the paramedics to the specialist heart unit at Derbyshire Royal Infirmary . After she was stabilised and settled she was given the seventy five milligram low dose aspirin the dispensing Doctor had totally missed the rare but possible reaction with the powerful anti arthritis drug, that was originally, used as a chemotherapy, Methatrexate. The combination of these drugs could start mini strokes and fitting which bedevilled Mum in her last days.

We were caravanning at the time and offered to drive up. Dad put us off as Mum was in the best hands and there was little to do, as she was stable. We were at Bashley Park caravan site, and our relatively rare mobile phone with its metre long aerial, and its two-kilogramme battery caused more than a few questions as to what it was. It looked more like a military transmitter than the mobiles we are all so familiar with nowadays.

Mum's condition was spiralling downwards slowly and despite all best efforts, she ended up in the City Hospital. Stable once more she transferred to Babington. This was a feared place to locals as it was in family memory Belper Workhouse. To end up there was akin to the destitute arriving at the poorhouse, so it was not going to be mums best-chosen option. We tried to visit about every fifth week but on more than one occasion were greeted by mother , not wanting any fuss , with why do you keep visiting , I'm alright . Has anybody decided to send for you? Because I am not going anywhere yet and I know how busy you and Barbara are. We were not happy though with the way Babington treated patients though. A woman next to mum had swollen legs with a variety of Lymphodema that more commonly known as Elephantitis. Her bandaged legs were oozing Lymph fluid that congealed and stuck the bandages to her skin. The treatment she received was rough and to the untrained uncaring eye inhuman, to the trained professional this was the best way to do a difficult task. We were returning home one Sunday morning and uncharacteristically called in to see mum outside visiting hours. The nurses were barracking her about not eating her breakfast in a condescending way, after all when you are, in pain and infirm, you do not want to treatment like a naughty child. The nurse was saying," now be a good girl Mabel and stop these silly tantrums." Mum knew we were on our way to see her and wanted to dispense with the difficulty of Breakfast, her mouth was sluggish and eating difficult. She was such a proud woman; she did not want us to see her dribbling food. I was aghast at this, but Barbara the always-quiet one of us assailed the Nurse," don't you dare talk to my mother–in–law like that, she does not have tantrums and deserves respect. "Wow! The red headed temper, slow to appear but loud and long when it did was well on show, Barbara and I was disgusted at such treatment. I spent some time delving through the Pharmacopeia and traced the aspirin and Methatrexate link; I gave several hundred pages of the research, duly photocopied to dad, and told him he had good grounds for an action. All the lawyers in the world cannot make your mother better though, can they? Was his reaction, but he passed the research to the nurses to show the negligence was NHS based .to. One nurse a large West Indian Lady was particularly nice to mum and Dad despite his normal prejudice knew of her, her husband had died whilst working at Glow-Worm and Dad asked her if she was happy with the excellent death in service benefit. She knew nothing of it her late husband's children from his first marriage had claimed it and hidden it from her.

It was then I saw the pure devotion that love brings as Dad spent his time at her bedside missing neither a morning nor a bedtime. He showed a love and devotion that left the promises of the marriage vows a pale shadow.

As children, the family moved to Rock House, 22 Brook Street, Nether Heage, Adjoining the house occupied by my mother's sister Elizabeth. Rock house was huge in comparison to Spanker Row and was reputed to be a former public House. The layout was akin to old public houses that I remember as a child so that story may be a true one. Uncle Charlie filled in the cellar under the kitchen before my time. There was a dual aspect, and a central corridor led from the front door. I never in my lifetime ever saw that door opened. The front yard had a low-lying wall with metal squares spaced every six inches; these were testimony to the wrought iron railings that surrounded this tiny patch sacrificed to the war effort. All the scrap iron could build tanks and battleships with no need to import iron ore and risk the Merchant Navy, out there fighting to maintain the supply chain, against the German efforts to sink them. Each side there was a large room. Uncle Charlie and Aunty Kit had the left hand one as their sitting room, and the right one was the sanctum of the front room. Weddings Christmas, funerals were the only time the door opened, except for the ritual weekly dusting. An upright piano stood next to the door and a large three piece filled the room .At the rear, the corridor led into the living room, here the dining table stood next to old leather covered Chaise Longue the leather cracked and worn as proof of age .A huge circular EKO radio stood on the table and crackled away constantly. Grandma's chair leaned against the outer wall next to the ever-blazing coal fire right next to the window, so she could see who was approaching the door. The ledger and brace door leading upstairs was immediately next to the back door and at right angles to it. This staircase spiralled up to the bedrooms.

Alongside the stairway lay, a huge kitchen dominated by a vast Belfast pattern stone sink with an ample sized wooden drainer each side, held prominent position under the window. The stove was grey enamelled New World model number 1. It certainly could have been a public house but I only remember the Spanker and Mrs Kneebone's Off-Licence as the village alcohol. Mrs Kneebone dispensed Draught beer into your own screw top bottle that she sealed with a paper sticker so you could not tamper with the contents.

Grandma's eleven children were down to eight when I appeared. Israel was the oldest although had not survived childbirth and his first few days .Jack was lost to mining and Effie to fire.

Lilly was the next, and she was married to Alfred Dennis, and had at least one child who I believe called John. They lived in Alfreton. Aunty Lilly had one son born out of wedlock; he was taken in and bought up by Grandma Hackman. Lilly was much older and we used to visit during the school holidays. She lived on the South Normanton Road from Alfreton, towards what is now Alfreton Parkway Station. We never stayed long, as the changes of bus took a short distance a long time to complete. We never seemed to integrate with the Dennis family at all .We would invariably visit during the Pit Weeks Holiday , when Derbyshire miners took off to the Miners Holiday Camp at Skegness , on a pit by pit basis , over the School holiday period . Therefore, your holiday week meant that you enjoyed an existence trapped with your workmates and neighbours. Alfreton pit was near Aunty Lilly's house, and the field would be full of Pit ponies taking two weeks, munching lush grass and racing around a huge paddock. Their day job suspended whilst all the men were communally bonding with their own at "bracing" Skegness. The posters implying that the sea air contained refreshing Ozone. Why would anyone want to breath Ozone, to the best belief I have it is toxic

Uncle Jack was married to Phoebe, Aunty Phoebe named Blanche but adopted her second name, and her maiden name was Carter. They had three children; Maureen, Terry, and Janet, .They all live in Belper. Uncle Jack injured and lost his life in a roof fall at Denby colliery in the winter of 1947. The year is well remembered because of the freezing cold and the deep snow .The weather had impeded the progress of the ambulance too .Uncle Mac had been working next to him at the time of the fall. I know very little of Jack but at the family gatherings Aunty Phoebe and Maureen usually represented their family. Aunty Phoebe, a spirit medium, delving into areas where I keep clears of .Did she do this to keep in touch with her lost partner, I can only guess. When her son Terry was in the Navy, she was invoking spirit assistance to help him pass his Killick's exam, and had managed to summon a dead sailor to provide the answers. I was about eight when that revelation hit the air, and it made me more than a little scarred of a woman who could summon up dead people and converse with them.

    Edith was married to Bill Brown, he was not well liked by the family, I believe he could be quite cruel to Aunty Edie; she had had two children but lost both shortly after their birth. They originally lived in Spanker Terrace a row of houses that ran perpendicular to the Spanker. There were three terraced cottages, long overdue for demolition; there was a single downstairs room .This living room was complete with a cast Iron range on the far wall that supplied the water and the cooking facilities. Off this was a small pantry to the side of the fireplace. .The stairs were opposite the door and led to a solitary upper bedroom. The small living room filled like an archetypal Victorian house, an upright piano, a stuffed brown trout in a glass case, the settee covered in old blankets. The stove had a kettle, large black soot stained iron device sat on the trivet .outside was a large home built garden seat in a rose bower, and the garden allocated to the three houses was solely in Bill's tenure. There was a huge tarred garage at the bottom of the garden, this doubled as shed and workshop. The shed was the storage area for the Norton Navigator 88, 350cc Twin cylinder motorbike. The garden not as well kept as Dad's one, Bill grew flowers and a whole bed of a flower that called the everlasting daisy. The vegetable plot was a little unkempt. These houses were to be demolished in the mid nineteen fifties because of the condition , and Bill and Edie bought a house at the Guide Post , next door to a Mrs Alsop who had great pretentions of a wealthy family that was little in evident . The move was done on Albert Wheatley's coal lorry, reversing in dad broke a side mirror, and bore a long-term grudge as the ten-shilling replacement was from his pocket and not Bill's. Their dog Jackie performed jumps and tricks to order. Aunty Edith died in nineteen sixty-six after a short illness and a convalescence at Etwall Hospital. Etwall league of friends must have impressed Bill, because, despite working hard on the potential of an inheritance, by doing a daily meal on wheels service Aunty Lizzie, cried that she felt overlooked and left a small £500 bequest, whilst the house went to the Hospital. It never really bothered Mum she never complained or looked to inheritances, but Aunty Lizzie was less than best pleased. Nice one Bill, you were full of surprises even after death, you still kicked the Hackman family that had spent a lifetime criticising you. Bill busied himself in his retirement by building concrete windmills , and wooden ornaments in the shed , heated summer and winter by a small pot bellied stove that busily consumed the off cuts of timber from his carving and toy-making . Bill related to the Stone Family in Heage by marriage. His sister Mary had been married to Joe Stone but after Mary's early death from cancer in the mid nineteen fifties Joe and the four Children, Arthur, Alan & Mary, the twins, and Phillip, moved into the Stone's family house. This is the first house on School lane at Heage. The conditions so cramped, as they moved from a more spacious dwelling on Bentfield Avenue as the solitary road of council houses in the village. Aunty Edie and Bill spoiled the young Phillip a little and just after the loss of his Mum, they bought him the top of the range pedal car, a Rolls Royce Silver Cloud, in a deep Maroon colour, I had never seen that level of quality in a toy, totally completed inclusive of its own transistor radio.

Ethel was a memory in the family and she had spent her life in service in Huddersfield but a tragic accident in 1932 curtailed her life and she burned to death, she lays under a huge Yew tree in Heage Church yard and Mum used to take flowers to her grave on a regular basis. It was a thought that laid deep in mind as each visit caused a reminder of the sister who burned to death. She was Aunt Effie who had unexplainably died by fire, the searched of coroners reports will one day give us the detail about the hereto unknown Ethel. Nobody ever explained the facts they gave you as a child , where why and when were immaterial , you didn't need to know .You therefore received the horrific unassailable fact " burned to death " that should keep you away from the fire . I must have been a nervous child, all these undisputed facts with no explanation ever given. The negativity only becomes evident in your dotage, the words do not featured large.

George the third son, who I recognised wrongly as the eldest had settled in Kent during the war and married Enid Seal from Penshurst. They had two sons John and Brian .John has two children Wayne and Susanne he lost his wife Janice in 1994. Wayne has a position with the Church of England he is working as a curate in South Devon.

George bought an ex Council House in Penzhurst village and their house was a regular holiday venue for other members of the family we visited Mum and Dad there on a couple of occasions. Uncle George had a retirement home-working job painting little Subuteo figures with small brushes and enamel paint. He did not like Aunty Enid smoking so she sneaked outside to enjoy her cigarettes with Mum. George had been a crane driver for a portable building company in Kent and if passing by Nether Heage a huge ex army Cole's crane suddenly appeared outside Grandma's house. Uncle George was also the first family member with a car and in the nineteen fifties would drive north to pay a visit to his mother. The presence of transport equalled a day out too. We would drive the back lanes of Crich and visit the Stand, Matlock, and the outlying Matlock Bath. Their garden was a super fertile one and the slightly warmer Kentish weather gave better growing conditions. The large Yucca plants that spear visitors to my door came from Uncle George's garden. We as a family visited there twice when my parents and the present Aunty were there. I took the children to Penshurst place, and surprised mum by calling in. We took the meandering route home via the Ashdown Forest and the A272 through all the small villages emerging north of Petersfield .Their visit coincided with our Christmas pilgrimage home to on at least one occasion.

Lucy was late marrying; she wed Samuel Pym a fellow Trent Motor Traction Bus Conductor in the mid nineteen fifties. Mum and Dad bought a beautiful porcelain coffee set in black outside, white inner with a gold leafed edge. Aunty Lucy had always promised that set to Kerry, from a young age, but like many family heirlooms it was engulfed by secrecy and deception when its time came. Aunty Lucy was a great person to be with .During school holidays when Mum took up a job at the Hospital on Crich Lane, Aunty Lucy who took me on the trips to Derby and Nottingham. Trips with Aunty Lucy were more adventurous than the trips that we took around dress shops when June was with us. When we went to Nottingham, there was always a Knickerbockers Glory in the Lyons cafe next to the huge slab square in Nottingham's Centre. The Knickerbockers Glory was the most expensive thing on the Lyons menu. It was in a tall glass with strawberries , ice cream , juice , whipped cream , correctly whipped from cream as opposed to the modern spray can equivalent .I think it was nearly five shillings the modern 25p but it would exceed five pounds today . Aunty Lucy would tour china shops, museums and the castle, never the mundane fashion houses for her. When explaining the Derby Crown ranges that she so much adored she would make objects come alive, she had learned an appreciation of fine things during a time spent in service at Butterly Hall in her youth. The alternative to this was the at least twice year trip to Derby for shopping. We could end up with June coming too and I think I knew every dress shop in the midlands, too well. Derby had its own charm though and we would be there the whole day. The indoor market hall was split into a pet area selling puppies , rabbits etc , a fish market , a poultry market , and a huge market hall , with , butchers , Haberdashers , bookstalls just about everything you could think of and cafes . The acrid smells of the animals and the fish filled the air chickens, puppies in cages, rabbits reared as meat as well as pets. Fishmongers shared a hall, the smell of sea and fish filling the air. The mountains of meat on the open butchery stalls dispensed to long queues of regular customers. Our next stop would be the huge Co-op, Midland Drapery, Ranbys, and a rotation about the city centre. We would always go to the main open market, adjacent to the Bus Station with huge vegetable stalls , a man selling china dinner services in huge wicker baskets , electrical stalls , clothing , shoes , bakery , sweets , every conceivable thing known to man was on that market , and at its rear a gateway to "Derwent Gardens " with an ornamental formal fishpond and access to the river . The smaller Cockpit Hill market had all manner of discounted items too and a slightly more risqué atmosphere too, and most exciting to any small boy a joke shop. At Christmas I would visit Santa in at least three shops. The Co-op always had a massive display, with an elaborate grotto. I think the Midland Drapery had a similar set up. We always had to get tomato sausages and a pork pie from Birds Bakery, coffee at the Kardhoma coffee house and lunch at Ranbys. The shopping for dresses was endless. Life on these trips revolved about the timetable for the buses home. We had to get the Belper Bus that connected with a Heage Bus so we didn't have long waits. Aunty Lucy always caught these buses at the Belper Mill, the rest at the front of the Bus Station .In Derby the main town square opposite the drill hall was the set down point, then walking down Sadlergate, through the Arcade the shopping began. Aunty Lucy always explained things and could make a trip really interesting with her wide ranging general Knowledge. The appreciation of the finer things was noticeable in her Edward Street house in Belper that had been the Pym family home. The walls were bedecked with oil paintings and sketches suspended from the picture rails that surrounded the high walls in each room. The top of the stairs had a five-foot high painting of Moses saved from the Bull-rushes. Next to the painting was an ornate stand with an aspidistra. The bathroom decorated in Black and white and was at the top of the stairs. Aunty Lucy tripped with us to Blackpool in nineteen eighty to see the illuminations. the heavens opened but as we had walked the three miles to Bishpam from the hotel , the foulness of the weather condemned us to a similar return journey again on foot , soaked we sat in the hotel and Aunty Lucy took an antidote to cold and damp in the form of a medicinal Brandy . Kerry peeled off her new jeans to reveal denim blue legs, Robert took to the hot bath, and the family found the side of Blackpool I disliked, the foul weather in illuminations weeks. To Alton Towers too despite her one functional lung and medical problems, she leapt to the rides, walked for miles and joined in everything that she wanted. After a trip to Alton Towers we were chided by Frank for letting her go on the river ride , little did he know it was her demands that overruled our concerns .Sam was a man born to a different era , his family were financially more secure than the Hackman's and the coveted gold jewellery and the finer things of life . After he passed his car test he bought a Riley 1.5 in Rose Taupe , 815 ACH became ours after his death and despite its less than 15,000 miles served as our family car for many years . We ceded the old Riley to a Riley enthusiast who was set on rebuilding it to a "as new" condition .Aunty Lucy was a great preserver, she pickled fresh eggs in an isinglass solution because the price fluctuated summer and winter dependant on supply. She made a fantastic Lemon curd too with fresh eggs, butter, and fresh lemons. There is no manufactured curd to match the homemade concoction supplied on our visits. Aunty Lucy produced it from huge volumes of fresh Eggs, butter, and Lemons .She save jars of all sizes and preserved fruit as jam, onions, all manner of things. Kerry always managed to get one of those tiny individual jars of curd for her own pleasure. When we descended on the ancestral cottage, we overwhelmed it so had to indulge in the dispersal of the children. Alison was a natural target for Aunty Lizzie, and Robert set off to Belper. Aunty Lucy had a Black and White television with poor reception, but she discarded Roberts's usual attention and introduced him to rummy for pennies. She was a skilful loser too .I can fully understand Robert's pleasure at stopping with Aunty Lucy she was a wonderful woman who put effort in to amusing children. It was sad when she began the onset of Alzheimer's in her eighties. She strangely, denied the required medical aid, Aricept, or the other newly discovered drugs, that would help her so much. There was some reluctance to involve the doctor and answers at best, were sketchy, and evasive, Barbara and I were given the impression that the doctor was showing no interest, When the truth evolved had her carers neglected her, and the family ignored her distress. The explanation was only evident when after Dad's death, the ink drying on Aunty Lucy's will codicil as we attended Markeaton Crematorium, I had enquired the day before Dad's funeral as to the possibility of Aunty Lucy joining the cortège. I was told most certainly , fact that she did not understand Les's death, so strange that she managed the day before his cremation to alter her will at the solicitors. To fail to understand, your brother-in-law has died, but to understand the word codicil is an amazing thought. The attempts to deceive little bother me as I know the Lord Judges all on the last day, and trust that the Lord God treats me fair on my misgivings. Moreover, forgive any deception against me, but leave to the Lord Almighty the final judgement of the deceivers who stay unrepentant.

    I always felt that as mum worked hard for the Women's section Ambergate British Legion, presided over the Ladies class at the chapel, devoted her time to helping others. Mum was a creative cook to, she though had dad to contend with who had very set feelings when it came to his meals. All meat to be very well done, the external appearance carbonised, and he then preferred the outer slices of this to ensure he had no raw parts. We never had pork, as pork rather foolishly disagreed with him. The tripe and other delicacies never did though. He did have a taste for the fried though .The huge onions , home grown , but never quite hardy enough to store throughout the winter , were sliced , fried in dripping from the Sunday beef joint , then as they browned . As they bubbled away, he would stir in grated Cheddar cheese. This was all fried together until the fat from the cheese started to separate and the cheese formed a crust at the edges calories, forget it, saturated fat, forget it, and salt, yes he added plenty. Bread similarly fried in the home rendered dripping, but on one side. The Cheese and onion then with the additional fat from the frying poured onto the bread. Salt was an absolute necessity, he had it drummed into him how essential a good salt intake was whilst a marine in the Far East. The advice never rescinded so remained despite the return to normal ambient temperatures in nineteen forty six.

 The family did some strange things though to save money, we shared a Derby Evening Telegraph with the Cuttel family from Grandma's death .Each weekend there was reconciliation about papers and eggs and bread money accounted for to the penny each Saturday. After the weekly shopping Aunty Lizzie would appear for her Saturday coffee 1/2 milk 1/2 water, boiled in an ancient aluminium milk pan with a stainless steel disc bobbing away to prevent boiling over. We lived with this weekly dividing painfully as we delivered the evening paper through rain and snow without thanks, a deeper bitterness that ran a full course embedded in the parental hopelessness of carrying on Grandmas legacy.

 Aunty Lizzie was next, married to Hector MacDonald Cuttel, with the one daughter June.

 After Uncle Charlie and Aunty Kit left, the family pile, sold on to the Taylor family who had a disabled daughter Ann. Ann was an accomplished artist and her father Stan marketed her pen and ink drawings as Christmas cards. Aunty Lizzie and Uncle Mac fell into dispute with the Taylors and remained in a state of animosity for over forty years.

Uncle Mac had an air of fragility that seemed to have happened after the roof fall of 1947. He had spent years sick, unable to work .He, whilst sick laboured for the nearby farm mucking out pigs and cattle, the Nicholls exceeded the generosity of Derbyshire farmers all by paying for the hard labour with duck eggs and goat milk.

June and Ron were divorced. .Gary after an expensive and elaborate wedding and four children split from Roslyn Ashley, his wife the notorious ex model.

Aunty Agnes was the next in order; she was first married to Leslie Walker of Parkside Heage. She started her married life with her mother-in-law, Mrs Martha Walker, a widow who had lost her husband in the First World War.

Leslie Walker

4976303, 1/5th Bn., Sherwood Foresters (Notts and Derby Regiment)
who died age 29
on 12 September 1944
Son of Charles and Martha Ann Walker; husband of Agnes Walker, of Heage, Derbyshire.
Remembered with honour
SINGAPORE MEMORIAL

Commemorated in perpetuity by
the Commonwealth War Graves Commission

She still cooked over the coals of the fire as opposed to using the pristine electric cooker that stood proudly in the corner next to the sink. The huge well laid out garden had a rear gate that led onto Heage recreation ground. I remember neat lines of redcurrants, white currents, and blackcurrants sweet and juicy as they ripened. Aunty Agnes lost Les during the war; He, killed by an American attack on the Japanese Hospital Ship that he imprisoned him .The Americans apparently disbelieved the huge red crosses signifying the ships status and sent the British prisoners to the bottom of the sea off Singapore . Mrs Walker proudly displayed her Husband's and son's war record and medals above her fireplace. We visited there for many years on a Wednesday night for tea. We walked and dad called later in the coal lorry, we went to collect Nielsen's brand Neapolitan ice cream from the store by the Black Boy .Mrs Walker also accompanied grandma on many outings as company. She was our Boxing Day centre, always there for tea. Aunty Agnes had an old-fashioned cocktail cabinet with a range of accessories that always fascinated.

Aunty Agnes remarried Dennis Brentnall a farmer from Selston, several years her junior, she produced her first child Graham just before Grandma's death. It was easy to understand why Graham was a delight to grandma's ears; she was seeing her widowed daughter enter a period of happiness. Aunty Agnes moved to a house ruled by another Mother–in-law, and became a busy farmer's wife. The new role as wife mother and chicken keeper was a far distance from the chic of the offices at Brettles hosiery factory. After Dennis Mother died, they built a new farmhouse in Underwood and set up the farm there. The old farm sold to the riches of a builder, and houses sprouted where sheep grazed. It was a good cycling journey in my teens to visit Aunty Agnes. My journey was via Condor Park and the old Toll Road that was a remnant of the Butterly family's fortune. The route was through Heage and Ripley along Nottingham road through both sections of the toll road, under the viaducts at Ironville and over the hills. It was a good twelve miles, but seemed to be a fleeting moment on a warm summer day. There was a small shop at Ironville at the coach roads end , on those far off days I would buy an ice cream and overlook the lake there that had been part of the canal feeder in days gone by . The ice cream choice was always limited to either the Lyons Orange Maid, or a Strawberry Mivvi, where strawberry ice, coated vanilla ice cream on a stick. Dennis permanently listed in that mental black book of failures that dad stored. During in his time at Granwood dad secured some Terrazzo tiles cut to shape for the toilet of the new farmhouse   , when asked what he desired as payment, the requested fertilizer never appeared, as the new stack tightly sheeted and not opened. That mental store recording firmly each debt; never were written off or redeemed. When I first set off to South Shields , dad produced a war time photograph ," that's "Tommo" Thompson" , he declared ," if you ever see him in county Durham I lent him ten shillings to get home from the troopship , as he had lost his money playing cards , and he hasn't paid it back yet ." duly instructed Mr Thompson never did appear

Dennis's dairy herd went at the height of Quota sales, a well-chosen time, and he concentrated the farm-fattening bull calves from local dairymen, as well as winter wheat and a few eggs. There was a butcher at Selston who was doing, a wholesale meat trade, when dad was at Granwood Floors, he would go to Ralphs Butcher on a Wednesday evening to collect the family meat. Ralph often had Dennis's cattle on sale. Dad loved Ralph's market approach, and never failed to return with some benefit or other, an ox-tail, or cow's cheek or other delights. He was partial too to home cured Ox-Tongue, and a large pottery dish, known as a pantion, would have a tongue laying in a brine solution, ready to be cooked, a weight added, o form the shape into shape, and then thickly sliced for tea. Barbara had a passion against this meat, and could never face the principle of having to eat a tongue.

Anthony soon joined Graham and both turned away from farming working in the local textile industry. In those last years of Mrs Walker's life, she would be with us on the Boxing Day trip, as we took off to visit Aunty Agnes and Uncle Dennis. Because of the numbers involved, Dad charted Albert Wilde's mini bus, Albert though one Boxing night totally forgot to collect us and late in the evening despite having ample drink dad became the chauffer and two trips in the farm van later we were all home, at a very late hour. Aunty Agnes was an extremely poor traveller, but she braved the nausea to be at our wedding, and shortly before her death, after a heart attack, she had said how all the years farming without a holiday, left her wanting to visit our house. Barbara welcomed that and it made her feels special, singled out as a destination for Aunty Agnes's first Holiday for thirty years. Aunty Agnes was also the solitary redhead in the family and to her siblings was "Gin", to denote her hair colour. Never a word Barbara would agree with.

Mum came next in the line tenth child of the twelve. She was the shortest of the brood, and shared a facial similarity with the majority, a beaming roundness. She followed the pattern of Ridgeway, and then Heage schools, then work. . Aunty Lucy had been clever enough to pass her eleven plus but the cost of the uniform prohibited her going. . As war broke out mum as a late teenager was a bus conductress at the Trent Garage in Belper, and started her day with a four AM walk over Crich Lane in total darkness .The buses collecting the workers being on the road before five, workers starting many factories in the dark in the early hours. Private cars were unheard of luxuries that were almost nonexistent.

She married dad on July 31 nineteen forty-three, and remained living in her mother's house at twenty-two, Brook Street, Nether Heage. When dad returned from Singapore, they moved into the cottage at forty-three, The Brook. In all mothers life she never moved more than five hundred yards from her birthplace. She worked in the elastic factory after the war in the evenings catching a bus to Ripley and walking along Derby Road to the gloomy factory .This on dad's tiny wages needed to be a better-paid position. She applied for a cook's job at Ridgeway Hospital. She felt a little inadequate, and feeling that her skills needed improvement, so took cooking night classes at Heage Secondary Modern School on a Wednesday night. This became a night to stay up late and enjoy a fresh hot supper, bought home after the class. We enjoyed beef olives, delicacies that we had never seen before too. One night she had to do Chicken Maryland, chicken was an expensive meat. As a small child, a "ten shilling note" gripped tightly in the hand I walked to, Fred Gadsby's farm. This proved the source of a fresh chicken. Money handed over he soon returned with a squawking bird and wrung its neck swiftly, the bird was despatched and Aunty Edie demolished the plumage and ripped out the innards and gave me the oven ready variety in return. Mum bird in hand set off to her class, frying the bird in its crumb coat, and we sat expectantly awaiting our first taste of Southern fried Chicken, as Chicken Maryland. Fred must have selected the bird because it had only a short life left, on the grounds of old age, the resultant supper; perfect in every way was un-chewable due to the stringy tough inedible bird. We enjoyed exotic Beef Olives and whole manner of different fare, as the lessons progressed. Mum then became the head cook for Ridgeway Hospital before taking an umbrage at some management practices carried on by Mr & Mrs Smith who were the administrator and Matron of the establishment . Mum, as Barbara had very strong principles of things being totally above board, and honest. The occupants were men, some with Down's syndrome, and some with behavioural problems. I suspect that many young men with Asperger's syndrome, and Tourette's, all the varieties of Autism, had been flung into places like Ridgeway to hide them from the nice families that felt so unfortunate to have them. Certainly, there seemed little family contact once the gates of Ridgeway closed behind them. With all fragile, shell shock and mental illness, not easily understood the answer was to put the patient out of sight so as not to offend the public's decency. There were some rules that Mum felt were petty and wasteful .Patients were to have soft-boiled eggs for breakfast, but their difficulties meant that there was egg everywhere and the cleaning staff were given an additional chore, so mum feigned her understanding of time and turned four minutes into ten. Mum was there for a number of years but did not always agree with the happenings, Fred Gadsby was one of the nurses who regularly hit the patients, and he was not alone in these practices. Mum had a deep sense of fairness and it reflected in the love some of the patients had for her Archie always followed her like a lost dog, but in the end preparing lavish meals for the governing committee whilst the patients got less than the best was not her way. There were some practices that the Smiths carried out that offended mums morals, so she thought it best to leave.

She left there and became a half-hose turner at Stevenson's Dye Works at Bull Bridge. She stayed there until her retirement sorting and turning socks and tights ready for the dying process. They were paid a low basic with a bonus for throughput in pence per dozen. When time and motion carried out their regular checks, half the team speed up so as not being seen as slackers, cutting everyone else's bonus. She enjoyed the team she worked with there too. Mum never attended the free pensioners dinners held for retired employees, but once a year passed through with the poppy box for the workers donations. The pensioners were just a lot of old folks still going on about work as far as she was concerned. Mum did not intend to let age catch her up. She and dad started broadening their horizons too, Scotland started the holiday bus tours, but Portland, Jersey, Austria, and Belgium followed. Dad would gather the deposits and set off to Matlock to book with the operator Slack's Travel. The Cuttles, and June with her friend Margaret (known as Sheffield Margaret, to distinguish her from any others of the same name), Aunty May and Uncle Ceph, as well as Mrs Betterton and others from the village took the annual holiday. Dad took his prejudices too. Whilst in a chocolate shop in Bruges, the proprietor asked them not to touch the goods, the shiny display of truffles lying before them. Dad reminded him if it was not for British hands touching the Germans, they would be making chocolates for Hitler now. Father never understood diplomacy, just British superiority. He also took umbrage in Blankenberg when the meal served to a German coach party was superior to the one received by them. The Germans had paid much more, immaterial to dad; he believed to the victor the spoils, regardless of what the others had paid. Mum took a great delight in her appearance and when Alopecia was starting to attack her, caused by the Methatrexate, Dad was looking deeply into the wig catalogue, but the concern being that neither the thinning hair nor a nylon substitute would suit mum. She would even on a minor trip out apply her lipstick, and powder her face. The permed hair was then set into place with a strong hair spray, that certainly was a great attractant to every wasp within a thousand metres. When we went out, on the odd Saturday when a borrowed van was available, mum and dad would disappear into the lounge bar, and alone left in the van with a bottle of lemonade and a bag of Smith's Crisps. Mum always seemed to prefer a family outing to the inevitable pub trip .This is what was good as we got the first car around the time I was fifteen, I had some premium bonds, and these cashed in to contribute to the car. We toured Nottingham with Dick Jones, and came back with the white Ford Anglia, only a few months old. The 1200 cc model with a bright red trim, and the Ford trademark, inwardly sloping back window. We would sally forth on a Saturday evening. Sunday still reserved for mother's Chapel attendance, Saturday evening tours of the countryside on a summer's day calling in on a far-flung relative on the way. Dad used to drink no more than four pints in those pre breathalyser days, reducing it to two when the option for the Police to ask you to blow into a bag came into force with the limit of eighty milligrams of Alcohol per hundred millilitres of blood. Mum enjoyed her outings and her family always.

  She enjoyed our children. A seaside Gypsy once predicted she would have six children, with Barbara, and ours, she got to five. She could be disruptive though. it wasn't the first time that Barbara caught her giving cigarettes to a sixteen year old Kerry , whose smoking was by that time against our principles .There were many similarities with mums tolerance of children and Barbara's . They both forgave a child when the benefit of doubt came into play. Barbara many times gave the benefit to a child, all children assumed innocent until she actually caught them in the act .They visited us several times a year, Christmas we tried to make it back to Derbyshire, but in later years, we were host more than visitor was. As our three grew there was always things to work around, and dad would aimed south. He dearly wanted to catch the train but soon reminded that the car was there for all journeys. We realised his reasoning many years later when we noticed how bad his eyesight actually was. Barbara was playing back a security video from our door camera ., when we saw him counting the cost of his morning SUN newspaper into his hand so he had the change ready , the video confirmed what was already suspected , his eyesight was much worse than we feared . He challenged by Aunty Lizzie to take Lucy home one Sunday night flatly refused to do it, despite criticism; His eyesight meant that night driving would render him so poorly sighted that he would have been a danger to others as well as to himself. Sometimes it is hard to admit your own weakness to others, and in dad's case to people that he barely tolerated. He and mum to some extent had built resentment to their dotage having Frank with them. Their personal together time was gone. We knew the thought was not a pretty one but they could never sit relaxed in each other's company in nightwear, or vest, as they were always waiting for Frank to return. The original arrangement was when I left to attend College in nineteen sixty-six, Aunty Martha, as Mrs Walker was known died, and Frank had nowhere to go. Mum rang and asked if Frank could use the room for three months whilst he found an alternative. The arrangement lasted thirty-four years. Mum asked once about the cost of digs, and when told she expressed surprise as it was twice Frank is contribution. At various stages of those thirty-four years, he was actually subsidised by mum and dad. Dad was excessively cruel to Frank, with a wicked tongue, that neither deserved nor needed, but the thirty-four year long, three months had tried Leslie's patience. He would tell us, mum and he had had no quality time together, whilst waiting on Frank. Frank's favourite sister, Lizzie, never in memory offered relief either, but was ready with the instant criticism in times of Dad's default. The need to prepare a third meal, or after mum's death a second one, when dad may have just chosen a simple sandwich, eroded and care that dad had. There were rights and wrongs on both sides but the background feelings always seemed to mark dad down. To some extent, we started to think that the bitterness escaping the surface was a resentful grumpy old man. How wrong, later proven correct at every accusation he made, one day apologies needed that will not be the easiest of days. The one thing that showed through his attendance at mum's side throughout her illness was the love and devotion he had for her, which alone made a proud son, despite watching sometimes petty bickering and stubbornness strike at both of them, but the love showed through at mum's final hour. After mum had passed away, dad returned south in our car. Barbara had sorted out her clothing into rags, jumble, charity shop, and such like. The bags were sealed and left for the various factions to collect. Mum had some nice things and dad had wanted to avoid the local jumble route, in case he saw some of the better pieces on a village scruff one day. We were surprised after he returned home to receive a call about some of mums clothes, Barbara confirmed they were bagged and ready, as instructed. what became obvious was that as we departed Aunty Lizzie had been to the back door and sorted through the clothes, taking cardigans a for herself, against dads direct wishes. She had then pretended that the items, were a gift from her dear sister years before. Culpam poena premit comes

    Aunty Mary (Dorathea) followed Mum; she wed Walter Taylor at Crich and lived at 1 Chatsworth Avenue, where she stayed with their eight children. Michael was the oldest, followed by Dorathea Lynne, Malcolm, John, Steven and David the twins then Margaret and Wendy. The house was always busy, so were the whole family, the boys took a keen interest in Scouting. It was as always a busy house. A large four-bedroom one with a corner aspect. The huge kitchen had a solid fuel "Rayburn "boiler in a prominent place. The main living room had a folding door arrangement separating dining and lounge ends. The front garden was a massive area of this large corner plot. The side and rear were no small area either.

There was always a welcome when you visited, we would walk to Crich on a summers day just for the walk. When calling one day with the new girlfriend Barbara, Aunty Mary changed the mugs for cups as being a Southerner she assumed Barbara had different principles, when it came to tea, Barbara would have preferred the Mug, but got the cup and saucer. We had just been to the new Tramway museum in the old Quarry, and had taken a trip to see the famous Sherwood Foresters Monument, "Crich Stand. " It seemed natural to call in to Aunty Mary's house, as done so many times before.

There was much pride in the family when John became the first one of the cousins to go to university and gain his degree in architecture .Michael not seen for years until Uncle Frank's funeral when we suffered a chastisement from June, for talking in Chapel, not June herself complaining but a Persona non-grata. I so wish they had shared the thought with me directly and I could have explained fellowship to them. Wake up! God likes noise in his house .I felt that Uncle Frank would have delighted to hear the buzz of people in the Church. Lynne was tracing her family lineage and we were surprised to receive an E-mail from Lynn Ablard about Dorathea Hackman, little realising that it was Aunty Mary that was the subject. Lyn was one of the few weddings that we remember in Taylor family. She had married a Railway Policeman; his preference be called "Ginger," to his real first name, which from memory was Godfrey. They moved first to Wirksworth, and we visited there for the well dressings one year, then from there they settled in Preston. Michael moved to a Flat in Fritchley, We visited once, and then the next time was as said before at Uncle Frank's Funeral. Malcolm became a Redcap. Military policeman, married an Irish girl, and the last heard of him was with South Yorkshire Police in Sheffield. John worked as an Architect, but later took up lecturing at a North Derbyshire college. The rest, we lost touch with .Wendy though married, Phil Elson, and lives near Deggie's old Garage in Swanwick, which Phil now owns. Margaret lives in Ripley. We had a lot of contact when Aunty Lucy was hospitalised. The local jungle drums had fell silent, and Aunty May let it out that Lucy was seriously ill in Derbyshire's Royal Infirmary. We were not able to attend Aunty Lucy's funeral, but one believe that things did not go well between Margaret and Aunty Lizzie who became bemused at Margaret's attitude, and as usual with these things became the victim, not, the perpetrator.

Uncle Charlie was the last of the in the line .He joined the Navy at the start of the War and was at the retaking of Jersey at the war's end. The day before VE day The glorious Channel Islands and their long suffering population , having lived under the occupation of Germany for so long were returned to Britain .the Islands being abandoned by Britain , as a demilitarised zone in nineteen forty . The Islands underwent some hard times for the eleven thousand troops, making up the German Garrison cut off from their supply lines after St Malo fell in August 1944. Despite Red Cross relief in December 1944, the Islanders struggled to survive until May 1944 when the first navy ship entered Jersey St Hellier Harbour bringing liberation. Of the two destroyers in Jersey harbour on liberation day there was HMS Bulldog .Uncle Charlie became a Trent Motor traction Driver and Married Constance (Kit) Wheeldon from the Butts at Belper. They lived, as the tradition deemed with His mother my Grandma. At Rock House, they had one of the front rooms and one of the bedrooms, all else shared. Uncle Charlie had one of the first cars in the family a split screen Volkswagen .They sold the house soon after Grandmas Death, forcing Uncle Frank to move to Mrs Walkers. Kit and Charlie moved to a sweet shop in Abbey Street at Derby, then a Pub at Fritchley and eventually stewarded Marehay miners' welfare. Uncle Charlie on approaching their retirement moved to Highfield at Ripley and after some years driving Prison vans, he drove the mobile library .Kit took a job with the Thornton Chocolate factory in Belper.

Uncle Frank bought up by grandma, and lived with her

except for his national service in the Royal Air Force. When demobbed, he worked for Rolls Royce in Belper, although his principle was to observe Sundays and he could not reconcile Sunday working. After Agnes's marriage and grandma's death, as Kit and Charlie repossessed their house for sale, Uncle Frank moved in with Mrs Walker Aunty Agnes's mother in law. He was there in Parkside at Heage for about six years until aunty Martha's death at which stage ,he moved in with Mum and dad He worked a Clothing Shop for Masterson's in Alfreton, and Ripley as assistant and eventually managed the Clay Cross shop until poor trading bought it to a close. The Masterton family had jewellery interests and the three clothing shops were trading at a loss, so one by one they closed. From there after unemployment for a long time, he joined Kit at Thornton's at B. He started as a temperature and became a popular member of the team, not only managing to master the Forklift trucks, but also conducting funerals and services there.

Frank ran and supported the Chapel all his life and spent time as a lay preacher on the Methodist Circuit in the area. Traditionally mum, and Frank attended the Chapel, and Aunty Lizzie attended the Church, in Heage. When Aunty May came to the village she joined mum at the Chapel, to add to the scarce Sunday evening congregation. Dad was a chapel trustee and treasurer for many years, it was one position he retained after not being re-elected to the Ripley Urban District Council back in the nineteen seventies. Nether Heage Chapel had by fate always held its own deeds, and stubbornly refused to yield them to the local ministry. These meant that despite low attendance, and poor village interest, the Methodist ministry could not close the chapel down. This would enable the district sell it for house conversion, to enrich the coffers of the district. The mainstay today is Josie who was the owner of the village hairdressing shop for many years.

Frank had a fantastic approach to children and would amuse them for hours, he never married despite there being a rare girlfriend on the scene, but he did spend an awful lot of his time helping others, and generally putting himself out for others.

The rest of the Hackman family , were never exposed to us , There was once a visit from mum's Uncle Harry , who lived at Loughborough , and worked for "Brush" , engineering company , the brass teddy bears , were cast by him as a night shift perk . Of the other Hackman's there was no connection ever made. The Nally family is though were a different proposition, there was my Mothers Aunty Lucy, who lived the other side of Nottingham and her family. We also had a branch that ran a Blackpool Guest House in the nineteen sixties, there was therefore a few still about The descendants of the Leam's scattered the village liberally , and it sometimes seemed that half the village was mum's cousins , the Beighton' Violet and Bertha ,Stanley and Hiram England who was a local Farmer? The Coopers, at number 24 Brook Street also related to Grandma to. That is what I would have expected from a family who had five hundred year of local residency.

Chapter 9 The first five years

Wednesday sixteenth of November nineteen forty nine, saw me into the world. As the first half of the last century closed I arrived by Caesarean section at Derby Woman's' Hospital. The hospital was a Victorian structure closed and demolished many years ago. I remember it as a sombre building enclosed by a high wall, situated on a street corner in a part of Derby, long crushed under the developer's machinery. Mum had an emergency transfusion of four pints of blood to make up for that, amount, she lost during my delivery .She became allergic to penicillin after the delivery and always blamed the transfused blood. The Doctor was one of Dr. Patrick "Paddy" Ryan's partners a Doctor Kelly, the "Lady" Doctor. Their practice attached to a vast mansion that was Paddy Ryan's Home. The surgeries were equipped in a Victorian attitude, with huge roll topped desks, hospital screens, a black couch, and wooden bentwood chairs, for the patients. The twin surgeries positioned down a short stair, angled doors filled with a mottled glass, separated them from the benches in the waiting room. The outline of patient and doctor hazily seen through this screen as the waiting patients, shuffled in time order waiting their turn. Nothing was that secret, if an examination needed the disappearance of doctor and patient behind the folded screens foretold of a longer wait. The waiting room and the consulting rooms were lit by old gas fires their noxious fumes hanging heavy in the air .I remember Doctor Kelly well into the nineteen fifties, until she was replaced by an Indian Doctor. Doctor Chakkrabbatti referred to by dad as doctor "bloody chuck a butty." He chose either Paddy Ryan or his son Bobby as his physician on every opportunity .That also minded me of the intolerant racialism that dad could have for the non-English. He had thrown words and phrases well beyond reason, directing one African Doctor back to his Jungle roots is hardly the way to achieve a sensible diagnosis. He regarded the Indian subcontinent as being full of ignorant labourers, and from Africa, he would, if he had been free enough to vote retained slavery, and opposed William Wilberforce to the best of his ability .I do know, nor wonder where he built up this intolerant dislike from. Nevertheless, it was never a desirable one. To have this air of racial distrust and ignorance is sad and sadly it took many years too lose it.

Dr Ryan. On one occasion, when dad was troubled by knee pain and deemed to consult on the painful joint .The tables were soon turned as he aged Dr Ryan consulted dad on the purchase of his winter coal. It all took time and soon some half an hour consulting with dad on the finer points of grade and cost had passed. Dad pointed out to the Octogenarian physician that there were patients waiting, Dr Ryan told him he was aware of that and "the buggers must wait. " Much to the see the surprise on those waiting faces   when dad strolled out red faced , he was looked at , in a what's he got to have been in there so long , look .

Of the Hospital, I remember nothing except the embarrassment of being born in a "Woman's" Hospital. The day I appeared Mum had four pints of the rare AB blood group that we share, to make up what she lost during my delivery.

I arrived by Caesarean section, so what caused the massive blood loss I do not know. Mum though was desperately allergic to penicillin and she had never been before this transfusion so she blamed someone else's blood as being the allergy factor. Dad summoned at the end of his workday by Grandma Hackman and borrowed a car to deliver her to the hospital to check on her daughter, and me, her latest Grandson .sixth of the fourteen that followed her. She had a matriarchal rule and rarely defied. If a day out was in the offing she would be ready, in coat fully buttoned, hat secured with hatpins ready for the off. Her long white hair plaited around her head in a timeless fashion. No matter how early you called, she was primed and ready to launch.

Home was now at forty-three, the Brook, Nether Heage. This one of a pair of semi-detached cottages, the second bedroom of ours over spanned the ground floor, front room of forty-five, next door. The cottages were the sort built for nineteenth century agricultural workers. The Hodgekinson family had been small farmers .The land that Walter owned had two pairs of cottages, one he and his wife lived in, a workshop and a large barn, . His brother Joe still farmed and his farmhouse was halfway up the hill across the fields, Joe was the only local farmer still using a horse to labour, all the others had little grey Fergusson Tractors. Joe and the horse wandered the village lanes, carting wood for fires and manure for gardens. The farm was steeply sloped and the horse plodded a single furrow plough across the fields at an angle that would have toppled a tractor.

The cottages stone built, and stand resplendent as a single conversion with all the conveniences of modern life now .After we moved out in nineteen sixty-one they lay idle for some time, but sold by the Hodgekinson family to be converted into a single dwelling with the novelty of a twee country cottage. The adjoining cottage housed the Cooper family Mr & Mrs Cooper and their son Keith who had a withered arm. Their cottage was dark and quite spooky with the walls painted with a blue wash as opposed to the more common whitewash. I was never sure of the story of Keith's deformity, but I think connected to a childhood illness. Keith was also somewhat a late developer and took some degree of ridicule from the heartless village children. Opposite lived the Holt family and they had a problem family member, a younger brother traumatised by the war, left with shell shock. There did not seem a cure and he was a quiet, introvert, so best left alone.

Built in eighteen eighty-four number forty-three comprised a living room and kitchen with two upstairs bedrooms. A single cold tap in the kitchen and an outside night soil toilet completed the services . The front door of number forty-three was direct into the living room and the cold Derbyshire winds howled along the valley and formed a focal point at the half-inch gap under the front door. A woollen snake from an old blanket and rag stuffing laid across the gap in a poor attempt to stem the whistling wind under the door. The wind howled in a constantly changing note. The door shrouded in a heavy velvet curtain that had a length of chain sewn into its hem to weigh it down against the prevailing wind. This made opening the front door a ceremonial chore, kick the snake away. Draw back the curtain, unlock the heavy three-lever lock with a clunk, and heave the heavy wooden door open. To close it took a reversal of this procedure, it was akin to a medieval ceremony. Most visitors arrived at back door no curtain and always open. The doors both external and internal were all ledger and brace construction. The three cross members braced with two diagonals sheathed in tongue and groove boarding of the same dimensions as floorboard. The doors nailed together and as they expanded and contracted with the weather the draughts between the vertical boards increased and reduced as the damp swelled and shrank the softwood. This split the paint and opened the gap in the tongue and groove wide enough to let the wind force its way through. No matter how you tried, the house self ventilated, the windows gapped too, so it was cold and a draft blew constantly, and without a damp course so we lived with a constant battle against damp. Dad on one occasion had the walls of the lounge re-plastered at his expense with a plaster that contained vermiculite and a damp repellent, in a vain attempt to improve living conditions. It may sound harsh on the property owner here but to defend his reluctance I would explain that we paid a magnificent sum of five shillings a week, today that is Twenty-five pence today. The rent was not a huge sum to keep an old cottage in repair, never minding being able make a living from the rent. Paint had   limited range there was Green, navy blue, sky blue. Pillar-box red, Grey, black and white, sunshine yellow, and the dreadful royal purple completed the spectrum. If you wanted, a different colour you mixed it from the primary ones above .The shade achieved by adding black or white. The secret was to mix enough in the batch, as you would never recreate the colour on a second attempt. The thinner was turpentine and the paint brushes a stiff pig bristle. Undercoat was always a grey matt and primer a bright matt pink. The internal doors were all in off – white, a cream colour that stayed the same throughout its life, unlike white that heavily based on a lead oxide that soon discoloured rapidly to a murky cream streaky finish. Wallpapers had a thin border and when you chose your paper, you removed one or both edges with scissors, or let the shop do it on their machine. If you left, one edge on you would end the paper with a lap joint, bulging at each seam. We had our cut and my aunty Alice came and decorated, it took a week of visits normally, and all done.

All the doors had a lever latch, one end curved like a hockey stick, the other flattened out and inserted into a handle that gave you a pull to the door whilst your thumb depressed the lever. This lever lifted a latch engaged into a hook in the doorjamb   the doors shut but never tight and as the wood warped in the damp, the effort to pull the door shut varied. The wind found all the gaps and provided all year round air conditioning with a cold front stretching across all areas.

The lounge was a large square room with a dining table, never used, under the window with a chair situated at either end. The fireplace took up the end wall and backed onto the kitchen wall. The chimneybreast heated the living room , kitchen, and the first bedroom upstairs. The fire grate was an excelsior the fire grate had a small bread oven to the left hand side , The brown stove enamel frame housed four six inch square tiles an integral tiled hearth with a stove enamelled fender surround edged the whole apparatus . A lever at the fire back deflected heat to the alongside oven. I never remember the oven in use it became warm store cupboard. The tiles were cracked and broken but the age of the range prevented matching replacements.

The fire blazed daily summer and winter. Twisted newspaper lay in the grate, the ashes dragged dustily to the bin. The chopped sticks laid over the top and cobbles of coal wedged in between. The paper lit and a sheet of paper placed precariously over the open chimney to draw the fire into life. If real care, not taken, the paper sucked itself into the flame and you held a flaming sheet of newspaper in your hands. Smoke billowed into the room, the short chimney never creating a sufficient draft to give the fire a good start, as wind circled the stump of a chimney a back draft blasted soot and dense smoke across the room choking the inhabitants and blasting a black dust over the surfaces. Once the heat built and the chimney warmed the fire started to blaze into life and self-perpetuated as rising exhaust drew fresh air into the bed of the flames. Once the fire started, there was a mad desire to stoke it with enough coal to heave a locomotive with a full train over the Shap. The summer heat made the room unbearable so the doors flung open to cool down; in winter, the heat sat in front of the fire and did not extend beyond the chairs. Ash filled the room as the ashcan emptied each morning and the cold ash toted out to the old steel bin. In winter, the ash scattered on the path as a non-slip coating. The coal lived in a ramshackle shed in the corner of the house next to the dividing fence. A galvanised iron roof and a door hanging on a single hinge finished the scene. The dirt floor covered in coal and dust. The door hung loosely on its hinges all the time I remember

The Fire was the Lounge focal point and a Utility chair sat in front of it. This was a dark Brown armchair covered in "Leatherette" To the side sat a wooden armed chair that lay flat to serve as a single bed. The dining table under the window was a drop leaf. and this matched the old sideboard on the back wall .The sideboard had two doors and the shelf inside hid the family valuables , the fish knives and forks , these would appear with tinned red salmon on special Sundays , but rarely . There was an odd collection of glasses too, including some stem- less tulip glasses that were very thin which Mum always favoured for her Harvey's Bristol Cream, Sherry. Mum always liked delicate, the thinner the cup, and glass the better. One reason behind buying the Derby Crown Cloisonné Dinner service, was, Mums assertion that if she ever owned Derby Crown she would use it, not store it in a cupboard somewhere. In front of the fire there was a rag rug , home pegged from rags onto an opened potato sack .Under the stairs a cupboard hid the blackout curtains left over from the war . The wall opposite the front window had a double door painted cupboard. This cupboard held the junk of life, Granddad Page's old pipes, a carved bulls head, with bones for the bull's horns. There was a horse's head pipe too, and a variety of other old smoking requisites. An old biscuit tin held the papers that detailed our lives, the old Identity cards, receipts, old driving licences the clutter of the years.

I used to lie on the rug, as the two chairs were not that comfortable and occupied by my parents. The old rag rugs were thick and strangely soft, a comfortable position easily found. I think blue featured heavily in the pattern. Blue the colour of overalls, the knees worn, left good material for rug making throughout the village. The overalls had a cotton twill cloth heavily washed so it softened with time to give warmth and comfort unseen. ? The fire would crackle and spit and when an ember spat out hitting the rug, it collected in the fire tongs and returned to the brazier .The rug stank and smouldered but never seemed to ignite. The joy of open fires never ceases to amaze me, a change in the wind, the draft would be lost, and the chimney would fail to draw filling the room with noxious soot and dust. This would result in the Daily Sketch, rescued from the toilet, and tightly flung across the chimney in an attempt to recreate the draft that was working so well, until the change in wind. The cleanliness of the modern gas, "pretend real fire" out classes its original format. The corner of the Kitchen had housed a fired copper to boil clothes, hams, and anything else boilable. The chimney soon removed, as was the brickwork that surrounded the old thick copper cauldron. The washing day modernisation had arrived in the form of a Burco Boiler, This grey monster was galvanised and held about fifteen gallons of water.

Dad worked as a driver for Wilson – Lovett the opencast site operators, and drove the old Bedford bus in the morning and evenings to collect and return the others to the Street Lane site.

In nineteen fifty three we went and bougha TV from the "Priestly" shop at the bottom of Oxford Street, We had a huge and expensive fourteen-inch one. When you consider that the measurement is the visible diagonal screen, my modern day equivalent is six times the size... To pick the TV we soon entered into a back room and there were five or six examples to judge. The most expensive had a tambour door to close off the screen during the day. We had that size and quality but without the doors, that one was those fifty years ago over eighty pounds. Wages were about five pounds a week so the cheapest television was four months wages. We had a huge "H" shaped aerial fixed to the chimney.

There was a small window that overlooking the rear

garden, fixed because of its small size, but it housed small plastic radio. We had the light program or The Third Program but most of the time the radio tuned to the "Home Service," night and day as it gave a background of noise. The AM frequency crackled in to life and faded away as the signal drifted. The programmes were daily the same, at ten each day we had "Listen with mother "each morning this was followed by "Mrs Dales Diary. "

The television though was a whole new world , the programmes started about Two in the afternoon and went on for an hour with programmes such as Andy Pandy , The Wooden tops , and Bill and Ben .We were still in the minority to have a television , and it stood majestically in the corner of the room . At about four, thirty it went off for an hour so children could have their tea. The BBC put a test card interlude on, and the potter day after day shaped a pot. I know there were other interludes but the potter's wheel always seemed to be there round and around forming the clay of life. Evening was the heavier programmes, Panorama; Thrillers like Quatermass were real entertainment, as was a young Bruce Forsyth at Sunday Night at the London Palladium. The prizes were tiny in comparison to today's give away, a fridge was a star prize on "Take your Pick. " The 405 lines of the screen were poor as I sit in front of today's LCD –HD screen and look back. Aunty Lizzie used to cover the screen when the TV was off. After all you would not want them looking in would you .A lamp sat on top, home made from a VAT 69 whisky bottle with a whisky label shade. That TV was with us for nearly ten years, built to last! At that time, many people covered the screen with a cloth, so that the TV station could not see into the room when the T.V. was off, unbelievable but true.

The kitchen was divided into two halves a large close boarded wooden pantry filled the front and the kitchen took the remainder. The pantry had a small front window, which opened and a fly screen placed over the open window, there was a large marble slab on this front wall and in those pre, refrigeration day's meat kept in a meat safe, wooden with fly screen for its sides and door. A sack of potatoes stood opened under the marble counter, and a huge Swede would lie on the top. Dad preferred his mashed potato with a blending of Swede.

A new world gas cooker stood on the floor on the end wall of the building   next to a huge butlers sink with a wooden draining board. Hot water fed from an Ascot gas fired boiler, cold from a vicious high-pressured tap. The sink was a washing and a cooking sink, a true multi-purpose fitment. A washing machine in the corner had a paddle on the lid and washdays were a whole day chore.

The washing machine was a green painted tub, the white sheets done first. Sheets and pillowcases boiled in a large galvanised copper boiler until the steam enveloped the whole kitchen. The soap was flaked with a sharp knife from a green bar of Co-op hard soap and the boiler frothed it. The hot sheets and a bucket of steaming water from the boiler dropped into the washing machine steam still billowing from them The lid closed and the handle stirred ten turns left ten turns right. This went repeatedly. The sheets pulled through a hand-powered wringer and a pressure screw on the top added the pressure. The wet washing went forward and back several times then was carried to the line were it blew in the wind until dry. The Initial white load into the boiler had a "Reckitts" Blue bag added to help whiteness. The water depleted as each sheet pulled out of the thick washing soup. However, the recycled water from the wringer fell into a white galvanised white bucket, the contents tipped back into the boiler and the heat and water both saved. The sheets were always white and always flannelette. Candy stripes were available but rather racy .At some stage brushed nylon came in which made the washing easier, but gave added warmth in summer. The boiler bubbled and the whole house filled with steam and the sterile smell of the hard soap. Everyone washed on Mondays, and only Mondays, wherever you looked the sheets billowed from the washing lines like an Armada in full sail.

A winding staircase obscured behind another hand built door reached the Bedrooms at forty-three. The sharp curve of the stairs bought you into the main bedroom. Two utility wardrobes and a matching dressing table surrounded the double bed, with its metal spring and wooden oak head and footboards. The dressing table had two outer raised drawer sections and a centre dropped area that housed a large mirror. There was a window front and back. A large carpet square covered the bare dark wood floorboards. A large China Potty secreted under the bed for night use. To save the treck across the unlit freezing garden to the also unlit privy this antique device was still in regular use,

My bedroom was connected to the main bedroom by a flight of three stairs and I had a large bed and a bedside chest .The front window was at ground level and laying down on the floor gave you an unobstructed view over the road and the neighbours garden , because my bedroom was over number forty five . The floor covered in lino and there were no carpets. Lino was always the hardwearing hygienic option.

There was no bathroom. All washing was to take place at the kitchen sink and a luxury once a week bath at Aunty Lizzies. Uncle Mac had Colitis, Which means when you have to go; you have to go now! , and the bathing routine would be ended by him hammering at the door with a serious urgency. A long soak in the tub was an unheard of dream .Fridays was torture Uncle Mac day. Their plumbing was poor and if you ran off the hot water to quickly their overflow ran onto the path and in winter this froze into a huge ice lump. That took ten years, at least before it ever became properly fixed. A new valve and float all needed to affect the repair. However, it never had the repairs.

The toilet was a night soil toilet, a large galvanised can like a squat dustbin sat nestled under a wooden seat with a hole cut in and a heavy wooden lid. You went, then treated yourself to the quartered section of the Daily Sketch, closed the lid and waited until the night soil men emptied it into the huge "DENNIS" night soil pump lorry every Wednesday night without fail, always in the dead of night. The lorry was dark green with a long angular bonnet and the two men who accompanied it dragged the bin to the rear and revved the engine to work the pump .the old slow revving long stroke diesel pounding away to herald the presence of the night soil team. We were to low geographically to get onto the sewer although all the other houses locally seemed to make it. I suspect the Landlord Walter Hodgekinson had a tight budget and did not want to pay for our convenience. It was eventually converted soon after we left in nineteen sixty-one. Mum changed her job and was cleaning for a Mrs Reynolds once a week in Ripley. Mr Reynolds owned Ripley Printers. The job at the Elastic factory became less and less.

The back garden provided food for us all year round. Dad was in a mental competition with his memory as Dad who had been a famed local prize-winner at village produce shows Dad grew huge Sturon onions that were giants, but the size sacrificed the keeping quality. They were however bigger than the ones his dad had produced so Pyrrhic victory achieved. Runner beans had the same effect huge but slightly tough, bigger than his dad's did though. I never understood the need to compete with history. I think the competitiveness was a desire to be recognised. A late statement made me realise how hard my dads' life had been he talked little of his childhood, but made a few scanty comments in his later years. He had suffered the loss of his mother as a pre-teenager and from what I can tell been left to get over it .in those dark long gone days. He once, only, referred to life as a stepbrother to the Pykett family in a negatively. He reminded me that as a child he in his teenage not only had his dad's chores in the garden to do , but was rewarded with bib and brace overalls as trousers and boots with hobnailed soles to wear , whilst his stepmother had provided her own with shoes and proper trousers . I had always believed that he had time and respect for all of them but there had been resentment dormant in his life. On reflection, which fitted with his desire for public office, he needed recognition on his own right. Sometimes I mused over his reluctance to exude warmth , but that was deep rooted in the loss of his mother and the inclusion of the step family .I understand the competitive desire and felt that applying science could do a bigger onion or a longer bean but never wanted to . That will leave dad as the best gardener for generations, and proud of it he would be to.

The front garden grew roses. Mum wanted a front lawn but requests were always greeted with, "you can't eat grass can you? ". No, we could not, but we never used the roses for culinary purposes either. There was a shrubbery to the right of the front door; this was overgrowing with a poisoness privet hedge. Delicious looking white berries full of juice sprang from this annually, but the eat one and you will be dead warning gave trepidation at nearing them.

Grandma's house was huge in comparison, and I believe it had an earlier life as a Public House. Uncle Charlie had blocked the cellar in the kitchen. He and Aunty Kit actually owned Grandma's house. Aunty Lucy lived there too until her marriage .Uncle Frank was there until Grandma's death .The house had four reception rooms and five bedrooms, one bedroom converted to a Bathroom. The coal fire in the living room provided heat for the whole house. The Front Room used at Christmas and was dominated by a large three-piece suit and a piano. The other front room was exclusively for Uncle Charlie and Aunty Kit. In grandma's front room, the ornaments were from another era. A strange pothouse, which on the insertion of a cigarette had a chimney that smoked stood on the front room mantelpiece there were fine glass antelopes and swans the fine work having coloured glass bodies' .These ornaments bought at seaside displays where you watched the glass artisan working so skilfully melting and stretching glass rods in a flame. The box room at the top of the stairs was Aunty Lucy's the front rooms, started with the smallest in the corner that used by Uncle Frank. Uncle Charlie and Grandma's rooms finished off the five bedrooms upstairs .The room that led into Grandma's altered to form a bathroom. The family links maintained by sharing the evening paper, paying bills for each other, eggs from dad, a completely interlinked system .The hens ran at the bottom of the garden in a hen house next to the old apple tree. The grass ran out from the back of the house to the hedge and the vegetable plot ran parallel to Aunty Lizzie's garden.

Everyone was coal fired, the village was a mining village, and the miners were now working for the coal Board that had taken possession of the mines from the much-maligned profit seeking mine owners from new years day nineteen forty seven... The first action was for the miners to take action against their new national owners. The village men must have been about twenty-five percent miners. The men returned home in the dirt they had accumulated during the days work. The faces blackened with coal dust. Washing was a strip to the waist at the kitchen sink. Moreover, in the older cottages a galvanised iron bath filled from buckets of water heated in the Burco boiler.

Stockpiles of the soap stamped PHB to show its Pit Head Bath Origins, these huge oblongs of soap spilled over a large bowl and jug that stood in the bathroom, Cracked and worth little it was lost to grave robbers, as the Millenium got underway. The Pit Baths had been resisted , as the mine owners were to impose a usage charge .Men returned home clean and well dressed .Many men still called into the pub on their way home for a couple of points , or more , then tea stood between two plates over a saucepan of boiling water to keep warm and moist . I believe the theory that hard labour needed that lubricating water before home showed, Dad though always was straight home, and never formed part of the early evening bar debating society.

Chapter 9 the days before School

On Mondays, we went to Grandma's for tea, all of us, Stew, always, the Sunday joint with the Sunday vegetables and the celery from the salad with any tomato boiled for hours with the Sunday gravy. Eaten with chunks of bread sat at the table in Grandma's living room the stew was plentiful but so filling. Monday to Friday Mum did a twilight shift at the elastic factory in Ripley on Derby Road. Therefore, I was in for tea then in for the night. She did not get home until the last bus at eleven o'clock at night. Money was tight and they both worked to get more. Dad changed his job first as the opencast finished; He joined Albert Whitely Coal Merchant of Crich Lane Belper.

Albert Wheatley was an arthritic old man with limited movement .He had a Son and a Daughter who ran his shop in Crich lane also but opposite the Queens Head Pub. The two businesses were interwoven. Dad shovelled coal into bags in all weathers straight off the floor in Albert's Crich lane field. He lifted them up onto the lorry and took them around the streets of Derby delivering in the terraces and outlying estates. We were not well off but the Saturday money collecting was an insight into what poor was. Some houses still ate from enamel plates and drank from chipped enamel mugs. At least one house used the bath as a coal store. We were in a tight situation but never that tight.

A new butcher took over the shop from Fred Gadsby, a Joe, and Josephine Hunt from Pease Hill in Ripley. Mum used to provide them with a hot lunch each day, and until Josephine learned to drive Dad drove her out on their Friday night mobile round through Heage. Joe cut many corners and his homemade sausage bore a resemblance to Howarth's of Openwoodgate, the plentiful amounts of fat it yielded did certainly. There was a Chip shop next to Joe Hunts, but it is only vaguely in mind as a wooden structure, long and dark green, and derelict. The butchers shop had two halves Vegetables and meat. It expanded over the years and finally fell into disuse in the nineteen nineties. Joe Hunt's son had a delicatessen in Ripley's Oxford Street, and as Joe and Josephine aged and became infirm, the business faded into oblivion. The post office in contrast was tiny, Mr & Mrs Gibson ran it, and they took mainly post office business. There sub post office status was lesser than the Heage unit was. It was from Heage that Telegrams came and Heage as well as being larger seemed to have more on offer. The post office had two bigger rivals for the essentials, Ripley Co-operatives store, that lives on as a band practice room and Mrs Kneebone's off licence, where she would draw beer from the barrel into an empty bottle that you provided, then she would place a sticky label over the cap to seal it. Some wives would collect their husbands bitter in an open jug and carefully carry it home with a loose cloth over the top to keep insects at bay. The beer came from the old Derby brewery Offiler.

Mum filed her life with a rigid routine until I went to School. Monday as I showed here was washday, Tuesday was ironing and putting away morning and women class at the chapel in the afternoon. Mum was president for many years. Hymns, prayers, a talk, then tea and biscuits every week two till four that occupied the Christian ladies f the village each Monday . Wednesday was cleaning and in the afternoon, her friend Gwen Ottewell would pass a few hours in heavy gossip whilst I played with the precocious Malcolm. Friday was Ripley Market by the Bus and always Fish for tea it was a good Catholic tradition that we strangely followed.

The meals well ordered too, Monday always stew, Tuesday a meat pie from the minced remains of the joint. Nice but dry, as dad did not like reheated gravy. Mum got around this on some occasions by preparing the meat with onions placing them in a deep dish, covering them with potatoes, then a thick flaky pastry, and having a meat and potato pie. Wednesday we went to eat at Mrs Walkers in the evening, and collected ice cream along the way from the shop at the Black Boy. Mrs Walker was Aunty Agnes's Mother in law. Thursday was liver, onions, and Friday fish. Saturday was a bacon roll for breakfast in homemade rolls, or baps to give them their correct title, Saturday tea was salad, Always ham, of the bone from Birds Bakery, Lettuce cucumber, half a boiled egg and tomato. The formula never faltered in forty years. Sunday was a roast joint Beef or lamb, never pork, or on a very special occasion Chicken, but only at Christmas, .Tea was the Salad but with tinned John West Red Salmon.

Friday morning was market day, a routine hardly broken in fifty years. Up to Ripley, and then sequential tasks developed to minimise walking. Home & Colonial Stores for a Quarter of Ham and a Pork Farms Pork Pie, then a quick visit to the Co-op supermarket, built to replace the old cinema in the early fifties. That made a resplendent row of Co-op shops, Furniture, tailoring, dresses and an Edwardian tearoom over came the whole run of Nottingham road. Shoes opposite sealed the square. There would be a stop at Taylors Corn Stores, to collect the Yeast and the loose bread flour.

Grosvenor Road ignored as Priestley's corner was rounded; Birds Bakery on Oxford Road replaced the Home and colonial in later years. Black pudding and sausages from Howarth's shop when established there in later years and then to the market for the Vegetables that Dad had not managed to grow. The Biscuit man with his cheap, if not so fresh biscuits and cakes, the sweet man with homemade peppermint rock and slab toffee filled both bags to straining point. We re-crossed the market and boarded the returning "106 Nether Heage and Ambergate Bus," which was a single Decker. Double Decker buses are unstable on Dungely Hill so the single deckers were there with their limited amount of seats.

The Bulk of the shopping was every Wednesday at eleven o'clock, off to the huge Nether Heage store of Ripley Co-operative Society. Mum got Dividend repayments of two shillings for each pound spent , paid six monthly , Summer and Christmas , The Dividend number 29916 being relayed at each transaction , and a tiny receipt slip was torn from its huge book and presented as a record.

We had a book similar to the recently discontinued Ration Books printed as an aide memoire. That list engraved in my memory, Butter, Bacon, Margarine, and Lard Cheese Salt Sugar. Tea, Coffee, Jam printed on each page. The Grocer filled in the missing gaps and you left with a record and price list of your goods imprinted in the books with an old HB pencil, which was stored in the space between the man's ears and his head.

The butter came from Denmark in fifty-Kilo tubs and was hand beaten into shape before wrapped in its greaseproof butter paper. The Huge Berkel slicer cut the Bacon into any of the twenty-eight selectable thicknesses; ours was always number eight, medium, not too thin, not too thick. Margarine was Co-operatives own Brand , The Cheddar Truckle coated in a solid cheesecloth forming a hard rind , the cheese sliced with a wire into wedges , these halved in height . Then in width, so the rind was equal to all. Lard was three-pig brand from Morells, Salt as raisins and sugar was loose and pre bagged at the shop, Sugar in blue bags, raisins in purple .tea we had Co-op 99, Coffee a rare luxury, always served in short mugs made weakly from half milk half water, always fresh boiled in a small milk pan. What is overpriced and branded as Latte was just coffee to us .The floorboards were bare and wooden the shop an ambassador from a resplendent era pre war. The aromatic blend of Cheese and hard soap filed the air.

Kneebone's' stores opposite the Co-operative was seen as a last resort, it did not do Dividend.

We kept a Pig at the farm most years and the week before Christmas it met its fate , The butcher who slaughtered and divided it returned with pork pie , ham , Collar bacon , which was cut to order with a sharp knife , and a joint of pork which was a new Year celebration the fresh Black pudding accompanied this . Because of the time involved in curing Ham and bacon, which as a dry cure took twelve weeks then I believe that there was a degree of swapping around, like a pig Co-op amongst a circle of friends.

Dad's friendship with Sid Gadsby also meant we had our own row of potatoes in the fallow field and a share in the huge Swede , The Swede were grown mainly as fodder , with Mangolds and turnips, this always led me to believe Turnip , as Swede was known was really animal food and not human consumption food . This left a huge sacking bag of potatoes in the kitchen at all times the larger ones would be presented as a supper treat of being Baked in their jacket in the oven for two hours then liberally coated in butter after being split and served.

We also regaled ourselves with supper most nights, homemade bread with cheddar cheese cut from a huge wedge. The cheese was traditional cheddar with a strong tangy bite to it. The cheddar had a rind formed by cheesecloth absorbing the outer layer. Onion needed always to take the edge of the cheese's sharpness the home-grown Sturon onions imparting a sweet flavour. Baked jacket potato with a huge potato and vast amounts of butter and salt were another alternative. There were occasional rare treats such as pickled tripe, creamed tripe, Calf foot, cowheel, pig trotter, and the only one that I ever acquired the taste for fresh muscles. These bought from Mr Palfryman the fishmonger in Ripley and prepared at home. This by cleaning, under the running tap, boiling and de-shelling giving a beautiful flavoured sauce, which discarded in favour of stronger stuff. We then placed the tasty fresh muscles into a jar of brine and vinegar to give them a pickled flavour. Why do this I do not have a clue. Dad though was a `great one for salt, he added huge quantities to all his food, before tasting it. Dad it is bad for hearts, I should have warned him!

Sometimes Saturday Dad with Ned and Maurice Wheatley would sally forth in Maurice's Austin A35 to the Peacock at Oakthorpe for Pints of Bass and an opportunity to put the world right the collective sayings of Ned are well known, to all of us. Ned had a simple solution to most things. The traffic problem of the nineteen fifties solved by taking all them off the road not fully paid for. This was one of Ned's solutions, so obvious, and so impractical. Empty heads vote labour in empty bellies votes them out explained the election.

Maurice was the owner of Whatstandwell Post Office and a smart well dressed character , he had a degree of affluence , after all not only was he a car owner , but he changed his car for new .We were invited there for tea once and were presented with fresh Salmon a fish that Mum adored . The Salmon then was line caught Scottish salmon that was wildly expensive. Farming salmon not considered in those distant days, so this flavoursome wild fish became more delectable to Mum. On the return after the home spun philosophising always at eleven o'clock , closing being ten thirty , drinking up time for the last pint purchased at twenty past ten was five minutes, and a twenty minute journey home, I would always get a bag of Nibbitts, a potato straw which came in plain and the new cheese and onion flavour,. This was opposed to crisps that were always plain and contained a small twisted blue bag of salt to sprinkle over the contents. This is how I have to stay up to see Quatermass, the scary television for adults after ten PM on a Saturday.

Saturday was baking day, Bread rolls, Cakes, sausage rolls. The bread rolls floured then split by hand fresh from the oven, butter sloshed in and cheese added to create a morning elevenses. Saturday Lunch would be similar rolls, preparing the way for the Saturday salad tea. Ham Pork Pie, sausage roll, lettuce, tomato, cucumber, celery always present each week .The salad followed the pattern laid out by grandma Hackman.

If dad had borrowed Sid's van or Wheatley's van we would sometimes go out on a rare Saturday, `trip to the pub with mum, I dare not protest at the boredom as I knew that would end the trips totally. It was only an hour sat there in silent obedience, no DS-LITE for me, just self amusement, writing down car numbers, stretching my imagination, protest was not on the agenda at all .Seen and not heard was the orders of the day. We lived on Dads preferences, he did not like Matlock , so if mum suggested it we would be offered Wirksworth or somewhere else with minimal attractions , Bonsall Dale was an alternative , but pre well dressing normally to avoid it , when its busy . Dad was not into busy, crowded, or congested, as long as it was empty and free we would have it.

Nevertheless, let me not denigrate those trips out, I savoured them. They were after all family time, and with the civic and public offices, that dad took on, that together time was precious, and appreciated. Mum was never a great enthusiast of public houses though and her reluctance showed. She would have to get to a full make up stage before leaving home no matter where we went .She enjoyed her family trips, we would see Aunty Agnes or Aunty Lucy. Aunty Agnes would suggest that Dennis got ready and tripped to the pub with Dad but he always took over an hour to get ready, this led dad to a low moan. If Dennis wanted to go out, he should have started to get ready an hour earlier. Dad had his unshakable opinions on everyone based on strict morals. One uncle had commented on a girl in a public house in an unsavoury way, dad immediately marked him down as a potential adulterer, and thereby marked, dad avoided trips out with him. The indiscriminate character assassinations were often though unfounded; my friends judged on where they came from, or by a random selection set with dislike as a default. Dad had an un-shakeable faith in his being a good judge of character so he applied his judgement to village and school. You must stay away from him! They are all no good, was the blanket assertion," .Well he is from Crich Lane in Belper; he will be no good then will he? "Was his assassination of one boy? I did not have the critical mental ability to understand the geographic designations of who was good or bad, so I resorted to surly a hem. Divorced mothers , scored extra bad points , as did coming from Alfreton , unemployed parents , un married parents ,poor folk , well poorer than us anyway ! . All these things scored in the hit list of life that became Dads mental bible of who was a bad lot and who was all right. I thought the scoring system based around, if they were a potential friend, then off with their head, they must be no good.

Despite all the pitfalls and woes, I enjoyed my time as a child in those post war days when the world was expanding, there was no unemployment, we were importing Caribbean labour to wipe the hospital floors and drive our buses. We never allowed for the fact that the sons and daughters of these migrants would want to better themselves; after all, they were the sons of toil. Dad had a total intolerance, and if the slave trade introduced, he would have happily volunteered to operate the transportation trucks. I have had a struggle with my own beliefs , after my formative years believing , black is bad , Abdul is a thief , the Indians curry rats , and the Japanese

, well they should be the subject of genocide . It was not an English superiority, which had been born of a superior race; it was keeping the buggers where they belong. Oh, dad never realised that they had taken our places as the poor labourers, and as we progressed that these economic migrants running from tyranny and oppression, with starvation and hopelessness equalised the vacuum formed as we climbed the ladder from the primeval pit. It has taken years for me to know that we treat humanity as kin regardless of colour, or creed. I ponder how the Christian missionaries were busily saving those black souls for God and beating them for their own good why can we not evoke equality, liberty, and fraternity across human kind unilaterally.

I hope that I have left this canker of bigotry a generation ago, but fall into the way and hate myself for it from time to time. Dad not all the legacies were good, racial hatred was the worst one though. Teach a child open hostility as the parental norm and they accept it as what should be, after all we create our children's formative ideals. We must take care to present good only, so that the next generations do not fall into our traps and pits. I certainly did and had to fight to lose the prejudices that I learned so early in life,

Chapter 10 Sundays

Sundays were totally organised. Sid would collect Dad for a morning cup of tea and a routine trip to Heage Hall Farm , every Sunday returning with several dozen eggs which Dad would then distribute amongst several others , charging exactly the same as he had paid per dozen . Aunty Lizzie and a few others would have their eggs delivered by Dad as a routine. Packed off to ten o'clock Sunday school finishing at quarter to twelve returning back at two for an afternoon session.

I regularly achieved one hundred and four attendances each year, and lost Sunday to Methodism. It unfortunately had the negative effect on me insisting that I would never send my children to such a Sunday ordeal. We used to get ministers with full on Adult style sermons that were well beyond our young minds. That negativity took many years to overcome and never damaged my belief in Christ, but did destroy my belief in the Church. I think the idea that exposure would leave a lasting impression was behind it but it was too much and too heavy by far. The interval between me remembering the chore of attendance and recovering my faith was some thirty years. If the chapel Sunday school had been Child friendly then the whole procedure would have been easier and probably enjoyable, but the default was Uncle Frank, or the visiting evening preacher. Uncle Frank's great devotion showed through but never really as fun. When you are for years old, you want the fun aspect. I always felt that shoved off there to get me out of the way. I bitterly remember the occasion when uncle Frank had a whole mass of 3-D pictures on a 3-D Stereoscope and was about to spend the afternoon showing off his exploits when I was sent duly off to Sunday School . Protests were futile and quickly rejected. I have lived to regret not sending my three but the scars of my childhood Sunday school coloured my judgement badly. It was solely the unremitting drive to send me out for the morning and afternoon to listen to dry as dust old Methodist preachers talking what appeared to be gobbledygook. If those preachers had taken the time to realise that we were children and not theology students I for one would have rebelled less and enjoyed more.

The Sunday school though did have attendance prizes if you made the requisite one hundred and four you well awarded a bible .Trips to seaside were a summer bonus, a coach trip to far off Scarborough or Skegness, Blackpool, or Bridlington took up a Summer Saturday. These trips did not stop at the Pub on the way home though. We all took a packed lunch and boarded the Bus outside the Chapel. The journey took about three hours wherever we went and three hours back, so left with about three hours at the seaside.

The first necessity was seaside chips, and tea in a cafe, a quick tour of the fair and back on the bus, and a long journey home. The bus sing – song was a chapel based repertoire. Tiredness induced by the seaside air reflected in the yawns and heavy eyelids until in those pre motorway days the bus wound around the country roads back to the village.

The driver's hat passed around to collect for his prowess at finding the destination the sixpences and shillings supporting his wages.

The other big Chapel event was the Anniversary. The Sunday school paraded through Nether Heage and Heage following Heage Silver Band. At each stop on the ambulation, George Beighton would open up his piano accordion and squeeze out a tune to the accompaniment of the Sunday school. Stalwarts of the Chapel would beat on doors, collecting boxes thrust forward, to gather in donations that kept the chapel running another year. The anniversary had a scaffolding stage that extended high above the choir stalls to hold the Sunday school for the afternoon and evening performances, to a bulging house.

There was a Fête in the summer, sometimes held on the field at the rear, which Sid Gadsby eventually gifted them to extend the grounds after the land was sold to build the adjacent bungalows .This was attended by the ladies class who held the tabletop sale in their own control. There was sweets and a tea stall, soft toys, perfumes, bric-a–brac and all varieties of things that nobody ever really wanted, but bought to fill Chapel funds. The entertainment could be Harold Copes Weight lifting group, or other local variety acts.

Christmas bought a nativity play where younger children produced the tear rending performance of their lives as dyslexia and spoonerisms fell innocently about the platform. The platform hastily constructed as with the anniversary one, above the choir stalls the expectant parents did an ever so sweet act as their offspring wrecked the original story in a thousand ways.

The huge organ was another feature that dominated the tiny chapel, with the diminutive Eileen Bamford dwarfed by the massive console. Mrs Bamford seemed to be a Chapel fixture and played for mum and Dad's funerals .She was playing well into her late eighties.

Sunday tea was yesterdays salad if there was enough left from the quarter pound of ham from yesterday. Sausage rolls would spread out the ham ration , but if all was gone then we dined in style with john West Red salmon , It was always dressed with malt vinegar and white pepper , bones removed and mashed up , with Mum's trade mark home baked rolls , smeared with Lurpak salted butter . When the one sliced tomato and the sliced egg added, the undressed salad was always a hard fought battle as there was a verbal advantage to eat more lettuce, eat more bread. Homemade cake, fruit, date would follow tea, Ginger all figured large in the weekly menu; cups of tea were also a compulsory addition always with the food, never after.

Mum would rush the tea things away by half past five and start to get ready for chapel, wash, change and a hat as she began her march to the evening service, back in time for the evening's television. Sunday Night at the London Palladium with the rotary stage was a highlight of our week

At this point in my story, I shall offer relief from the monotony of myself indulgence and offer an insight into what I broadly regard as my bloodlines.

Chapter 11 Leslie Page

Leslie was born in Horsley Woodhouse in nineteen twenty one, although a temporary lapse of memory seemed to have convinced my Mum that he was, like her born in nineteen twenty. The pensions department found him out and he worked an extra year until he was truthfully sixty-five .Leslie was the seventh Child of seven. Hedley his next senior Brother Pre deceased him in the late nineteen twenties and after a weak childhood had failed to thrive.

Thomas worked from the age of thirteen for sixty years as a miner, running his own gang, finally at Denby at what I believe was called Page's Face, due to the multitude of Thomas' children hewing coal there. I lost some of the trails but Thomas's mother was Mary Jane Page, Daughter of Benjamin, and Clara (Nee Cook). Benjamin came from 148 Bell Street Pensnett Staffordshire; Pensnett is in the Parish of Dudley. In the early nineteenth century, this small rural idyll transformed into an industrial town with the pollution and grime that it brought. Chain-makers, factories, iron works, and the terraces that housed the workers filed the green fields with an industrial sprawl this expansion turned this into an ever-expanding urban sprawl that overdeveloped in the pre Second World War days of community house building. His wife was a Pensnett girl to and was born Clara Cook

Mary Jane vanishes in the eighteen eighties and I strongly suspect that shortly after the birth of her second Child Isaac .She possibly lost to consumption. The TB was raging across the land, but childbirth alone saw so many young mothers and their offspring to an early grave. We therefore await further research to find great grandmother's fate. .She and Isaac left the lone Thomas to his Grandfather's care, and I suspect that Thomas's father George, also a son of a George left the district. Mary Jane had at least a Brother Stephen and Isaac as well as Sisters Elizabeth and Sarah. Stephen seemed to be a Denby and then Kilburn man until he moved to Ilkeston at the dawn of the twentieth century to carry on the family coal mining traditions. His offspring were Samuel, Jane, and Ellen.

The Lamberts took Thomas in and at the tender age of nineteen ads the century departed, he wed Alice their daughter, and shortly after, she produced Maud, the first of the line that was spaced at three yearly intervals until Leslie in nineteen twenty one. Maud, Harold Cyril, Alice, Cephus, Hedley, and Leslie followed.

Alice had a medical problem and in nineteen thirty three lost her life post operatively at Derby Royal infirmary, leaving her family in Thomas's care. Thomas soon married the Widow of George Pykett, and Amelia became the Step Mother that Leslie did not ever want .She bought her only children, Amelia, George, Lizzie, and Alf who because of his late father's serenades to him universally became as Sonny, from the Al Jolson Classic, Sonny Boy.

The family moved from Horsley to the new houses built for Miners by the mine owners the Drury Lowe family. These houses built on a thousand yard plot designed so the miner could feed his family from his back garden. This is reminiscent of the Greek land area, each thousand-metre plot being a Strema, is that the ideal size for a man to feed his family off. An orchard backed onto the mine spoil heap and the apple pear and plum trees filled the area at a high density , this is the end that the pig and the hens were kept , these were fed on the household scraps reducing the bin to being an ash bin only . The garden led to a tiny courtyard that found the single story kitchen. This kitchen led to a living room, then via a hallway into a front room. As I previously explained, the best room was not for everyday use but for the special days

 Dad enjoyed the Scouts, with the added attractions of football and boxing, and took to laying in as if he never could have explained to me. Alf confided that Dad called for school would rattle his boots against the floorboards to reassure all downstairs that he was not only awake but up and dressing. Alf sent by Mr Dicks the Headmaster home to remind Leslie of his non-attendance.

 Amelia produced Royston and he eventually married Ivy and produced a son Royston they remained for many years at the Rykneld hill house that had been the Family home. Amelia Page , Les's step mother moved from Royston's home to live with her eldest son George who had the solitary detached house next to the pottery . We visited there regularly, the house had no electricity, and the gas burners provided a yellow light from the mantles. The air had dampness about it and the woman that I always knew as Grandma Page sat awaiting the end of her days. Doctor Ryan suggested that she move to a sheltered accommodation near Ripley Hospital but by the time her mind made up, that home was full and she ended her days in the Glebe in Alfreton. I remember visiting in the middle of the nineteen sixties and she was chiding some of the others for not pulling their own weight in sharing in the homes chores.

 The only member of the family that we were ever in contact with was Aunt Amelia. She worked all her days at Denby

Pottery and in the days before the Pottery began its shop and outlet used to have boxes of second quality goods, all at staff prices, and part of Dads empire of trading was to buy, collect, distribute and sell the same. Never though at a profit, always at cost price was Dads motto, he could not profit from others. Dad had a set of unshakable principles and being straight and honest with people was one of his undying principles.

Les Left school at fifteen and started work at Slater's Brickworks making drainage pipes, the work was extremely hard, and no concession made for youthful inexperience. He met mum in nineteen thirty eight as they perambulated the streets of Ripley on a Friday night circulating the town in an effort to attract a mate.

When war broke out the papers, calling Dad to arms arrived and after a trip to Derby to sign on, he returned a Royal Marine. Not to the battlefields or the landing grounds but fresh from training at the marines Devon home at Lymphstone Barracks, where he honed his skills in marching and boot polishing, trained to Blanco webbing and keep smart at all times he ventured to Cardiff. He, soon, appointed to a Garage in the middle of Cardiff for trade training. HE had an accomplished set of hand written notes that explained carburetion and electric ignition, which he gave to Darren Wilkinson. I would have loved to thumb the pages of those old books and remember how he started a climb to a skilled trade. He quickly learned to drive and trained as a vehicle mechanic. The newly trained tradesman was then to predate my arrival in Hampshire by defending Hayling Island from a machine Gun position in Hayling Island from which he flew the Blimp shaped Barrage balloons .From here to Westerham in Kent and soon to embark on his world tour at the expense of King George

India became his next home after passing through the Suez Canal and more acclimatisation and training. He was preparing for the big push to retake Burma and Singapore. The war in Europe almost won and Dad was with the spearhead of troops that were to attack the Japanese in our colonies. The scientists saved him the danger by releasing an atomic bomb a week before the Tank landing craft ferrying them to attack Singapore from the sea reached the shore. The second bomb unleashed its destruction twenty four hours before Dad was about to see action at very close quarters, and the Japanese surrender saved him the risks. As he landed, the armed Japanese were still on guard and as he was in the party that released the prisoners from the notorious Changi Jail the sight sickened him. There was no sympathy for the Japanese who disregarded all Geneva conventions and entertained their captives with slavery.

On one occasion when an ex prisoner dropped to a Bren gun and destroyed the lives of an unarmed Japanese working party , the damage was done totally before the man was removed from the gun . Dad's job was as driver to Surgeon Commander Vincent-Smith who he taught how to drive, and used the massive Plymouth V8 as les's personal transport. His tie up with the hospital was because of his officer's position as Principle Medical officer. On one occasion, a senior nurse asked dad if he had ever done injections, and then taught him how to administer them on a ward of Japanese prisoners, treated badly, as a reflection of how they had treated the British forces, when they likewise suffered incarceration. The Geneva Convention seemed too applied with a degree of interpretation, as the despicable starvation and enslavement, had taken an effect on the victors, who had become sickened at the emaciated state of their brothers at arms, now rescued from Japanese torture.

He returned for de-mobilisation and went to work for Wilson Lovett, with his new found driver mechanic skills .It was at this time that he applied to join the Derbyshire Police Force, but failed the mathematics exam .he was told he would get straight into the Metropolitan police but didn't want the adventure of the relocation that it meant . The sorry point is that his mathematic exam failure was probably an error of the moment rather than a failure. He never went back to try again though .Regret remained with him though throughout his life, and the mathematics never failed him as a trustee and treasurer of the Chapel.

I also felt that as the Brother who did not go down the pit, he did not follow that family success trail of Granddad as an underground ganger employing his own men. The others had their own houses and dad refused the chance to but the pair of houses at the guide posts for £300, solely because he would never borrow money. . Regret was the failure to purchase property, which he instilled into me .How much simpler it would have been after Uncle Frank's death if the old cottage of 28 Brook Street Nether Heage had been ours.

He suffered hard labour for this bad start with so many years as a coalman delivering a hundred bags of coal a day in one hundredweight (fifty kilogramme) sacks. Working for Albert Wheatly with the promise of inheriting the coal business left dangling over his head. He was working for his future, the golden egg from a not so golden goose. Albert Wheatly was infirm and riddled with crippling rheumatoid arthritis. His son and daughter ran the shop, and dad ran the coal yard, serviced the lorry, loaded and weighed the sacks, delivered it, collected the money, worked six days a week, all on an unfulfilled promise. I remember Albert well on the Saturday collecting round , using an ex NATO left hand drive dark green Austin A50 van , he always gave me a shilling (Five pence) for helping .

The Saturday round involved collecting money on credit for coal from the poorer back streets of Derby, it made the week a long one for Dad. Some Saturdays we would have football tickets and would take a seat in the Osmaston Road end of the now demolished Baseball Ground, to watch the second division club in a battle of what I saw as uninspiring football. The half time pies disallowed on the grounds of you gets tea when you get home. The back of Abbey Street and the streets around London Road and Sinfin the old pre war terraces of Normanton and Osmaston were all on the weekly coal round. The coal was delivered and paid for over the next few weeks until the next due delivery .The coal was taken down a long passage between the terraces , or sometimes tipped into the coal hole , a grid on the pavement that led directly into a cellar , where a large section was earmarked as the coal bunker . There were still some of the small yards. Houses on four sides around a small yard with a double size entrance formed these ancient yards. This, the remnants of the pre war slums, t pulled down and replaced with modern council housing. As the tenants removed to newer council, housing the on modern Chaddesden and Markeaton and Mackworth estates the standards of these estates dropped.

There was a Saturday call too at the Wholesale market where Dad paid all the shop bills, often from the coal takings. He visited Bellis & Meeks, Johnsons, Johnson Brothers, and paid the weekly account. Here he collected our weekly groceries. I armed with a half-ounce plug of tobacco saw Bill in charge of the Banana ripening stores for Johnsons. I exchanged the plug for a full hand of ripened bananas, cut from the huge stalks hanging on hooks in the gas-heated rooms. The bright green bananas warmed to a golden yellow with open gas jets replaced with bananas in plastic bags stored in cardboard boxes in the middle sixties. Bananas always were a problem as refrigeration blackens the skins and turns the fruit off. The specialist reefers hauling these bananas from the Caribbean had to keep the holds at a constant fifty five degrees Fahrenheit , and only had a half degree tolerance in either direction , The art of the Banana ripener has joined many of those lost trades in time forgot. Bill's job was to control this ripening with the varying heat, then to cut the hands and place them in the long heavy wooden banana boxes.

Our fruit and vegetables put into a large cardboard box and Len, Mr Johnson's manager calculated a price, a few shillings, but always paid for .Loaded into the van we finished of the calls for

When in my Primary school years Mum was working I spent, my holidays sat in the lorry cab whilst Dad shovelled and heaved the coal, filled the lorry back and headed to Derby. I ranged around the coal yard passing time, trailing through the undergrowth and the scrub.

After Albert succumbed to a second attack of pneumonia, forgetting conveniently to write his will after the first attack, his son offered Dad continued employment. Disappointed bitterly Dad took off to a delivery job with greatly enhanced pay and better conditions with the National Coal Board, delivering the miners concessionary coal. They were entitled to six tonnes a year but handed back a tonne to give the pensioners from the colliery a half ration. The delivery team was a two-man effort and although the tonnage was greater, the work shared. Dad had a lift each day with the car pool that ferried men from the village to the pit, or he caught the half past five bus. The lorry was more modern, and it maintained by the garage instead of dad being the unpaid mechanic. Albert's son Jack found his inheritance hard work and despite Dad having left the business in good order, Jack was struggling with the work and the round. He offered dad a partnership, but, still slighted by the broken word, the offer left to fester. After all the offer came out of desperation and not any sense of fair play. Therefore, by nineteen, sixty the ownership of the coal business was but a dream, a dream that I am glad never came to fruition. I can only imagine how the hard work would have slowly worn my father down.

At the NCB the lorries were loaded under the coal washer , this was where the coal was rinsed and washed , where the lighter "Bats " floated off with the dust and the good coal graded and the dust washed away . The huge rope and canvas bag was held under the chute and the lever pulled the coal thundered into its new found home .It was one of these huge lumps, some filling a single bag to the limit , that escaped its new home and struck Dad across the knee that was to plague him all his life onwards .

When Redundancy came in the middle nineteen sixties, Dad now a National Union of Mineworkers part time representative accepted his pay off gladly. The Union and the antics of philabustering to gain a second union negotiating day , which invariably doubled the expenses but always finished by eleven am , meaning a half day on full pay had sickened him . From that negotiating skill learned there he stood, at the behest of Joe Hodgekinson, Schoolmaster, as Labour candidate, for Ripley District Council. I have noticed over the years that many a stalwart of the left is not the man with the pick and shovel, but the man with the pen, and the words.

 . Dad had received his recognition, as Councillor Page, he was chair of Heage School Governors, member of various committees, but as avid, a conservative voter as you would ever meet. Why not show your true colours I once enquired, "Not whilst the NUM pay my electoral expenses I won't "was the final answer.

With the closure of New Denby Colliery Dad and the rest of the workforce made redundant. This was in nineteen sixty-seven and the hard work and the labour on his now frail knees was over. He applied to Securicor for a job and spent several Years with them. Glow Worm eventually took him on **in Mil**ford force. The conditions were better and there was a small pension so he moved there and stayed there way beyond his sixty -fifth birthday, relieving the others for their holidays. The rest of his story I shall tell later.

The years on the council were complimented by other

unrecognised public service; Dad was the Ambergate and Heage District Poppy Day organiser for over Thirty-five years, from nineteen sixty-four until Colin Pickens took over in nineteen ninety-eight. He spent years looking for his replacement and arranged his old friend Colin Pickens to take on the job. Dad awarded a Gold Legion badge for his good service and I felt that it was best if we returned it so it became available to reissue to another worthy member, the badge thus returned to Ambergate and Heage branch for further service. This seemed to anger Aunty May in some way. I had done what my heart told me, not what my relatives expected. Barbara and I attended the 2001 Annual Dinner at the branch's expense to return this coveted badge.

Dads prized medals, the service medals, and the Burma Star, I gave to Robert, to enjoy. Dad spent over thirty years in public service, he took many hard working legion posts, as well as the Poppy Day organisation he was secretary of the Service Committee that ran the hardship funds for ex servicemen and widows. It was in this role in the late nineteen-nineties that he was reunited with his step brother Alf (Sonny) who was suffering from a second World War injury , gained as a paratrooper , shot down whilst landing at the bridge too far at Arnhem .So in that famous drop we had relatives . Uncle Cephus was at the Battle of Monte Casino in Italy, The elder brothers stayed hewing coals alongside their father .I know Dad resented the BEM never reaching his father, because of his death before the award actually granted, despite it s gazette notice . A medal for Sixty years service in Mining, that took some earning, and shame was we never have it to hold.

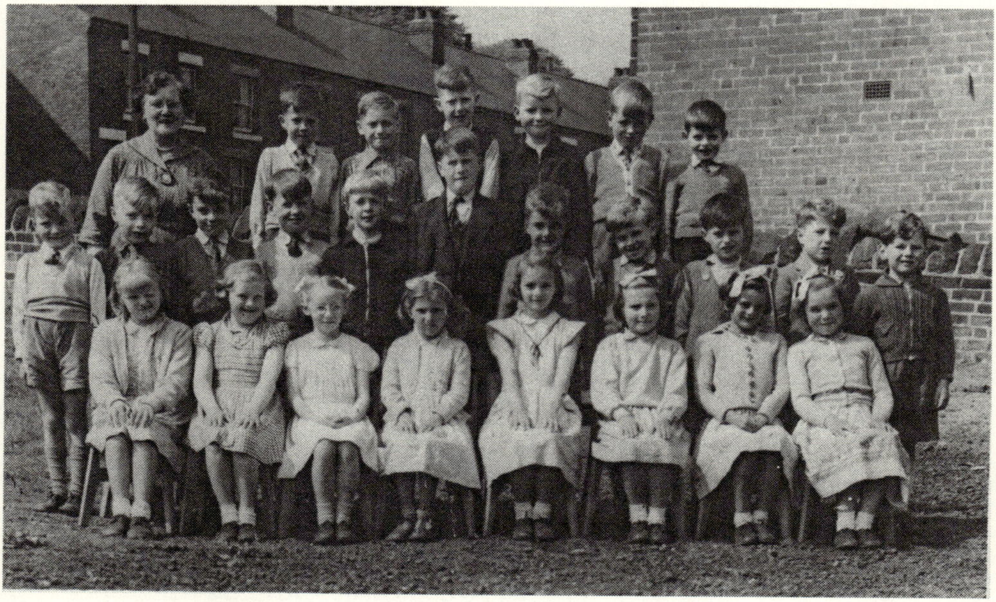

Chapter 12 the First School(s)

The first School was Nether Heage County Primary, known as "Ridgeway." I spent 1954 to 1961 there in all the classes. The school was Victorian stone construction, the huge windows high enough to prevent you staring out of them .This was the school that had educated Mum and all her siblings in their early years .From Lilly to Frank , who was known as "Kipper " , not sure of the reason behind that nomenclature but I suspect it may be sleeping in class. The classrooms heated with hot water warmed with an ancient Victorian coal fired boiler, the water was pumped around four inch pipes that fed huge hot water radiators made of heavy-duty cast iron. Hand stoked during the Day. The toilets were outside and in winter open to the elements and ice formed on the concrete floors. The water pipes lagged with sacking to keep the supply going in all but the coldest weather .Toilet walls and the large single trough urinal were tarred; this gave a contrast to the thick whitewash on the upper walls and cubicles. The doors painted in a universal pale grey , that liveried Derbyshire County Councils , premises and vehicles

.The playgrounds were tarmac covered , and the boundary walls scaled up to twenty foot high from the entrance gates , as the school grounds were cut into a steep bank . Playgrounds segregated into Girls and Boys to keep the sexual segregation in the Victorian spirit. The washing facilities were located in the entrance porch of each of the younger and older entrance porches. There was never soap or towels and the rush in discouraged use of the sinks, they were though massive, and the lone cold-water tap sat centrally. The central hall divided into two classrooms reunited only at the Christmas party. If you were in the Head teacher's class, you would line in single file and await Mr Hustler lurching forward to ring the bell and call you in from the biting weather. Miss Saint's class and Mrs Swift's Class queued at the rear porch for their entrance. Coats hung in the relevant porch and you filed into your individual desk, each oak desk grouped in pairs. . Silence encouraged , and work was a driving force , play was not part of the mainstream curriculum .Mr Hustler's class was adorned with a black plastic Ink well filled with a violent red ink, found in a storeroom somewhere and doled out as an economy measure. This ink had been found in an old store cupboard, it was in quart brown glass bottles, and each bottle diluted to a half gallon, of this blood like fluid. The age caused the ink to have fibrous threads in it that required cleaning from the steel nibs, normally with your fingers, the ink then being wiped from them wherever you could find a dark place. In Miss Saint's class, one had slates, these were scratched on with scribers, when there was no more space a sponge cleaned the scratched slate, and the process began again. How the environmentalists missed that paper saving exercise. In the other classes we used pencils, but in nineteen sixty as an introduction to the adult world , led by Mr. Hustler's condemnation of the ball point pen , as an instrument to encourage bad handwriting we dipped nib pens into ink wells, just as our predecessors had done a hundred years before. The cheap paper sucked it wildly from the nib, soaking it through to the other side of the paper; this made any of the scribbling very unreadable.

The whole school ran on a reading, writing, and arithmetic, There was always art and in the first classes a variety of play through learning. You would take a pile of assorted blocks and stack them in size order, or there was a ply house with its pretend cooker, where girls played house. The first class also had a ten o'clock treat, "Listen with Mother" put on the radio tuned to the home service, and by this, the daily story read to the whole class. Radio was AM and the frequency would drift so the radio would crackle and fade in and out. The wobbly radio transmissions the normal quality for the day we just drifted with the signal quality. The FM bands with the stable transmission was a long way off , as you got older and more sophisticated , in my case 11 , there was the new invention the transistor radio . My Phillips one was eleven pounds in nineteen sixty one , equivalent to over one hundred and fifty pounds today , The money to buy that came from ten pounds Aunty Lucy gave me for passing the eleven plus . The small desks and chairs arranged next to each other so that there were two long tables and you faced the child opposite. One double width long table ran down each side of the room and the large central area was clear. The walls were painted cream and the woodwork a pale grey. The schoolyard was male in the one by the gate and female in the large yard overlooking the farmland.

At the bottom of each yard a solid brick built air raid shelter with bomb proof doors and a solid concrete roof resided ready for the Luftwaffe to return and attack the under tens of mid Derbyshire . The heavy blast proof doors were secured with a clamp arrangement that held them tightly shut and kept the doors firmly closed against attack. There were no lights in these shelters , and the PE equipment was stored in the one in the girls playground .These dark dusty structures housed fifty years of old desks and broken chairs awaiting resurrection. We were bought up with the make do and mend philosophy that had been the rules that were imposed upon our parents for the last decade. You never know when you might need it was the motto of the days. The Air raid shelters were a no go area for pupils, as was the craft room, a shiplap wooden structure that had been a centre of woodwork in the days one's parents attended here. This room had too fallen into disuse, it now being the home of a stuffed fox and its evil eyed companion the stuffed owl. The fear that those glass eyed monstrosities could inspire was immeasurable. The stone built toilets were in the appropriate playgrounds. These backed onto the boiler room which afforded a minimal amount of heat to these companion structures .In winter on the cold days the pipe-work , thick and lead , covered in strips of sacking to defend the pipe from the cold managed to just resist the ice forming winds . The water level in the water closets often had a thin ice film forming over it. The urinal was a half four inch drain pipe with the walls over it heavily tarred a lagged pierced pipe was isolated in winter leaving a heavy blanket of urine's acidic odour sticking to the walls and choking the small child rushing to escape from the odorous surroundings . The cubicles were less inviting the Izal toilet paper with its non-absorbent gloss sided paper starchy and sharp edged. Poking out from the roll hanging of the wooden pole suspended from a wire hanger firmly attached to a nail beaten into the heavily whitewashed brick wall.

    The playground's tarmac and painful if you fell, it being totally covered in a fine flint dust that carved flesh like a hot knife shaping butter. We did not wear protective trousers but a flannel short trouser. The design had evolved over decades. The wear parts below mid thigh were flesh, after all a little pain taught you not to fall. It was usual for all boys to wear shorts for school and play, until you went to senior school. The grey flannel was a thick heavy weave, lined against the weather. The waistband was a rubberised band to hold your shirt in place. The sides had adjusters that enabled the shorts to cover two sizes. The waistband also had buttons to take braces, the leather attachments to the webbing braces helping your shirt to stay in place. The braces webbing was slightly elastic and adjusted with a steel loop at either side. In summer in queues for school admission, the clever trick was to ping the braces of the person in front. The shirt to complement this ensemble was a grey flannel, coarse, and cutting when wet. Socks hung off an elastic garter that bound the wool tightly to the calf .slowing circulation to the feet. Any slackness in this caused the wool to slide to the ankles and the call of "pull your socks up "the defeated sock laying baggily around the ankle. Socks required garters, this elastic band a quarter of an inch wide, sewn together to form a tight gaiter about you. These were always getting lost, and unfortunately replaced. Shoes were robust and Oxford brogues. Shoes were all too often a dark brown colour. Dad would take me to a shop in Belper's High Street on a Saturday; he liked Weaver brand shoes, which were emblazoner Weaver for Wearers. The choice of colour was brown, I so wanted Black, but for an untold reason that was not to be, "Brown!" it was to be.

The teachers were graduated too as you got older conditions got harsher and teachers aged proportionally. The first class was Miss Saint who was gentle, young, and fresh ; she made attendance at School desirable. After the age of seven and through until you were nine , you crossed over the back road through the brickworks , endangered yourself across the major road in front of the aqueduct , lost long ago , that carried the Butterly to Cromford canal across the road , forming a narrow damp low bridge . A short walk bought us to Sawmills Village Hall. This was school Monday to Friday for the seven to nine year olds. Mrs Jean Bowden ruled this independent unit. Unfortunately, when she went to visit her sister in Australia on the P & O Arcadia we got a supply teacher. She was less than bright. I did not get on with her from day one and ended back in Mrs Swift's class earlier than the rest of the group. Mrs Swift got on with the education she not intended to waste our time. The last class was the Head-teacher Mr Hustler. We had trips out in Mr Hustler's class; we toured York and its emergent railway museum. We walked to the brickworks where the class soon grounded in how bricks started by exploding from the rock as dust, ground up reshaped and baked. The exploding rock in the quarry being the highlight of the tour .We spent weeks on an unfinished art project, when we all made a chess board, and none of us ever finished it. In the half hour assigned the first fifteen minutes were spent setting up and the next fifteen minutes putting away. We constructed a Cruck barn out of twigs, which remained an unstable pile of twigs. I asked Sid Gadsby if we could play football on one of the fields he agreed and we trooped off to play football on the Barn Croft. Malcolm Ottewell kept trying to take umbrage by telling me that as Sid was his uncle he could have organised the loan of a field. My retort of " shame doing was not as good as talking about it " resulted , as I walked past him with a swipe across the back of my head with the cast brass school bell resulting in five stitches across the back of my head . Typical Malcolm, to cowardly to attack ,but not from a face to face position he came at me from the rear out of my vision , what a horrible spoilt child , but weren't we all . The five stitches resulted in his banishment from football. I found sympathy hard to find when unlike mere mortals it trumpeted that Malcolm had won a place to Oxford, which he then within his first year achieved "sent down" status as he failed to reach the standard. Oh! How the mighty fall, so pitied !!!

We endured the eleven plus to escape the primary system direct route to the Secondary Modern School at Heage. This school had delightful craft lessons including an afternoon on gardening. That, I considered being a total waste of my effort and time. There seemed to be an emphasis on the life skills, needed to build a family, to start a home. The educational standard of Heage was sadly lacking, although a further escape was available after the first year when a thirteen + exam was available, but much tougher than the eleven + equivalent. Two take the Secondary Modern route to secondary education did not preclude anyone from, a university education, it just made the work required twice as hard. There is always in any group a defined set of un-teachable, these then become the disruptive , taking a grossly unfair amount of teaching time , thereby watering down the education available to brighter pupils . I see this today as children pass through the comprehensive system where a supposedly homogeneous group of abilities, means that the brighter children will encourage the less able. I sincerely believe that there is a streaming process that couples the better pupils by ability, to the better teachers. It is easy to condemn teachers, when there is no inducement that could bring me to stand in front of thirty something children and try to drag them into line.

The "Eleven + " a two-part exam that had a first, tick box, straight tick box IQ test, ticking odd ones out, ticking the spot the differences in a picture type of questions. If you passed part one you have to part two, a maths and English test, you then got out of going to Heage School and languished amongst the eggheads of Herbert Strutt's or went to the less popular Ripley Technical School. I in my enigmatic fashion ticked the box for Ripley. I thought that Ripley being a relatively new premises, would be a more enlightened and progressive establishment. The curriculum at Strutt has still retained Latin and Greek, and concentrated on the classics and arts. Ripley concentrated on the Sciences and Engineering.

The afternoon walk across the fields to home not missed, the morning trip was by Trent Bus, and cost three pence which is just over a penny. The Bus conductor had a clip of priced tickets, which they took from a rack, mounted on a neck strap, and ceremoniously punched a hole in it, then handing it back. Either the return trip was by Crich lane then over the fields to Nodin Hill along Gun Lane and down Shop lane, or we took a turn of the road by the new telephone exchange and cut across the fields to Gun Lane. The foot and Mouth outbreak in nineteen fifty nine ended that an s the fields became out of bounds and we all walked the long journey that followed the road.

Summer and winter we took the long walk but in winter were all protected by Duffel coats with the hard wooden toggle fastenings and thick woollen hoods. To protect ourselves from the severity of a Derbyshire winter we wore a liner to the duffel hood of a balaclava helmet and woollen gloves, these became wet and cold as the journey neared its end. We left School en masse, and David Jones left the party first, at his grandma's farmhouse on the dangerous corner at the start of Ridgeway. The rest of us lived in the village, those few short years we walked in oblivion to the world falling in and out of friendships almost at every step. John Key , David Whysall , Malcolm Ottewell , Peter Jones , Wappy Wainwright as John was known , a tall ungainly sort , The crowd who dwelled on the Avenue as Bentfield road was universally known struck off across the recreation ground , which used to fill the triangle between Shop and Spanker Lane . Those names are dim in the past ,Malcolm Edwards , who never learned to read and write throughout the formative years , he was late blinded in one eye by his wild brother Dennis , Terry Sheldon who became a ten pound Pom at eighteen and set forth to Australia , Kelvin & Ann Lineker . Shirley Taylor, the girl who suffered from nerves, resulting in wet underwear, regularly, sent home to the inhumane chorus of her peer group chanting Shirley Taylor has wet herself Miss! Shirley Taylor has wet herself. What a cruel monstrous crowd, we should have been stopped before we became total bullies. . The splashing on the floor resulted in a totally silent audience that amplified the effect into a gushing torrent akin to the Colorado river breaking down the Rocky mountains .Ann Powdrill , a pretty girl whose port wine birth mark covered half her face , leading to her being known as beetroot . Cruelty never bothered us as children, in today's climate, we would acquire a councillor, and a social worker for such biased taunts. WE were horrible children, but all horrible to each other. We in the eyes of our parents knew nothing, after all, we were the first generation of the post war babies, and we had not seen war. Most of our parents had not either, but hey! In those days children had to speak only when spoken to. Strange behaviour in adults was to be whispered about, the strange Mrs Murden who wandered the village muttering to herself, the shell shocked war wounded at the Hoult's who wandered in a daze, waiting for another barrage of Nazi shells to fall, there were many flawed people.

The Spanker used to assemble the old miners on a Friday night who would gather in the Taproom to recall tonnes of coal, roof falls, pit ponies, the wonderful foreign travel awarded by King George in the War that followed the War to end all Wars. The music was not from the dusty old piano in the bar , but was the shuffling of dominos in that Tap room .Old men in flat caps, faced with grey stubble, drinking Mild Beer, the cheapest available, spitting onto the wooden floors, black dust impregnated phlegm as the mine atmosphere still hung in their lungs.

Beer was one shilling and three-pence a pint or sixpence in today's money ,when you compare though the sixteen pints for a Pound , a week's wages would but 80 pints of beer for a labourer , not much different than today , in equivalent terms . Bitter was more expensive and best a penny more than bitter. The Brewery was Brampton's, taken over by John Smiths in the late nineteen fifties. Frank and Lilly had remarkable memories, order a drink once and they automatically started to pour in on your return, there was no draught lager, but Skol was in half pint bottles, with the nut brown, IPA, light, specialist flavours that have almost vanished from our local public houses today. There were many combinations of bottle and draught. Black and tan, brown split, light and mild, the hand pulled half was always generous into the pint glass, so the added bottle gave measure well over a pint.

Heady balmy days, days when riding a bike by trying, falling off, realising that hurting yourself really is painful and to be avoided that a good day work growing by experience. Summer we would treck off with a war time gas mask case , a bottle of tap water and a jam sandwich and picnic all over the woods and ponds in the area . There were several natural dens in the hedgerows, the bank alongside Dungely hill provided a deep cover for our observation posts, and the bank had a natural gulley that you, on dry days slid down, into the road. A dangerous occupation then and now the bank as gone, with the addition of a pavement, the chance of sliding in to today's heavier traffic would be fatal. Charlie England had a field bordering this, just rough scrub, but if spotted on the wrong side of his hedge, he gave chase in his van as you fled down the hill. The windmill field had a spring and a stream that led into the brook .this had a hedge both sides and gave natural cover for hide and seek as well as a variety of other games that we dreamt up daily, . We stormed the banks of this tiny rivulet, as soldiers, as cowboys, as the secret service, floating sticks and watching them race along the tiny stream. We munched on our crude sandwiches and bottles of water there too, as though it was a palm strewn tropical beach.

We played Cowboys and, well no one would ever be Indians, we could never play war because no one would play the Germans. We played all these warrior games but always without opposition. The juxtaposition of the first and second finger formed our six shooter , and a twitching thumb the trigger , Shouts of "per-clang " simulated the small arms fire , aim and someone died . Most serious invasions required the automatic rifle, or Sten, or even on violent days a Bren gun, they consisted of two clenched fists and a "too, too, too," noise. This weaponry was superb, and you could never lose it, it was always to hand. Other weapons in this simulated armoury were the huge bullwhip, and the bow and arrow, all imaginary. It gave a timeless sense of equality you needed no wealth other than that of an imagination.

The whole village our play zone, with the wide network of footpaths we had a freedom to roam the hills, some no go areas though, we kept out of Bessalone and Thacker woods,

"Trespasses will be prosecuted "areas these, and we couldn't read to well . Bessalone housed a vast underground water storage area on behalf of the Severn Trent water company . The windmill and the Malthouse both derelict and a fear of dangerous masonry, well no, fear of getting caught, made the adventure a risky one .When you live in a small village of a hundred houses, you are so easily identified, and so easily reported, across the Post Office counter and the chapel pew. The sound of foreboding rang when you heard the cry of I will tell your Dad, It was never worth getting caught, or more importantly spotted, for to my Dad accused meant guilty, tried, and found wanting. Strange, sent off to explore, to take walks through the fields, but you are never to deviate off the path... With the network of aunties and cousin's spread over the area, you became easily to trap, and it was often a fair cop, when wrongly accused though protest was useless.

Winters always used to provide enough snow for a short toboggan run from the windmill to the bottom of Dungely hill. I think it was the winter of nineteen sixty-one when there was snow on Boxing Day that lasted to Easter. Sledges were homemade; mine the slowest, as dad never fitted the metal runners that added speed, so I slid on the crude wood slowly. Dad was always busy, he was keeping long hours at work, in the garden, visiting , British Legion , Ripley Council , Committee meetings , If you offered help., you were told to weed the garden , but never what plants were weeds . I miss that time that we could have spent together, which was lost as dad scraped together the things that his meagre salary could not buy. We did well though and were never hungry or cold. There were a lot worse off than us in the village. The food was always plentiful and the best quality expertly cooked. The repetitiveness and plain menu never questioned. Mum cooked the food dad wanted and liked.

Summers were days we walked, and wandered the hills and vales. We took train-spotting trips to Ambergate station, friendly drivers would let you climb into the huge cabs, hissing, spitting steam combined with steam oil, and coal fumes to give a special smell. The vaporised steam oil had a distinct smell that I recalled years later as an engineer on steamships .The huge engines pausing at Ambergate as a lay by whilst express trains hammered through the Toadmoor tunnel to Sheffield and beyond. Trains had names too, The Palatine, and the Midland Pullman, ran exactly to time. We diligently wrote the numbers and the names of the Engines, the faraway places of the Jubilee class, "The Gold Coast" ,"Bechuanaland ","Union Of South Africa, the colonies sped by cast in the brass nameplates of the engines. The new Diesels were being tried and tested too D1 "Peak District, "leading the vanguard of oil engine trains .The new diesels were badly designed and often underpowered for the work. We rarely saw the huge Deltic engines built not by British Rail, but by English Electric, The triangular engine boasting six pistons to each three cylindered bank, and the banks formed up to eight long to give a twenty four-cylinder power monster. When a Deltic spun into life it could scream to full power in seconds, no slow build up of revolutions, a howl of the wild power greeted the driver as the throttle pushed forward. The classes of engines bore names, but most of the class diesel electrics were Peaks. The technicalities did not matter the huge steam engines breathed a life beyond their mechanical parts , fire and steam seeped from their orifices , sparks flew as the first stroke of the cylinder caused a better draw on the fire as the exhaust steam blew into the funnel . The drivers in their dark blue cotton jackets worn over bib and brace overalls had a plastic topped peaked cap, resplendent with a British rail Badge. The old identities still emblazoned the porters trolleys, liveried in the LMS maroon. London - Midland and Scottish, the engines built at Derby and Crewe were led by the Princess class hauling the biggest, fastest trains with their giant tapered boilers and their shiny black paintwork. To see that paintwork now replaced by the original maroon has breathed a new life on the few preserved leviathans.

Ambergate fell at a triangle of London – Manchester, London – Sheffield, and Sheffield – Manchester trains .Freight mainly across the Sheffield to Manchester link, but the rest took the express trains through the picturesque dales .The Ian Allen books listed the numbers and we ticked them off when we saw them. Not much of a hobby when compared with Nintendo's virtual world but it amused us for years. The Midland Pullman, thundered twice daily on its London to Manchester service, the small tables in the open carriages enjoying an individual table lamp to illuminate the diners high-class menu. Breakfast on the way to London was porridge , Kippers , Egg, Bacon and a full house of accompaniments , Dinner on the return leg a much grander five course spread , of Soup , Fish , Main Course and pudding , with the obligatory coffee and biscuits . The windows curtained not covered with the standard roller blind, and the executives commuting daily from Manchester enjoyed a splendid degree of luxury as the Pullman brand demanded. The train was a regal Blue and the powerful engine had to slow for the curvature of Ambergate junction's elevated track. The whistle of the turbo blower heralded the onset of pure power as the engine exited the number one platform , passing the signal gave the driver an urge to abandon Ambergate as though doom was attaching itself to his train . The acceleration was visual as well as vocal, pure power, pure roar. At Ambergate, the intellegencia from the Railways based in Derby began the experiments with all welded rail. The fishplates that had allowed the metal rail to expand replaced as the rails were pre tensioned to allow the temperature and length to self compensate. Finally welded together the rail was silenced forever .The trains ran clacketty clack as the wheels ran over the joins, but after leaving Toadmoor fell silent as the new technique took hold of the metal wheels.

Ambergate held its own fascinations, it had two chip shops, and a rickety arrangement perched on stilts to bring it from Ambergate recreation ground to a road level and as second hidden behind the White Hart Public House. The village followed the path of the Derwent River as it forced its way from the Dales to Derby to spill into the mighty Trent. There was a Cyclists cafe, specialising in beans on toast, a wooden hut that has given way to a brick structure with toilets. Three garages dispensed petrol. The Jet Garage had a car Auction site attached, The Shell garage a Caravan Sales. The third garage now long replaced with a fast food restaurant.

We walked over a low river bridge where the Gas Works stood in later years, and passing a lime Kiln, we scurried through the canals Hag tunnel. Dark and dripping with water the canal teemed with fish and we tackled the Roach shoals with maggot bait, and the Pike with a small roach trapped on the line. The fish we regarded as inedible and, except for the captive live bait returned them to the water. Fishing rods made of split cane and some had a flexible end that twitched when the bait suspended taken; within a hundred yards, the canal river rail and road crossed each other intertwining like a wild bunch of cables. Summers seemed so long and I left to my own company from seven in the morning until Mum returned at four.

Buses featured a lot, as did trains. Dad didn't get our first car until nineteen sixty six. We would go out on summer evening bus trips to the peak district, Dovedale, Monsall Dale, sometimes dubbed mystery tours but always to the same areas. We also in addition to the School trips had on one Saturday per year a Chapel trip to a seaside town, this was always by coach.

The coaches locally were Mike Horton Coaches from Ripley. We would go to Skegness or Blackpool, Bridlington once as far as Scarbrough. The trip was the whole day. Three hours travel in each direction and three hours at the seaside. Sometimes the trips would be inland to the pre huge funfair days at Alton Towers, to see the gardens. To Dudley zoo, Drayton Manor Park we didn't have major holidays but were well blessed with days out.

As a child holidays were a rarity and I only remember four. One to Brighton to the Sea view Butlins Hotel at Saltdean, another to Birkenhead to visit Mums friend at Bebington. A week to Blackpool, to a hotel owned by one of mum's cousins, a John Nally then a week in London with Aunty Lucy and Uncle Sam

Brighton, we set out by train from Ambergate. The luggage was sent ahead with the railway man. Who collected it on the Friday on a flat truck pulled by a three wheeled Scammel truck .We set off with a walk to Ambergate Station with Grandma and Mrs. Walker in tow. We caught the train to Derby, and on to London. We changed stations in London by Taxi and were soon on an Electric Slam Door train to Brighton. It seemed odd to have no engine, as we settled back into the luxury of Southern Railways Green liveried carriages, the Guard joined us and this luxury was First Class. Dad dug deep and paid everyone's excess so we could enjoy the trip. At Brighton we had tea at the station fourcourt café .A scruffy establishment, the teaspoon had a hole drilled into its bowl, and a bolt secured it to a chain attaching it to the counter. Then the inevitable bus trip on the Southdowns green double Decker to Saltdean and the Biggest Hotel I had ever dreamed off, Swimming pool. Dance hall and a television screen the size of a cinema in black and white. Here were some multi story rooms. We were domiciled in one of these blocks beyond the swimming pool. Whilst we were checking in a Southern Railway lorry arrived with not only our but everyone else's luggage. Those ultra manoeuvrable Scammel Scarab three wheeler lightweight Lorries, pulling a trailer, half side boards, half canvas tilt were at every station delivering the railway's parcels. We set off to the room that had an inbuilt radio in the wall. The announcements were constant. You were awakened by a "Good Morning Campers call. " There was a local unusable beach, but all the facilities needed were on site. The children were enrolled in the "Butlins Beavers" club and supervised by redcoat entertainers. There was a morning and an afternoon set of activities. Roller skating, adventure walk in the local area, crazy golf, art, many things to keep us all busy were available every day. Gran and Mrs. Walker were happy just sitting. The meals were set and there were three a day. We even had supper one evening. Dad for years afterwards used the size of the cod as a yardstick against which all other fryers failed. He also spent time trying to make me swim, but Dad was never the best teacher of anything. You were given a few chances, but if you didn't understand what he wanted then he could get very frustrated .The evenings had entertainment, Top entertainers too. We had the comedian Arthur English and dozens of redcoats whose names I'll never remember. The entertainment ran a string of contests that had Knobbliest Knees, the most glamorous Granny, and the prettiest girl contest. The evening was then filled by the contest, the Star act, then a Sing – Song. The old war time songs were belted out. There were songs like, Tipperarry, Quartermasters stores, Bluebirds over the white cliffs of Dover, The early evening television on the projected black & white screen. A wonderful unique time that first holiday gave to us all. Brighton so far away the other side of London seemed to be at the end of the world. I was nine years old to .The rules of Butlins said that only children over eleven should go to the hotels but no one seemed to apply the rules. Dad thought the Holiday Camps to awful. He had been ensconced in the Sunshine Camp at Hayling Island as a wartime barracks. He obviously thought that the cooks and staff had not been de-mobbed. A fantastic time, it must have been it is still a clear week over fifty years ago .I must have been an ice cream junkie in those days, in the afternoon we would go to the first floor café for tea. I would have a Banana Split, A single split Banana with banana and vanilla ice cream, double cream, cherries and all for three shillings and six pence, in old money, today that would be seventeen and a half pence.

A few years later were the London adventure. We stopped in the hotel just off Russell square. I had my own room, but in those pre en suite days the toilet was along the corridor.

All the bedroom doors looked the same and I was scared I couldn't find my room again, so I am afraid I shared with Mum and Dad had the single. We breakfasted in style, then set forth to explore London. We took in the Planetarium, The Tussauds Waxworks. We even went to the Chamber of Horrors. The Tower was a wonderful experience .We queued for ages to see the Crown Jewels. The British Museum was within a few hundred yards of the hotel. The vastness of the Egyptian and Greek exhibits didn't seem as interesting to me then as they would be now; we lingered amongst the Elgin Marbles, so exquisite, saved from the pollution of Athens by philanthropic Lord Elgin .The trips to the Science and Natural History museums weren't as long as I would like to spend now. I never felt that dad was not a great lover of architecture or museums and his boredom threshold showed more than once I think. We explored all the highlights. I always loved museums. Aunty Lucy and Uncle Sam were with us the whole week. Aunty Lucy loved history and was good with enthusiastic guiding.

The vastness of Hyde Park amazed me that such a huge space was in the centre of the city. We tarried here for a whilst and became lunchtime idlers as we heard from dad how extravagantly costed the ice creams were. We fed pigeons in Trafalgar square, admired the architecture of the City, sat in Piccadilly Circus amazed as the neon signs performed endlessly , all trying to grab our attention , as they glittered ever changing before us . We walked and bussed and even took a river trip, from the Tower Pier. We boated past Battersea's elegant power station , the Houses of Parliament looming their A.W.Pugin designed gothic spires piercing the skyline has we motored towards the turning circle of the tour opposite the " Cutty Sark " at Greenwich .

We took in the whole city. I vividly remember the Pakamac, The thick nylon stand-by coat to protect against rain. The Pakamac rolled into a large sausage so it would stuff into a handbag, or blazer pocket, we lugged them everywhere, but what a talisman, the rain keeping off us.

The hotel was huge and was to the best of my memory on Russell Street, there was an Edwardian elegance about the area in sight of the University Building and the British Museum, and it fitted in with the elegant terraces, metal railings protecting the passing public from a plunge into the basement. We walked everywhere .and trod the streets like a tourist army. Lunch was usually a sandwich in a Lyons Corner House. Dad was always mindful that the average cockney was about to inveigle him in a scheme, simple in application, a con trick designed to fleece unsuspecting country boys of their hard earned cash. You can add Cockneys to dad's list of people to avoid too.

Regents Park Zoo was very fascinating in those days. They had the most un-politically correct chimps Tea Party. No-one would allow the humiliation of chimps that the tea party consisted of. Today I would much rather see Monkey world, but then to see the chimps perform was wonderful. The Elephants were huge, Guy the Gorilla was still there and there was a scruffy concrete bear enclosure, and a glass walled snake enclosure. The Zoo was nearly a whole day on its own. We lunched there and watched as the chimps performed to the delight of the tourist. Dad had no interest in the Victoria and Albert or the War Museum, as he remembered the war and didn't need a museum to remind him .London always seemed overcast and smoggy in those pre smokeless zone days.

The third Holiday was a trip to Bebington in Cheshire. This is just outside Birkenhead. Mum had a friend who had been evacuated to Heage during the war. Her friend Pat was married to Cyril. They had a daughter who was about three years older than me. We trained to Liverpool, changing at Manchester. The ferry to Birkenhead from Liverpool pier head crossed the, then had to catch a bus to Bebington. The house was near to a large golf course. A three bedroom council house, situated in Brackenwood Road , opposite the Brackenwood Golf Course. The great entertainment was walking and an evening trip to the pub.

It was the second time I had caught a boat from the pier head in Liverpool. We had had a school trip at Ridgeway School to Llandudno in North Wales that included a sea trip. The school caught the Liverpool train a school special from Ambergate Junction to Lime street Station .We walked to the pier head , boarded a Llandudno ferry . There was a whole fleet that plied around the north Wales coast the excursion ships were owned by the Liverpool and North Wales Steamship Company The steam engine had a wonderful smell of hot oil and all the olfactory pleasures that I associate with steam. The "thump, thump "of the engines pounding from the hot smelly, "No Admittance "doorways into a dark hot subterranean cavern. I did want to explore there then but armed with the knowledge I have now I could probably spend days exploring those old Ferries. We didn't have long at Llandudno. There was a coach there to take us to the base of Snowdon and via Snowdonia. We didn't have time to catch the railway up to the peak. We took the coach for a late return home.

Our Fourth Holiday was some years later in Blackpool. I think I was about fourteen then. We set off as usual from Ambergate station via Manchester luggage in tow .We got off the train and walked to the Hotel. It was owned by the Nally family, mums cousins .The week away was the normal for holidays in those days. We spent days on the beach and walking along the Golden Mile , the arcades and auctions , fish and chip shops , and what dad referred to as Catchpennies , places selling " kiss me quick " hats, , plastic jokes and those funny seaside postcards . We always had to send postcards on day one, postcards to Gran, to aunties, to friends. Postcards were a compulsion; you were condemned if you didn't send them. The sticks of rock were the next thing on the menu, followed by the essential presents for gram. The souvenir, cheap pot marked "present from Blackpool."

Hotels in Blackpool were the comedian's epitome of the Seaside Boarding House, with the strict landlady. The doors were locked at eleven thirty. There was a sign in the bathroom demanding tidiness. Mealtimes were to order, exact timing was required. The day started with the morning walk to get the paper, Breakfast was a slender version of full English, with a top up of Toast and Marmalade. Eat plenty, it will save on lunch was the day's requirement. Once you were out, by ten o'clock. You were out for the day, not to return before four o'clock to be ready for the five o'clock tea. As we were family we weren't subjected to the full assault of these rules, but there were enough left to make life ordered. On one day we went to the pleasure beach, we played prize bingo too. I remember winning a dartboard .More to carry home too. I had then a five-pound camera from boots, if I took pictures, but cannot remember any. It was a 35mm so the prints were small .There was a trip to Fleetwood, where there was a market on a Friday. The beach was a daily happening , cool winds blew in from the Irish sea , and we spent the time at the beach fully clothed protecting ourselves from the sand ballast of the onshore winds .Dad searched for pubs that served Bass Best Bitter , and then bemoaned the quality , It wasn't like Bass at home .

The summers over and the Eleven plus passed new green uniform and long trousers, signalled the passage to growing up.

Chapter 13 At least it wasn't the Pit

At that tender age of Eleven and three-quarters facing, what was to be the foothold on the future the "big" school? Short trousers, at the fashionable below on the knee style were no more. We would wear a tie , the long flannel trousers would hide the grey woollen socks , held in place with elastic garters , that failed more as the day progressed ,garters that incurred no complaint , or a refashioning would take place that would act as a tourniquet around the ankle .So alive and fully grown having escaped the county primary school . That summer seemed so special with anticipation in the air. Had Thomas Page felt that same anticipation, at the same age his forecast was sixty years of drudgery and hard work, I awaited my satchel he awaited his shovel.

The schools system of the nineteen fifties had, the returned warriors who had lost their youth fighting for world freedom and equality, the promises of no more war, and the United Nations brokering peace and freedom from poverty. They had retrained as teachers the others were bright young things that had been the first of their own generation to lift from harder backgrounds and fight their way, using their own intelligence as their sword and shield.

The air of the soft-palmed socialist, establishing a comfort zone, educating the sons of working men to lead them forward lay abundantly along the senior school roadway. We looked on teachers in awe and respect; we trusted them to do their best for us.

I , remembering the hard times I had , sometimes unfairly given my our children's teachers , when their teaching was poorly researched , wonder back to those days , and think of the rarity of the natural born teacher , and the educator . I was often quoted as saying " Graduates who can do the job get a highly paid place in industry , the meritocracy teach ".I still believe that to be true , but fortunately some of those dedicated professionals , spatter the body of the profession .

There is a degree of regret that the opportunity presented by secondary education is never appreciated when you are there. Effort was doled out as to what was needed not what was wanted. I wasted my chances there. I can sit and blame others, poor teaching, poor inspiration, poor facilities, but the bottom line was my poor effort. I caught up but later when I could have been enjoying my life with Barbara, I stuck to my learning.

Chapter 14 Ripley Technical

The new green Blazer and grey flannel trousers were a completed with a green and silver striped tie, and a green cap, metal badge a miniature replica of the blazer badge dangling above the peak secured by three metal loops. These loops then sown to the cap. A new leather satchel completed the ensemble. Mum had gone to Snooks a large independent warehouse , with Mrs Smith from Ridgeway Hospital, and paid , a lot of money , eight pounds , for a satchel with a briefcase handle, she wanted the best for me and was very proud of the eleven plus pass . More than I knew at the time. The blazer, non –standard, mum wanted the best, even if differences got you spotted, the blazer made to measure from the Co-op in Ripley too.

When you look at the Co-op the area at the bottom of Grosvenor Road , housed the Co-op butcher and Baker , Opposite a large co-op that sold the bric-a-brac and records at the Nottingham road junction was Co-op Shoes , Men's Clothing , Ladies' Clothes , Children's' wear , The Co-op Cafe , Banking facilities , The Co-op undertakers . The first Supermarket in Ripley built by the co-op on the site of the old

Empire Cinema, all these local owned. They all supplied from the Bakery, Coal yard and Dairy situated less than a thousand yards in each direction. There always appears indifference in Co-op movements; the lethargy of the members leaves unguarded trust with the management committee. A prime example was the ability of those committees' members to take interest free loans from the organisation. There was then no check in place to stop that good socialist from, lending further at whatever rate he could extract. How can one be a socialist, when socialism carries so many parasites inflicting their diseases on it?

We on the first day had issue of a bus pass to take us free from Nether Heage to Ripley, because it was over three miles travel in each direction. Derbyshire County Council deemed distances less than three miles were a walking distance, the pass given, and the future set and a date to start embedded in the calendar.

The school was only three years old and we were four hundred pupils strong. The second Head Teacher J.R.Burns was still finding his feet; the teachers were all still fresh. The deputy head a prim woman with a severe bun called Mrs Strong, what an apt name for that woman, for by her nature you would have avoided argument with her. The rest a complete mixture of young old, enthusiastic, and indifferent , some seemed to think that the two best reasons for entering the profession were July and August . Some were dedicated; Millward was an excellent Mathematics teacher, not as well qualified as poor Mr Miller, but not as vulnerable. When watching are run of" Please Sir" the sixties comedy, there is a poor bumbling greyed teacher there that strikes a strong personality resemblance to the dithering much maligned bubble

On The first day we assembled in the playground , as the tennis courts were better known , and we were sorted into alphabetic order , A- L were 1X and M- Z were 1Y . Our form mistress was Gillian Hayhurst the music teacher and one of the few that did not wear her gown as a badge of office. Burns stalked the school in a mortarboard too. We all received a new Rough book for rough work, and timetables that divided the day into forty-minute interludes spaced by a maniacal room change at the period end. For the main, the first years based in rooms one, two, and we did little changing of rooms our desks being our main base.

The day started with and a registration in the base classroom, followed daily by assembly at ten minutes to nine. There was a hymn, a reading, a short prayer, an address from J.R., addendums from any other teacher wanting to waste time speaking, a second hymn, and then wild abandonment as we all ran to attend the first class, late. The first two periods followed. A break when a rudimentary tuck shop opened spaced out these lessons, there was potato puffs or wagon wheels as a nutritious choice, the option of take it or leave it as the second way. Girls from the domestic science class wheeled a teacher's tea trolley, from the domestic science room to the staff room, where the teacher's tea was served to them. Fifteen minutes was like no time at all, as the bell recalled us to the lessons, and the next pair of forty-minute distractions led us into lunch at noon.

We had a huge dinner break to take in two sittings of pupils. The afternoon began at one thirty and three periods and a fifteen-minute break filled the afternoon. Gent automatic bells signalled each change, a single strike at quarter to the period end and a long ring at period end.

Lunch itself was two parts, dinner, and pudding. Dinner was a meat dish collected from the hatch , and vegetable dishes collected by table monitors ,whilst the queue was being dealt with a short benediction was said by the teacher , normally , Lord Bless this food we eat and make us truly grateful . The main course, could be mince beef pie, savoury mince, casserole of lamb, braised Ox liver with onions or similar, all easy to eat and with little residue. The vegetable tureens always had mash potato Swede and a green, often boiled cabbage or cauliflower. Puddings often steamed with a thick glutinous mass of yellow custard, except when the sponge was chocolate, when the sauce tuned a vibrant pink .Tables cleared, and the second sitting were visibly forming a disorderly queue to attack their portions. Teachers dined free as a supervision benefit, and headed most tables. The Head teacher J R Burns always sat at the same table at the same seat in the well of the hall .The mumble of diners was overshadowed by the clatter of knives and forks on the plates. Dinners were subsidised and for the week cost twenty-five pence. The monies were collected on a Monday, with the exception of the handful of people entitled to free meals; this was less than a per cent of the school roll. The table always had a water jug, with thick glass tumblers at each space. To look now at current trends in school dinners, we had proper food cooked on the premises from scratch. The alternative was to get fresh air if you were not eating at the time, so dining hall or playground was the choice. If the weather was bad, and above drizzle, we were allowed into classrooms, herded like cattle into rooms 1 or 2. On cold wet days the playground being the choice as it was not really rain, just drizzle, soaking your clothes, the library became a cosy option. We were all supposed to have coats and outdoor shoes, so suffering the weather was self-inflicted.

Some lessons periods doubled, Woodwork, and metalwork alternated around terms. Eric Woodward took the woodworkers and Doug Ambrose the metalworkers. In metal work we did really interesting things like make metal name tags , solder a tin tray , make a mild steel , case hardened screwdriver, all pretty useless, but nevertheless good practice . Woodwork was similarly useful; the compulsory pine pencil box was of such proportion that it needed wheels to move it. The designs were basic, to show us the skills needed, but the results impractical. Art took two periods, and likewise had sculpture and painting as term varieties. The teacher was a small stocky man named Mr. Samson. He did his best to enliven our philistine sense of the artistic, but the clay he had was un-mouldable. We though made figurines and sketches all of sufficient quality to enrich the school dustbins. Mathematics was a favourite subject , although it became a merciless opportunity to torture the incumbent Mr "Bubble" as Mr Miller was renamed, his rotund figure and shiny head gave him an all round appearance . He was though with his master's degree one of the most highly qualified teachers, he had problems getting his classes disciplined though, and occasionally they fell into total disorder. We rode cross a curriculum of geometry and trigonometry, expanding into the calculus that was much needed at college, in those pre calculator days. In later years at the school we were taught by Mr Millward, Head of Maths, a different proposition, in terms of discipline, unfortunately none of these was inspirational. English with French featured daily. The French teacher was a witch of a woman called Mrs Williams, who was poor at her subject and not well attributed as a person. I once had the temerity to ask a question and suffered her indignant disgust, what! question what I say !, I was not questioning her teaching ,just asking her to expand on the reasons you would use a word , I am easily put off , and as my father before once committed to being put off stay minded the same forever. In the second and third years we were graced with Emma, Miss Edith Hemesley, in her fullness of middle age and facing retirement, her approach was ferocious, unequivocal, and she came armed with a handbag that was leather, and huge. That bag was reminiscent of the Handbag , so lauded by Lady Augusta Bracknell , in " Importance of Being Earnest " the Oscar Wilde play , that Barbara and I so enjoyed at Chichester's Festival theatre , when the formidable actress Miss Patricia Routledge bellowed forth . Miss Hemesley's version though appeared in her hands as she slid behind your chair, raised the offending bag, and firmly landed it on your head. The contents never saw the light of day in the classroom, but the inflicted pain indicated that railway lines, or Smith's Anvils, may be appropriate descriptions. English we had the delightful Mr Wilson, who had a passion for drama that he enthused to his students, I regularly, during his tenure as drama master took part, albeit small, in the annual play. His great success was John Flanagan who has spent has life as a professional actor, often playing police officers, a role model from his father I expect, the formidable sergeant Flanagan of Derbyshire Police. How a teacher can make a subject come alive in their hands is truly a gift, and one that Mr Wilson, with his love of literature bore out. I still remember well the Mark Antony speech from Julius Caesar, being illustrated by John Flanagan to the amazement of the whole class, a fifth year pupil was bought out to read us a play, how strange.

The science subjects were one of the school's stronger points, and the facilities were far ahead of any other school in the area. This reflected in the teachers and their qualities. Physics in the early years taught by an ex Rolls Royce engineer called Mr Reay, he had the knowledge, but not the ability to engage the young minds in his care, and Physics was lost until Mr Barry Cope taught us in the third year. It is such a pity that reflections tell me of fine minds coupled with poor aptitude to educate causes poor teaching. I became convinced those years ago that we, as pupils today, were taught mainly how to pass those ever so important exams and not the subject. Chemistry and Biology were under the jurisdiction of a young teacher called Marie Christine Jones, who had absolutely no idea, how to control a class. She was just fresh from teacher training and prone to short tight dresses that were a distraction from the test tube. Eric Webster taught woodwork, but also drawing, the technical kind where pencils were chiselled to a point and paper guillotined to A3 to save resources. Our schoolboy hands dragging pencil carbon and ingrained dirt from our hands across the paper .Eric had the flair and skill, having taken a diploma at Loughborough to enhance his skill base.

He was one of the few teachers that actually had humour is his skill set, which he used to enrapture us in his subjects.

The fragrant Miss Gillian Hayhurst took Music. How Camille Sans-Saëns Carnaval des Animaux sped through its fourteen movements to lead is into an oblivious sleep state, as the years Tromped along, we graduated to **Peter and the Wolf** by Sergei Prokofiev , which was even less understood.

We had the teachers who were well equipped to guide us past the Head's goal of five O levels average for each pupil, but the skill was lost to some of them in how to impart that knowledge. P.E teachers were the worst, had they become PE teachers because they were ill equipped to do little else, I often wondered. Jeff Foulks imparted his athletic skills and was demeaning if you could not manage to does the tasks. I remember reading of his heart attack at a relatively young age, and pondering on how his fitness regime had failed him. He left Ripley Technical. . Michael Walker arrived as the replacement he took geography and PE for two years before he also left later replaced, after two terms teacher less, by Jeff Grattan.

I see how the curriculum binds teacher's hands, but rigorously following the subjects chosen core and applying the selected book, did not teach us the subject. The object was never to understand Biology, but to pass the exam in it. If that explanation had been a public information issue I am sure, compliance would have been easier. Our peer group excelled as compliant sheep grazing the path, but I always want to know why. The thirst for knowledge is a disaster for most teachers, for it disrupts their program, to pass the O level is their sole goal.

That was then, times may have changed, but I see little evidence of it. Dr, Edmund Kraal, took our class at South Shields for a few short terms, the first time I came across a natural born teacher. He made you thirst for the knowledge that he had there to give .We was in those far off school days shown that on heating metals expand. A metal ball, a Bunsen burner, and an iron hoop, showed when cold ball passed through hoop, when hot the ball was too big. Why, Mumble, cough, and pass to the next subject. Thermodynamics years later provided the answer, but school alas failed to explain. This hardened attitudes to the whole profession, and endorsing the thought that those who can do! Do! Those who cannot do it, teach about it. Harsh but it so often true. In assisting Alison on one of the rare occasions that she appeared with homework, I explained that water had phenomena whereby the transition from zero to four degrees caused a contraction. She was marked as wrong, much to my chagrin why, solely because the teacher lacked knowledge and was following a proscribed course, read from a book. That teacher hid on parents evening

Therefore, five years starting now to lay the foundations of life, fail here and all the roads out of poverty and serfdom denied, not quite, but the hills are be steeper ones to climb. The first goal was five years starting now, get five o levels! Easy, did that! If the goal had been nine, I would have aimed higher but five was the requisite amount, so five I got. If Dad would have spotted the soft approach he would have bemoaned the lack of effort, but fortunately, running the Urban Empire of Ripley took up much of his time that left after the Coal Board demanded the first forty hours and he took little interest in either school or the efforts required . The approach of the teachers is what's called the tick the box approach, here is the question remember to tick box B, exam passed, easy is it not?" Nevertheless, why box B Miss? "you may ask," don't be stupid child, you tick it without question, or you don't pass the exam". Simple answer, subject exam passed, quota met, child educated .Teacher! Good result, promoted a step up the Burnham scale, more pay, all satisfied. Child though does not have a grasp of the fundamentals, "doesn't understand

Miss "oh! Just pass the exam and if you want to know go to university and study it the answer.

Cynical; but there was a small minority that actually enjoyed an understanding of the subject, the majority were carrying out a job. Colin Alan Swain, head of Biology, tormentor of boys sadistically dishing out punishments with a folded rubber tube, I remember well, when Mum informed me that" Annie Swain's lad who used to teach you , Has got six months incarceration for interfering with a boy at Belper Parks School" . I punched the air in a victory salute; we had only endured his sadism, not his perversion. That complete animal was formative the opinion of educators, and homophobic attitude in my mind. Annie Swain's boy Alan, got porridge, what good news for justice, not taking a Christian stance of forgiveness wished him a liberal sprinkling of broken glass and body fluids as an accoutrement with each serving. That animal singly put me off school for life, when in a conversation with dad I related this he said, "You should have told me! I would have sorted it! Alas, he would not have, I did not resort to parental interference because the parental opinion was "the teacher would not tell a lie!" From there on life would have been impossible so I took the beatings , and made a mental note to find him one Friday Night in a Belper Pub and seek revenge , I no longer countenance violence as an answer to any problem , but a trip to Derbyshire Royal infirmary would have awaited Swain. I felt that I would have a good defence in court, and the case would drop rapidly rather than Swain risk exposure for his crime. The court though beat me to it, and I accept that justice seen, as done , his pillory was public, and the system worked , the bully mentality hides an inadequate personality, and still feel that the one at the front of the class the worst School Bully of all .

The first year over , and the summer bought me a disaster , the first week of the school holiday , playing on the old recreation ground , now a building site , where I hasten to add I should not have been I slipped off a soil bank and fell badly. This resulted in a Potts fracture across my ankle .A trip to Ripley Hospital was blessed by the gentle hands of Doctor Ryan, who without, the assistance of any pain killer thought a gentle tug and twist of the ankle would pop it in the right place. It did not work, but it did hurt .Derby Royal Infirmary, for a week and then twelve weeks on crutches .Dad was not too harsh about the inconvenience of me being at the Royal infirmary, and they managed the arduous ten-mile journey once during my stay. For at least the last forty years, Dad reminded that disobedience, causing the break, had, after all become a major inconvenience, him having to get back from Derby late at night. To add to my distressed condition I was twelve years old and on an adult ward, with lots of scary sick people.

On return to school in the September, a leg was complete with a plaster. A warm autumn helped the discomfort by causing itched in the unreachable places deep in the splint. The second year found us in the Annex that had originally been the primary school , that predated the main building .These were a temporary wartime hut , shiplap construction ,and cold in winter warm in summer . The class was now 2Y; a progression from 1Y .Our standard of teachers seemed to improve. Miss Edith Hemesley taught French, English was the domain of Victor Wragg. Vic expelled as a tape recorder sales representative in Generalissimo Franco's Spain, for why we did not know, but it gave him an air of secrecy. As 2A ensconced it the draughty cold annex we languished in our separation and isolation from the school, now some four years old and too small. Biology went up a gear and we were taught by Miss Thwaites, the Girls PE teacher , Human reproduction with its John and Jane films was introduced , one girl fainted as the flickering screen showed a baby taking its first look at the world , and the cry of I'm never going to do that !!! Echoed from an enclave of girls. Miss Thwaites had a gusto and flamboyance, and was not easily phased by the disruptive boys .She was also not capable of being embarrasses. In discussing puberty her up front approach, was hands up who hasn't developed pubic hair yet. Hands glued themselves to pockets and not one admittance came forth. All we wanted to know about reproduction in a term explained and delivered. The History lesson involved remembering the date not the detail of the events and consequently fulfilled the oft misquoted Henry Ford , as being "Bunk , as taught in Schools " . Mr Powell tried his best, but distractions were common and the mêlée that accompanies them a normal feature.

The caretaker found he Annexes a chore and they had a stale air of neglect. The Caretaker was Charles Lamb, he was known as Legger, as in Leg err Lamb, or more often as Wiggy, for all the obvious reasons. He headed up a small team of cleaners that appeared at four o'clock and scurried about the empty classrooms with powered polishers. We as an end of day chore had to mount the chairs on the desks as an aid to the cleaning team .The toilets stank of industrial pine disinfectant, and the much-avoided San Izal was replenished by the roll. Paper towels, always out by morning playtime were topped up and a red carbolic type soap was left to rot into sludge on each sink. This team did not idol through the summer, at each September, the school shone after a deep clean and the paintwork had been partially refreshed.

It was at the end of the third year that we had "options" to drop or to take subjects. Mathematics , English language and literature , French and RE were compulsory , as was PE .We had to choose from History and Geography , or ,Physics and Chemistry , and any one from Woodwork , metalwork , needlework , and Domestic Science . Technical drawing was an added option, because there was a juggling of classes' problem, we were formed into a new boy's only group of fifteen known as 4J. We did the engineering subjects. I thought as I did my six-hour drawing for a Department of Trade and Industry certificate of Eric's scornful comments on the untidiness of my drawing. We had drawing tables especially to aid our skills; Eric however forced to use drawing boards so we did not mess up the tables. The fifteen at the core of the group were the remnants of the old Three "j , This had been a catch up class for the eleven plus failures that had sat and passed the much harder thirteen plus , and had been a hard working group . There was a sort of misfit element that came with this assorted band.

We were based in the Drawing class room and relished our freedom as the elite. We were an A stream class of standing, and had to divide between the other classes to fulfil our quota of subjects. We took nine in total, and were aimed at an O level in each one .My nine were English Language and Maths that were compulsory to all, then Physics, Chemistry and Biology, Metalwork and technical drawing. English Literature too was a good choice but French which was a requirement for university entrance, was not a droppable option. Religious Education, Music, Art, Woodwork, Geography, History all fell by the wayside; Physical Education remained as a non-examined compulsion.

It was stood waiting for the toll of the entrance bell that bought David Beighton to carry out another of his bully tactics , backed by the already six foot thick Gavin Lord . I was part way up the stairs, and the late Beighton started kicking me. I grabbed his ankle and strode up a second step. Toppling David over the balcony rail, whilst still gripping his ankle panic set in. I was more scared of dropping him that he was of landing on his befuddled scull. Tears ran down his cheek as his cries for help totally ignored. My classmates held Gavin back, as Beighton asked for mercy. The thought of dropping him did appeal, but on hauling him back, he remembered that bullying was a potential hazard that gave him time to turn to bullying younger classes.

The fourth and fifth years bought us senior status and the right not to wear our caps into school on the bus each day, what freedom. The girls could were stockings, or ankle socks, as opposed to the knee high white socks of the junior years. It was an either or choice, much ignored by one girl Joyce Wilkinson, who always appeared with ankle socks over her tan stocking legs. She was the fourth years wow factor , I remember seeing her a few years later in the Co-op record store where she was a shop assistant , with blue horn-rimmed glasses as popularised now by Barry Humphries persona dame Edna Everidge . The class sex Bomb to Mrs. Frump in such a short time. I from the first year hung around with Alan Mee, who spent the first few weeks at school, whilst the teachers learned their new charges, answering Mee Sir! , every time asked is name, yes boy you, and was the answer, yes sir I the reply. I used to sit with Terry Elliot, known as Dall, in those far off days nicknames so easily formed. In an early class, Terry hit his thumb with a soft faced Thor hammer, and at the time, Thor Heydall had just completed his Trans pacific voyage, so hey dall turned to Dall, Odd thoughts that kids have. James Moss and Jim Neary were in the first few years as friends, but as the J group split away, I think of Colin Wheatcroft and Grahame Williams as classmates. We had open lockers in our classroom as opposed to the un- secured desks elsewhere. We bored a hole in door and frame, and then inserted a wire to form a magnetic catch to secure our belongings. This meant magnetising a bolt so you could open your own (or anyone else's) locker.

The mock exams soon came in the early fifth year and then the real ones were due in the July , In those days pupils awaiting results were not discharged the requirement of attendance but were in school each day either for revision or a few extra classes that were deemed required !. We had the Youth Employment man in, what a wasted effort. The department though had an added bonus of employment meetings and exhibitions off site. It was at the Alfreton Drill Hall with the need to get three stamps from three stands that before I could go home, albeit with the travel from Alfreton.

The Derby Evening Telegraph would be no earlier in the doors of Nether Heage. Not knowing what I wanted to do I search for the obvious, empty stands, quicker stamps, quicker out? Two stamps on my card and the man from The Merchant Navy, was begging an audience. Hi, stamp my card and we can both feel fulfilled was my thought. The man was interesting , climb this ladder and in ten years you could be Chief Engineer on five thousand pounds a year .School Head teachers got about three thousand , so this was serious talk . The money trapped me.

A repeat performance of a career day on the school premises left me looking at the world travel offered by the Royal Navy and the commercial world of the Merchant Fleet. I was soon on my way to Manchester and the Shipping Federation Office in Salford. I had a new aim, to run away to sea, well I thought it was less dangerous than joining the circus, I did not read the fatalities though. In those days per capita, the Merchant Navy had more fatalities than the dangerous occupations of mining and farming.

Mum accompanied me to Salford, how I escaped the Old Man, I shall never know. He caught me though and stayed firmly by my side as Clan Line star Superintendant W. K. Mabbett did his best interview techniques. Dad had a wide knowledge of all things nautical having been on a troopship to India had broadened his horizons widely. The trip to London was a chore though, as British and Commonwealth became my first choice, solely based on the diversity of its fleet of over a hundred ships. They had liners, cruise ship, general cargo, reefers, tankers, bulk carriers, containers, and even a large fishing vessel. I applied to Regent Oil whose quota for the year was full and got as far as reading the P and O application form with its printed heading , dear sir . I beg to apply for the position of... Interview over, job in the bag, college selected, six months to wait. The B & C options were Warsash, where full uniform was the order of the day, and a six o'clock run began each morning as a not avoidable option, Stowe in Glasgow,

Plymouth. Which was a milder form of Warsash or Poplar College in London's East End, the choice became obvious South Shields. This was the college with the reputation for the best engineering tuition. September nineteen sixty-six was booked and arranged, a year to waste, but the future set. I returned to school to finish a failed Physics O Level, and took woodwork, and general studies to fill each day. I re-sat the physics and by February was equipped with passes and grades required, so took my leave of School

Goodbye school, hello, big wide and never-ending world, my new life lay ahead of me f or me to do as I will with. So Engineer Cadet Page, six months, of what to do get a job save some money, and that became my next priority .There ,the answer Ambergate brickyard here I come, Cliff Radcliffe seemed an easy going guy, and I had worked the last summer for Bowmer and Kirkland as a crane driver's mate for about twelve pounds a week. Dad approved and I set off, he knew Cliff, as a Denby man they all seemed to know each other.

The Brickyard produced two kinds of Bricks, press bricks and handmade bricks the clay dynamited from the quarry wall and ground into clay in a huge mill, water added, the clay made and bricks formed. Like toothpaste, the raw clay spread across the press, the press banged down the wet clay brick ejected from the mould, loaded onto barrows, pushed to the kiln, and stacked ready for the thousand degree of the fire. The handmade ones, men took the clay and it then pounded by this team of bruisers into wooden moulds and each hundred paid for as a batch. The hard working makers could earn phenomenal thirty pounds a week pay packets. They were crab like in appearance, bulging biceps, and triceps from forming the clay into the moulds and skinny legs .I was a loader working for Ron Melrose. The money was good and I banked ten pounds each Friday, the change took me to work the next weekend for eight pints of Double Diamond on a Friday night with Ron's youngest son Peter. We would only have one or two at each pub, but toured four or five different pubs. We normally went along Nottingham road, having started at the Butterly Club on Alfreton Road. I had not revealed my future plans to my workmates, so took a lot of flack when in conversation , a lump of uneducated lout said what are you doing here if you are so clever, I stupidly mentioned the six o levels whilst pointing out I could prove that I wasn't totally stupid. The ensuing brawl left me a poor looser and I decided to move on.

I passed my driving test around this time on my second attempt. The first was a nervousness caused by getting a test in Ashbourne on a Market Friday. The market quadrupled the traffic in the normally peaceful Ashbourne. Four weeks after my failure came my success when the same instructor trialled I on the previous errors and I got through. Driving ambition led to J W Smalley, wholesale fruit and vegetable merchant as a seven and a half ton lorry driver. I could not afford a car so I chose to gain experience with someone else's vehicles. I soon assigned an Austin of England flat faced wagon that was beyond its sell by date. I perfected gear changes; it had a non-synchromesh gearbox and crunched from gear to gear as I practiced my technique. The Smalley family were an odd bunch who a few years later managed to bankrupt the family company, turning the wealth to dust. A love of sports cars and a poor business acumen lost them their family fortune .I had my first accident too whilst playing at truck drivers. Whilst reversing the truck into an entrance a van parked behind out of mirror sight, I ran over it. The person was a total pillock but a friend of Mr Smalley's. I told the truth to the insurer and they fairly apportioned the blame ,But I had one week to go , so when Smalley started on about his friend's van , I reassured him that there was apportionment of blame , and invited him to take his job and put it in a suitable position . The work done and playtime over, now to start the real job, the one that was to take forty years to learn , all lying ahead , awaiting .

Chapter 15 South Shields calls

The time came to get ready to run away to sea. Dick Jones had his car at the ready and on a fine September Sunday headed North, or North East, to be more accurate, kit packed, papers signed, and Rover three and a half litre ready to go. The black six-cylinder leather bound luxury saloon purring as we sped north. The A1 road took us to Darlington where we had lunch with Dick's in laws who were caretakers for the Ropner Shipping family at the corporate headquarters in Darlington. Dick and Dad were to call here on the return leg to have an evening meal as they split the three hundred mile journey. The A1 in those far off days being single carriageway for long stretches made it a harder run than today's motorway network would let us believe. The road-building program stretched out from the capital, and on the A1 the M18 was still under construction, with the Northern stretches of the M1, the road that was to form the network's backbone. Leaving Darlington, having had a tour o the shipping offices and the grounds, as well as inspecting the old Alvis that was much Mr Ropner's pride and joy having been a twenty first birthday present it was time to drive out of the huge gateway and the then North again to Doctor Winterbottom's Hall of Residence in South Shield's Marine and Technology College grounds. This was run by Major Evans a Welsh Regiment retired officer, with a Matron, and a small domestic staff .The catering was poor cargo ship standard, more akin to school dinners. We were curfew at eleven o clock, and had to be self reliant in all our needs.

We were assigned rooms on a company by company basis , there were four of us in the intake , me , Harry Entwistle ,Alan Usher , and a guy who left in year two , to become a fireman in Bolton ,whose name is a total loss to me Some of the previous year's intake were there to greet us . Namely Jim Austermule, always known as Bill's favourite and Daisy, Bill's nephew, who was the only person Bill ever sacked. Despite being threatened with mum will not like this warning that's your SISTER Uncle Bill! W.K.Mabbett as Bill was better known was an ex Union Castle sea going engineer .His memory was failing and all apprentices were nominated as Joe.

The short cut to the college was through the house grounds and we familiarised ourselves with the shared rooms, mine with another British and Commonwealth apprentice Harry Entwhistle. We were all in the OND class, and set off to allocated groups on the Monday to take the next two years of learning to heart.

This was not school, the lecturers were quick to point out, we wrestled with the mathematics and statistics, Electro technology, thermodynamics, Materials, chemistry, the complexities of mechanics and the technicalities of drawing. For at the end of "year one " we had to pass the OND stream and Part A of the Department of Trade and Industry's Certificate of Competency in Marine Engineering,

Alongside the education in the subjects there, was a practical element where we learned fitting, machining, and electrical fitting as well as dismantling and rebuilding marine chunks of machinery? We then had sport as a subject, and the strange Liberal Studies, that was to teach us management of men and ourselves.

I forget with the passage of time the Liberal studies lecturer, but his wife took maths, so in delivering her to college he had taken an appointment. He was a retired senior RAF officer who had been as Air vice Commodore involved in the education branch, but he had started as a lowly Spitfire pilot, so he had our attention from day one. Dr Edmund Kraal, who felt that electricity was too complex for marine engineers, taught us plumbing, whilst leading the Electrical department. The cable was replaced with pipe, the voltage with pressure, the amps with litres, and all else was revealed, as resistance became a valve, parallel circuits became hydraulic grids, capacitance, conductivity all became glaringly obvious. Dr Kraal did not suffer fools either , when the old question of electron flow really opposing the positive to negative flow was thrown at him , instead of the flowery explanation that I have seen in the past the pupil , was told , you don't need to know , and you are not clever enough to understand . The chemistry class held in an old school building in the centre of town allowed just enough time to avoid lunch and walk to the old school building. The classroom shortages overcome by the new facilities under construction in the corner of the huge playing fields. New classrooms and workshops, under construction, and one workshop to house the single cylinder Doxford J type prototype seven hundred and sixty millimetres bore engine, which when rebuilt thumped away at 105 rpm turning the massive 10 tonne flywheel. We were the only marine school with a full size slow speed diesel to play with.

The year flew by and Easter came with a voyage from Liverpool to North Shields for the three-week College break on the TSS Kinnaird Castle. We joined in Liverpool's Bootle docks, and allocated the old officers cabins, the ex passenger cabins were now occupied by the ships regular officers. We stood engine, bridge watches, and dry-docked the Ship. The TSS Kinnaird Castle was a twin Screw turbine ship built as the SS Clan Ross, and then loaned to the emergent Safmarine as the SA Scientist, before returning to B & C as the black hulled Kinnaird. The electric power was from three 750 horse power Ruston Diesel engines , of which one ran in port , two at sea , three on standby .The electricity was 220 Volts DC current . That three short weeks was only a brief memory, but the Second Engineer was Davy Cadenhead, known as P***head Cadenhead and the third Engineer ,South African, Brian Yeo. Brian was an odd character who practiced self hypnosis , and would push pins through both ear lobes , then ask which one you wanted to see bleed . It worked every time, a party trick I never tried. We were alongside in Liverpool with the Clan Menzies. which had a contingent of deck apprentices as the companies training ship , for five deck apprentices and a training officer in charge of them .We sailed for North Shields in Ballast , heading for the dry docks there . The crew were Zulu on Deck and in the Engine Room and Durban based Indians in the catering department. We had an uneventful trip passing Scapa Flow, and rounding the top of the British Isles before sailing up the Tyne and into North Shield's " "Smith's Dock" .That voyage was the only time that I ever stood a bridge watch, which at night must be one of the most boring ways of passing time.

Summer bought examinations. In addition, eight weeks of intensive training at the college in welding and pipe fitting electrical wiring and all aspects of the practical that could be forced into a ten-hour five-day week, with additional Saturday mornings. The next term began in lodgings, only the naughty ones grounded to the hostel.

I lodged with Kathleen Lavrick in Osborne Road. She took eight students, and her Father "Pop" lived there along with Sandra Gates a child Kath had taken under her wing .Pop was ninety-seven and filled our ears with his stories as a ships carpenter in the early days of steam, when the engine used if the wind failed. He told of the search for the Tierra del Fuego lighthouse at night. The light had stayed unlit because local natives had made a meal of the keepers. The wooden propeller kept breaking and as carpenter, the engineer enrolled him to help build a new one from spare timber. He was deaf and the great sport was to mime words until after much beating of his deaf aid he would resort to new batteries, at which point we all talked loud and deafened him. Regrets I have a few, but it seemed fun at the time .Sandra was twelve and surrounded by eight late teen and early twenties men could act very silly and giggly, but a swift elbow to the ribs normally sorted her out." I'll tell me mam " her great cry , and if Kath upset her , she would get , I'll go off to my real mam , This stopped when John Waterman , having watched Kath reduced to tears , got up , got the car keys , told Sandra to pack right now and he would take her . Kath worn out by the child on this occasion failed to protest and Sandra facing a possible return to her Real Mum's burst into tears and apologised to Kath for her behaviour .John was the Second Electrician of the SS Andes and was studying his electrical T4 and T5. It was through John's love of motor racing that I spent time with him tuning his bright shiny, new blue MGB convertible. We put a lot of work into that car, and spent idle Sundays Motor Racing at Croft Autodrome at Darlington; we toyed with the sports car racing of the BRSCC and took unsuccessfully to the track n a few occasions. John was designing and building a Formula Ford, and we spent hours on the design of the Neutrino, eventually built and raced at John's native Kent circuits.

Last heard of John on a Russian Cruise with the Andes was marrying a Russian Bride and spending his time trying to get her out of Communist Russia, which was proving quite hard, I often wonder if he succeeded? We also had a larger than life Australian, Norman Patterson, Norman worked for ANCO chemical carriers, and I believe died at sea in the early nineteen seventies shortly after marrying a local Shields girl, who Norman's best friend Fred married less than a year after Norman's death. There was a couple of Deck Officers in house with us. The second year sped by so quickly.

On the first Friday after payday we would, being in the once monthly flush of money go clubbing. If only I had been money wise, I could have bought a Tyneside slum and started a property empire .South Shields had no shortage of nightlife and as shipping company apprentices with our keep provided. We were better off than those shore based apprentices who had to pay their mum's from their £4.00 per week .The clubs were all different, The Latino had big acts, the Chelsea Cat, had many girls, the Club 27, live music the Beach Club was a little rough and gambling
.
The Chelsea Cat and Latino were part of the Bailey Club Empire, a group started by an ex Reyrolle's Electrician from a Cellar in Beach Road . Strangely enough I think he was called Dave Stanley , and he had named the clubs after his mother's family . That club moved to new premises and renamed the Chelsea Cat .From those humble beginnings rose the Steering Wheel in Sheffield, the Dolce Vita in Sunderland, Newcastle and Middlesbrough, all those Northern clubs belonged to the Bailey Empire. Beer was three shillings, fifteen pence today, a pint instead of the half-a-crown or two shillings and sixpence paid in the Public Houses and entrance was five shillings, equivalent to twenty-five pence today, but probably an hour's wages to an average working person. To students, luxury lunches consisted of a pie and two pints a day in the Westoe Arms. The cost being half -a-crown, twenty-five pence, and two shillings, ten pence, for a huge round mince beef and onion pie, delivered in hot and freshly cooked from a local baker at half past twelve each weekday money soon ran out each month. On the poorest weeks we drank at the County Hotel opposite the college on the main Sunderland Road , the Landlord was well known for watering the Charrington's bitter , but it was the cheapest pub in town , until trading standards prosecuted

him and he lost the licence ,. The Wednesday attraction there was a candle lit folk club, and beer you could not get drunk on, but the atmosphere was fantastic. The cinema had a midnight matinee on Saturday nights but tiredness normally overcame and the money wasted as you slept through the film. The alternative to clubbing was one of the town pubs followed by a curry at the Shah Jhan, curry house in Tyne Dock. We did the vindaloo. Tindaloo and phal specials , became an hot food eating trial to see who could eat the hottest .Little did I know of the delights of Clan Line cuisine , and my return for the third college year ,made these Bangladeshi hot curries taste in the mid range , to the early morning specials that awoke the taste buds of clan Line Engineers . As the summer approached I started going out with the young chemists' assistant from Akams chemist shop in the Westoe Road .The approach of a ship put that to a quick end.

The examinations over, work beckoned. I bought my new uniform to the provided list and headed home. The big suitcase for uniforms and overalls the small for my stuff .Train home await orders. South Shields was on hold for the next thirteen months.

Chapter 16 off to Sea

There was a shriek at the door, for the first time since world war two had closed its books on death , the Telegraph boy a man in his eighties, but still boy by rank stood at the door .Telegrams meant loss of life or as Mum soon realised Orders to join a ship. Panic over I am still alive, the "boy "rewarded with a tip, I do not know why, anyone would tip the harbinger of bad news, but we did. The bags packed and the train waiting, I was off to the commercial docks in London, to the SS. Clan MacTavish. I had two new matching suitcases; the smaller one held my clothes, the larger my uniform.

The heavy doeskin cloth with two shiny georgettes at the collar outlines with the purple cloth that designated the engineer officers. The purple was a rumoured to be a legacy from the sinking of the Titanic, from when the braid was reported to be first used. The gold braid insignia of rank worn by British Merchant Navy marine engineer officers on the sleeves of their uniform jackets has a purple background. There is a long held belief that this was decreed by King George V in recognition of the heroism shown by Titanic`s engineers. Although it is a fine story and that heroism certainly deserved recognition, it is incorrect. In 1865 it was decided that British naval engineers would wear a purple background to their gold braid of rank in order to distinguish them from other officers and that colour coding transferred to the British Merchant navy engineer officers when they started wearing uniforms. Although engineer officers aboard passenger ships wore uniforms the practice was not common was not usually seen. As more engineer officers wore uniforms the purple background became common and the myth associated with the Titanic developed. What was true though was from time immemorial we have had our seamen, a motley bunch of men, fearless, hardworking, unpretentious loyal only to their ship exploited by governments and ship-owners alike, In 1836 a House of Commons Select Committee was set up by the government of the day to look into the affairs of seamen. Forty year later in 1876 Parliament passed the Merchant Shipping Acts after which seafarers were collectively referred to as the Merchant Service. In recognition of the service given during the First World War by our seamen, King George V in 1922 decreed that the Merchant Service would henceforth be known as the Merchant Navy and that the Prince of Wales would be Master of the Merchant Navy, hence the title MERCHANT NAVY. A title hard earned and well deserved.

I on arrival at St.Pancras realised that London Taxis did not do "Docks" or "South
Of the River," and it took several attempts to get a taxi to the commercial docks. At the end of Commercial Road, we passed the dock gate pub "The Blue Post" cleared security and entered the impressive gateway. The docks were full of commerce and not a berth lay empty, as ships were queueing in the Thames to off load. The taxi ousted me at the gates as the driver didn't do docks , I took direction from the docks police and hauled both suitcases several hundred yards past ropes and trucks until the black funnel with its twin red bands became visible .

A nineteen forty nine built twin-screw triple expansion turbine ship, Clyde built. The chief engineer Peter Wilson, second engineer Stan Simpson, junior second, Mervin Roberts. Stan's wife found a spy hole drilled from the ships office where Mervin spent considerable time, Mervin became known as "Mervin the Perv." from that point on. Whether the drilled hole under the sink was his we never actually knew, but before Stan's wife left the costal voyage, she associated Mervyns red Eye with a dose of hairspray squirted into the freshly drilled hole, the Third Harry Robson a Geordie, who kept a quiet life enjoyed his beer after watch, but drifted throughout his time. The fourth engineer , an ex Gibraltar dockyard apprentice Alfie Bonichi ,Fifth Engineer , Peter Johnson , who had turned down the opportunity to play in his mate , Eric Burden's band , and taken a safe apprenticeship with Parsons , and Jack Maidstone a fiery short person from Poole with a huge chip on each shoulder . Keith Agar and I were the Apprentices. We familiarised ourselves with our surroundings and the team of guys that were to be our 24/7 companions for the next year. The cargo was almost all off loaded and the holds had a few crates laying in the deepest holds marked for Immingham and Middlesbrough and as the oncoming crew we were to finish the discharge before we reloaded and steamed south.

We set of for Middlesbrough to Dry Dock, then Hamburg to load car parts for Africa. The return leg saw more car parts loaded on to the deck in huge plywood crates in London. These and whole Land Rovers were destined for South African factories, where they would be quickly re-assembled. The huge crates universally known as CKD, cars knocked down. The holds were carrying whiskey and other UK spirits, as well as a whole variety of boxes containing all manner of things; a huge One Hundred Ton sugar boiler was strapped to the deck by the hatch for the number three hold, making the hatch difficult to work until we reached Mauritius. There stood a one hundred and twenty ton derrick by the hatch that would easily off load the boiler into a barge on arrival.

Mauritius had neither Dockside nor cranes, so we discharged all cargo into waiting lighters.

Broad planks, three tarpaulins, closed the hatches and wedges to hold the tarpaulins in place secured the openings against all weathers. The Bangladeshi crew, who were still Pakistani, as the independence of East Pakistan had not yet occurred, secured the ship and we set off South, The first port of Call   was to be Las Palmas for fuel, this was the cheapest fuel port so we as a company topped up there.

The Babcock boilers were bought up to their four hundred and fifty pounds pressure , the super heaters circulated , the condensers primed until they saw twenty eight inches of vacuum , and as the first dry steam hit the blades the turbines started turning the propellers slowly as we entered the locks and once free of the docks we steamed down the . Thames .Turn right at Dover and head west for a day at eighteen knots, to past the port of Brest, we were deep sea, at last. The 220V DC electricity produced by three Ruston six cylinder generators, running singly until we were on standby. Keith was with Harry Robson overhauling the off line one of these, and I was day work with the Electrician servicing the Clarke Chapman winches.

You started work at seven, and took an hour for breakfast at eight. We kept clean in the first hour making the change into uniform, to enter the officers Dining Salon. Breakfast was Juice to start, orange, or the tropical delights of Guava or mango .The "fish course", followed, Haddock Smokies from Arbroath, Kippers from Aberdeen, or just plain smoked cod bound with rice as Kedgeree. Main course , had one egg , never more , it was against company policy , bacon , sausage , tomato, beans , and then a third meat which would be devilled Kidneys, minced Collops , a savoury mince for the brave , or sliced liver . The next course was sliced fruit, then toast and jam to finish. Back to work until Smoko at eleven, when the cigarette and coffee break, with cakes fresh from the coal fired galley ovens .The duty mess always became host to Smoko, until the warmer weather took hold and we would find a shaded part of the deck. Always silver service at each break, the coffee provided in the morning by a liveried steward, silver plated Mappin and Webb coffee service and the fresh cakes on a plate stand. Coffee was for the morning, tea for the afternoon, following an age-old tradition.

Twelve was lunch which started with two pints in the Officers Bar , and was a Soup , from huge packets of Maggi soup mix , a good lesson in French soon told you that Potage Parmentier , was potato Soup , and the rest seemed to come in grey or green dependant on what title was honoured on them . Fish followed , then Curry course , a good daily choice always with chutneys , chopped tomato, onion , cucumber , and Mango , Lime Pickle and Mango Chutney accompanied their fresh companions , pompadoms topped this off .The main course followed as did salad referred to as Cold Cuts and green Salad . Pudding finished the meal, but for the hungry, there was always Cheese and biscuits. The cheese range always Edam, Cheddar and Danish Blue .Work resumed from one o'clock until a second Smoko at three, with Tea and Tab Nabs, as the Bangladeshis called the little afternoon cakes. At five we stopped work, showered, retired to the bar for two more pints, and settled into the evening meal, which was a re run of lunch, back to the bar. Read a book, play cribbage, listen to music, or the old Eddystone radio, and try to get world service. The Radio Officer, Norman, a rotund bald Yorkshireman, could never tune it to world service of the BBC so we stood little chance.

Cabins were on the weather deck and were sealed in port by a huge hardwood door , at sea and in warmer climates this was securely hooked back and the inner door , a lighter affair with louvered panels top and bottom was shut into place . At sea even this restricted airflow and was replaced by a curtain drawn across .The twin port holes were pegged open except in bad weather, when were capped with steel deadlights. The fresh air fiends amongst us split a five-gallon drum diagonally and forced it into the ports, this scooped air in as the ship drove forward. You removed it in port in case the ropes sheared it from its flimsy mountings .The desk was a chest of drawers, but the top flap folded as a writing tablet. There was a daybed and bunk, a single chair, and a wash sink. The catering boy did laundry, for a few shillings. The Bangladeshi pay rates were twenty pounds a month and two shillings hour overtime, that is ten pence in modern money. The Tindal and Cassab, the PO's in charge of their departments, got half as much again. The first four months pay saved from their twenty-four month engagement as baksheesh for the shipping agent who procured them their job; this meant the next job easily purchased. By this system, they kept seniority and the better-paid jobs, Failure meant a lesser paid more menial job on the next trip. This regularly done by bribing the shipping master to "sign them on "at their home port of Chittagong, this a daily part of their lives. The Northern European Shipping unions took great objection to this cheap labour, and rallied against foreign nationals, paid a pittance. The protest backfired, as ships took on British crews for a short time before ship-owners sold ships to third world flags, then chartered back. This lost the prized jobs and the tonnage, how socialists easily follow George Orwell's ideals direct from the pages of Animal Farm. The socialist leaders never able to understand the global picture are parochial, and look to their individual ambitions and recompenses.

The poor robbing the poor seemed an odd concept, but centuries of this happened before the British Rajah ran the government, post partition the old ways returned.

Having bunkered the fuel at Las Palmas, where we bought the duty free binoculars and watches, a good Seiko was less than Ten Pounds. a good Omega under fifty pounds and Rolex from a hundred pounds   for the stainless steel Seamaster

.The other favoured purchase was Bacardi Rum at under five shillings, twenty five pence a bottle, ignoring the companies ruling about bringing spirits on board. We resumed our South heading and at a steady 16 knots were soon across the tropics and the equator. I was still polishing and overhauling the winch controls, scrubbing the salt licked copper terminals whilst sat on the hatch combing. The electrician was struggling with his health, and was inclined to do no more than supervise. I supplemented the days with the occasional watch, to give the juniors a watch off .I normally stood the eight to twelve watches that entailed the horrific task of soot blowing. The soot blowers positioned around the boiler and as you rotated them sprayed the boiler tubes with superheated steam to clean off the debris of the day's oil burning. This was an extremely unpleasant job as the soot often blew back and covered the operator. We always saved this until twenty to midnight so a fast pint of draught lager quenched the taste of acrid soot before the shower and post midnight relaxes. The bar normally covered in the freshly showered watch in boxers and the thick white Clan Line towels. Socially we played cribbage, or Ukers, of which I now have no recollection of a single rule, drank about four pints and went to bed. Peter Johnson had his own entertainment, we were all smokers in those far off days, and peter as he struck his Ronson varaflame lighter would break wind. One night he forgot his boxers, blasted away, struck the lighter and singed his pubic regions badly enough to require treatment from a Chief Steward / Purser who was more than a little irritated to be called by a crazy bunch of engineers indulging in odd early morning practices.

John was another Yorkshire man, son of a Farmer who had escaped the farm and learned his trade amongst the Hotels and restraints adjoining Central Park in New York, until Uncle Sam decided that a spell in the army, bogged down in Vietnam would be good for John's citizenship. Eidlewild Airport beckoned and the American experience ended. The sheep farming stayed in John's blood though as his nickname of the Good Shepherd indicated no religious connection but ability to divert the crew Moslem Killed Mutton to our table. This meant that it was easy to divert our precious stores ashore, where unscrupulous chandlers quickly converted it to cash, which was part of John's benefits. Our food became his investments. The thirteen shillings and sixpence, sixty-two and a half pence that was our food allowance well spent. The amazing Seven shillings and sixpence, Thirty-two and a half pence   allowed to the Bangladeshis was even harder to maintain, their allowance was by measure, so much Jappatti flour, so much mustard oil, ounces of herbs and spices, pounds of lamb and so on. Chicken was a speciality purchased live and ceremonially killed on board, all parts including head and feet used in the food. . If there was ever an impoverished Purser / Catering officer, I am yet to meet him .The allowance meant we could all eat well. If the funding not firstly diverted and then converted to the benefit of one man, it seemed strange to me, especially when on passenger ships that the catering department were so lowly paid but so individually wealthy. The tips could not be high enough to allow a head bar man on a passenger ship to renew his jaguar car yearly. The higher "the caterers " climbed the more affluent they became. The tips alone could never achieve this, even at the highest level; the thought lays doubt about the true honesty of the men.

The Cape soon appeared with the magnificent first view of Table Mountain and the low cloud that formed its tablecloth now we start the off load. The engineers took to the shore for a meal, we ordered what we wanted and the bill split equally `. This was in a way unfair to Jack Mainstone who always craved for the pig liver never seen on board, and therefore was the cheapest order, most wanted Steak, never seen on a Clan Line menu, with at least two fried eggs skating across the top. From Cape Town, we transited the Cape ports to Durban Port Elizabeth and East London, just short one night stops along the way to the Transvaal port that lay serenely in the Indian Ocean, its Whites only beach secured with shark nets, other beaches less protected.

Durban always seemed an East West junction where the huge Indian population, transplanted there by the British Colonialists had become, Lawyers, traders, skilled clerical and commercial sector. The majority of Mercedes-Benz two hundred series not Taxis were Indian owned. The taxis distinguished by the illuminated NET Blankes, whites only sign on the roof.

There were three main calls in Durban, the Officers Club, where the Crayfish Thermidor introduced me to how excellent seafood is so easily ruined by a chef with a sauce, secondly the four seasons Hotel where the bar was fully air-conditioned and thirdly, the New Smugglers. This bar replaced the old one that had two bars, one in and one out of the docks with a custom post at the dividing door. The smugglers did a twenty four ounce lean steak, lean because all the fat had been walked off on the arid Botswana plains I tried that steak, for its one rand price tag, in those days ten shillings, the modern fifty pence, in every way possible but it was always a dental challenge
    The beer was good though and we illicitly topped up our Tennants barrels at the Lion Brewery .with the excellent Lion Ale, a superior beer to its better known stable-mate Castle Lager. It was here the ailing electrician taken off and flown home due to ill health. a couple of months out and I was ships electrician, on the grounds that I knew more electricity than the ex-dockyard guys that had become engineers in the mechanical sense of the word .We headed north to Lorenço Marques, the hometown of the pleasant pop radio station LM Radio. The stop here was short and we carried on our Northwards transit to Dar el Salam, which I think means harbour of peace in Arabic. Here the Chinese were working hard on the Tanzanian infrastructure and movements around town were restricted. There was a Hapag Lloyd ship import off loading German aid to the government. At least ten stretched Mercedes Benz 600 limousines were off loaded, so the government could move around in comfort, the rest were Deutz military trucks the populous could gain from a highly

mobile army. The atmosphere was uncomfortable to say the least, and we rarely ventured ashore. Next port north was Beira, which was in the firm grip of the Portuguese military. The main bar was the Moulin Rouge, the seats cut from tree stumps of African Hardwood, and despite several vain attempts were un-steal able. The only other ship here was an American Naval vessel taking Africa in on the way home from Vietnam. The Americans had an unfortunate habit of sending men on extended antibiotic home by sea, so they were more wholesome when getting home to their wives. The charges in the bars for all available commodities doubled, and anyone tempted by the dusky maidens prevalent in the Moulin Rouge instantly put off by the US prescience, for wherever they were diseases they were slowly curing followed. As a diversion Jack Mainstone put off an approaching girl , with a camp attempt at humour , insisting he only liked young boys , bad timing we thought as the girl reappeared with , a boy she claimed was her younger brother and very good . It was here too that an American, who in the kindest of ways suggested that" if you could not afford it Limey "as he heard Jack protesting loudly at the price rises " let Uncle Sam buy you a beer", Wrong move. British Merchant Navy 1, US forces zero. Here we also picked up a supply of mailbags for HMS Devonshire, which was on the Beira Patrol, stopping shipping breaking the Rhodesia sanctions. The sanctions used against the White minority government of Ian Smith, who was locked in conflict with the Zanu PF Guerrilla army of the hugely popular Robert Mugabe. The insanity of The Royal Navy patrolling the coast was , the Blister copper bars we had loaded , came from trucks at the port's Railhead , the markings of RR for Rhodesian Railway was Still showing under the white wash that had been hastily applied to cover them . When we left port, the Devonshire appeared on the horizon and a boat put into the water, the effect the mail exchange. The red official bags replaced on the rope with a flagon of rum, for the blue crew mailbags, we received a thank you. Mail exchanged, a tot of fiery rum and then we turned east to Mauritius,

Now after two months I had a replacement electrician, and could revert to being an apprentice. I, soon told to show him around, but as a mail **boat** third electrician he soon made it plain, he needed no help especially from an apprentice. I looked forward to this relief, as now I was not required to stay aboard to drive off loading winches. I looked to my day off and hired a local guide with a beaten up old car to take me around the island. He drove Peter Johnson and me around the coast. The local delight was a fresh Green Coconut, the top sliced off, and the gel like juice that had not yet ripened into coconut diluted with neat local white rum, topped with ice and drunk through a straw. You only needed one of these to bring on a euphoria .The lazy day rounded off with the boat trip back, dusk was falling and the boiler over number three hatch was hanging six inches off the hatch and swinging precariously. I was greeted by Peter Wilson, with the hail of where the XXXX have you been. Day off Chief was the answer , XXX the day off get that XXXXXXX boiler off before we sink in this god forsaken hole , that xxxx is clueless , pointing at our electrician , the one who needed no help . I stumbled on the winch platform , looked to the mate who was in charge of off loading , shouted ready to lift , engaged the hidden heavy lift button concealed under the winch control , " I have done all that , screeched , my bright replacement, Lift shouted the Mate ,and as I rotated the control the boiler raised . I then swung and released it to the awaiting lighter, the vast amount of rum and coconut milk helping my bravado, with such a difficult lift. The clever replacement slunk away, Peter Wilson growling behind him as he slouched back to his cabin. Moment of Glory I thought, but it was short lived, "Next port you are duty cargo electrician and that xxxx can xxxx off ashore," the Chief barked.

Our cargo now quickly loading marked "Cadiz," "Seville," "Livorno," and "Genoa." I realised now that it looked that the return leg was not as straight forward as first thought we were heading home via the Mediterranean and a second leg to South and East Africa. We started the return journey part one by sailing due West, past Reunion and Madagascar towards Mombasa to finish loading for Durban and beyond.

Christmas was approaching, but we would be back out at sea by then. Mombasa was a real eye opener, the beer was White Cap, with picture of Mount Kilimanjaro on the label, and the bars read out British naval history, the Nelson Bar, The Anchor Bar, and the others started off the street which led to the castle and the old Arab quarter. The beer was cheap and the bar Girls would entertain you for less than five 5 shillings Kenyan, twenty-three pence I had the immortal warning of Leslie ringing in my ear, so had another beer. We toured the town with the aid of a local guide. Fort Jesus was starting to become derelict in those days and little done to conserve it. The old Slave Market still stood where less than eighty years earlier Africans traded by Arabs for vast sums of money. Good slaves of both sexes were up to a hundred pounds, which was three years wages to the average person in the eighteen eighties .We toured the mosque and the Hindu temple, then drank the Coffee and Fig mixture traded by the Arab Coffee sellers in ancient handle less cups, of exquisite china.

We began re loading hides and coffee for Durban where it was to be. Transhipped he holds were filling rapidly. An old friend the HMS Devonshire appeared in harbour, with an invite for pre Christmas drinks in the wardroom. The display of coloured lights about M·Tavish's upper deck was quite resplendent, as we thought until the Royal Navy with its unlimited resources switched on a mass of colour in a fanfare of light. We spent the whole day dipping 60-Watt pearl lamps into paint pots and running festoons .As dusk fell we switched on a display running through the rigging, to be overshadowed by an illumination worthy of Blackpool. Topped with red painted plywood Santa Claus, peering from the top of the funnel we knew we did not have the resources to play this game, in either work force or equipment. Therefore, in the time honoured British way we sallied over there and drank the officer's expensive beer. There were second Lieutenants cringing at the impending bar bill as the steward opened can after can. Enough diversion, the steam was son back to its required 450 pounds per square inch, the ropes and wires released the hatches battened down our cargo and that for the homeward bound Mail Boats of our Sister company the Union Castle Line secured, we started south.

Christmas consisted mainly of a pre dinner drink session which involved a large   glass of Drambuie and an excellent 25 year old Chivas Regal Whiskey ,that had been to damaged to land , for the attention of the Commander HMS Naval Station Mauritius . He would not have wanted a crate with a smashed bottle , so we disposed of it in a fitting manor for him .Dinner unusually at lunchtime was an elaborate affair , with a whole Salmon carved at the table and roast Goose with all the trimmings to follow . Each course interspaced, not with sorbet, but with a whiskey and cigarette break. The ship ran as an unmanned engine room for part of that day, with the Bangladeshi crew watching the boilers and engines. The brief was juniors looked below at least every ½ hour and the seniors watched their drink levels .Durban and Cape Town passed quickly as we headed to Walvis Bay in South West Africa , as Namibia was known   , under South African Rule , here to load canned sardines . The mission padre took us on a desert trip to Windhoek via the sand dunes and the oasis at Gonacontes .Here we had a mission barbeque and the off taste of the supposedly fresh lamb was due to it being a tough old Billy goat. The coal fired tugs and railway engines of South Africa's Harbour Board and Railway were constantly active.

Back North, across the Tropic and the equator and to Dakar for fuel, we carried vast amounts so the company had opportunity to select the cheapest ports for Bunkers .It was here that Jack went ashore and bought a watch, like his friend Peter's. Jack had coveted Peters Roles Seamaster, which had been a present from Peter's old school friend Eric Burdon, of the Animals group, famous at the time for the old standard, the house of the rising sun. It was an excellent look alike , and it looked just like the one Peter had removed from his cabin whilst on watch less than an hour before .Peter demanded the watch back, Jack demanded the £20 he had paid , Peter wouldn't pay him , although without Jack's purchase his watch would have never been seen again . They never spoke for the next six months.

We were soon at the impressive old town of Cadiz and after discharging a few crates, we entered the Mediterranean through the straits of Gibraltar. We had cargo for there but because the Spanish were having a border tantrum we could not leave Gibraltar for a Spanish Port, and we had Seville and Valencia to follow. A stop at Marseilles, led us to Livorno, and Naples as we headed to the main Port of Genoa where most of the cargo was destined. We were to spend six weeks here and a small change of crew as Keith flew home, as did two deck officers. We fully entertained by the Padre's assistant at the Genoa Church of Scotland Seamen's Mission, The person spoke. thirty five languages including Gallic .Here we found dial-a-pizza ,a long time before the Pizza Hut imitators spread like a plague across the UK in pursuit of the burger, and chicken nugget . We paid the ships security man to collect them for us , delicate crisp based with pungent tomato and herb topping , covered in stringy molten buffalo mozzarella , pepperoni to top it , we saved the chief steward a fortune as these delicious take away became regular features . I would have the Walport films in the box that we carried swopped with any British ship I could find, to make the film nights more frequent. The wet hides , dry hides , copper and crates ashore , we loaded shoes and ceramics , baths , shower trays , tractors and their parts , fiats and Ferraris , closed the hatches said our goodbyes , and set off for Barcelona . I found the Ramblas fascinating as the throbbing street of cafes bars style shops and a bullring. I only ever saw one bullfight and realising that the toreadors half kill the beast with their spears, weakening it before the matador shows his art with a sword, I felt the fight so unfair.

This was not a contest of man and beast , because the result was known , the bull looses , every fight , get a new bull , fight again .|Let the odd bull kill the odd matador and win his freedom and interest would rise . There was a restaurant off the Ramblas called las Caracoles, which was memorable for the age of the building and the spit roast chicken that rotated by its front door.

Gibraltar called and we harboured under the massive rock, taken by Britain's Royal Marines from its Spanish occupiers. The town more British than Plymouth or Portsmouth .I got a lift to the top of the rock and a tour of the caves from some Squaddies that were taking the crates from the Dockers and delivering them to the military base. Through Hercules's pillars and turn left as we aimed south once again. Cape Town was the first call, then around to Durban non-stop. This leg of the voyage was passing rapidly, except for the two junior engineers having their enforced silence. The boat berthed at the Bluff across the harbour from the main town, which made the journey into town a long one. There was a pedestrian tunnel across the |Harbour, but a lone drunk Peter arrived back one night stood in a pair of bedraggled y-fronts, having had, all his clothing including his shoes and socks stolen, and his wallet. The infamous watch, he had left by accident in his cabin. Beira next for Rhodesian copper , that was off loaded quickly in Durban , again on the bluff , and we set out with very little cargo for Walvis Bay .

What delights awaited us here, fishmeal, thousands of tonnes of the foul smelling rats delight, Bags and Bags from the sardine fisheries next door neighbour the fishmeal factory .Straight to London. One port one load an easy run home lay ahead. The smell was horrific, but by day two, we noticed it less. The rats were in party mood and measured over two hundred millimetres in their body length. We have to sort this out. Roy the mate declared, I'd buy a pint for every dead one you can get. Free beer has always been an attraction, and I spent that night watch fashioning some spears, cut from the bronze condenser tubes. A pint at our ever duty free, and not real Tennants beer bar was seven pence, three pence in today's money, fair thought, we approached the engine room hands at a penny a rat, and quickly reimbursed the Cassab, as, the store man was known with £2 for the 480 rats he had in six large sacks. That equalled six ten gallon barrels paid for, until the mate on inspection tried to renege on the deal. We settled on two barrels, and let him feed his new prizes to the water life passing at the time. When he found the deal we had done, he was less than happy and engaged the bosun at a much more favourable rate to do rte dirty work for him. London soon reached and we set ashore to taste a pint of proper British Beer, The Blue Posts was the first pub from the dock gates and as we strolled in, greeted with screwed faces. Are you bleeding lot of that bleeding fishmeal carrier, the proprietor challenged? We were all showered and respectable, but the lingering swell of fishmeal had stuck like natural glue. We off outside had a free pint each delivered by the proprietor, who politely, in the charming east end way, suggested that, we found another boozer and frequented it till the smell went. We were now late August, so without further leave I called home, dropped off my uniform, collected my books and took the train to South Shields.

Thirteen months at sea bought me home with a week's leave and a return to college at South Shields .Forty weeks engineering Technology and I would only have few months sea time to finish the four and a half year apprenticeship.

The college was mainly practical for the forty weeks and it flew past, we spent many time stripping and rebuilding engines including the single cylinder Doxford that lay in the new workshop specially built to accommodate it. I was back at Kath's house, and bought my first car an Austin A40 Somerset .The cellar club had had its trendy make over and was the Chelsea Cat. Sandra had a new best friend, the old one warned off by Kath for her liking for the older boys in these digs. Susan Bulley bought a new chore, since Sandra had found a flasher in the short cut behind the Osborne avenue chip shop Susan needed an escort home each evening. The college day started at eight thirty and ran until five o'clock, and there was a lot of work. We had machining, materials, rudimentary naval architecture, advanced electrotechnology, systems, boilers, motor engines, and so much practical. There was only one classroom day the rest was workshops. Easter bought a short voyage on the Clan Alpine, joining at Avonmouth, and going via Dublin, Liverpool, and Belfast, to end in Smith's North Shields once. The Zulu crew were prone to enjoy a drink and one night in the Jungle pub on the North Shields Quay , I spilled a local's beer as I pushed my way to the bar ,The guy took offence and wanted a full replacement for the 20 ml that I had spilled , or !! He would teach me not to spill his beer. His aggression faded when he lifted by his lapels a clear foot from the ground by an indignant Zulu Storekeeper known as Tiny in respect of his full six foot seven inch stature. You not speak my Boss like that, say you sorry! The local humbly apologised, bought his own beer, and did not mess with Zulu's again. I used to talk to tiny to see if I could ever understand the African Politics brewing subversively in the South African Republic .I remember his stance on Apartheid , "any of my daughters brings home a white man for a husband , I kill him whilst she watches , then I kill her" . I rather stupidly asked what his reaction would be to a Bantu or another tribe as a potential son – in – law, "I kill him first just the same. Nevertheless, much slower "was the reply .We had Wilbard Moshe a Kenyan, with us and he had considerable trouble working with the Zulus, I could not understand, were they not pleased at a black man progressing? He is not a black man, like me, "tiny quickly retorted," he brown same colour as I defecate," I altered the words slightly for the sense of decency, but hopefully the gist remains the same.

  The forty weeks over and the McTavish's sister the M^ctaggart was awaiting in Immingham, train to Hull from home then taxi to Immingham docks. This was a whole different game, the Chief Engineer was Stainless Stan Steel a Scottish Bigot of the worst sort, He hated Catholics , English ,and anyone clever than him in that order , so Tony Hickman the English Catholic third engineer started on a losing wicket . Stan's introduction to Tony, "your an ex apprentice, your all rubbish." Tony grinned sheepishly and in a broad Wolverhampton brogue, said, "Well thanks Chief it is only a reflection on the skills of those ex dockyard Chief Engineers that have trained us." Stan was not quick enough to work out, if he enjoyed complement or insult and his ignorance showed. We were loading here and carrying on further to the port of Hull. Hull behind us, a week finalising loading in London's commercial docks saw us underway this was not a happy ship at all. The second Engineer was almost as bigoted as Stainless Stan, another Glaswegian, and Tom by name. There was constant bickering, and stupid petty rules. Stan wanted the fuel bunkers three times a day. This was a messy job as the fuel was heavy furnace oil, and it was stored in quite a few of the double bottom tanks. The long weighted dip tape gathered the oil wiped clean on each dip. Stan liked his little tasks to underwrite his authority .I used to ullage the readings , which made it an easier task then , have a smoke by the mast house to waste the time , this way Stan was not bright enough to work out that there was an accurate but easy way . Bunkering was at night in Las Palmas, and Tony was late with a tank change, losing about ten tonnes of fuel to the harbour and the adjacent beach. We corrected the figures over the next few weeks, and Stan has reported consumption of tonnes of fuel per mile was never in the range of his predecessor .At Durban he made a real Pratt of himself when he banned Tony Hickman from going ashore, after he found that Tony had attended a Catholic mass one Sunday morning. We were all looking for out of this ship as we steamed north .The skipper was as big a maniac as Stan was. Whilst we were working on the main stream powered whistle at sea , my co-worker one of the juniors chirped at the budgerigar , hanging adjacent to the skippers port hole . An angry face appeared at the window, dinar tack to me budgie lad, that is a captains budgie and he dinar want to tack to the likes of you. Was this serious, or had I signed on to the insane club? We headed north praying that this nightmare did not turn into the Clan Line famous, home after the double header, and enjoy a Mediterranean cruise, type of trip.

Stan's second love, only slightly behind his adoration of his own ability, was football, and Stan at each port of call North of Durban would via the local Padre. Arrange ship-to-ship football matched. We were not able to win a raffle never mind a football match, and each defeat saw us plying the winners with drink at our expense and Stan reaching new depths of self-disbelief and anger. In Mombasa, the final game we took on a Dutch ship that was worse than we were and as the winner, returned with them to enjoy a party at their expense. Stan returned to the Clan M^{c}taggart annoyed, because despite the victory we had only scraped through, and should have played better .On the Dutch Ship we were entertained with Oranjeboom beer and from their Galley, which was Chinese crewed my first taste of Chinese food, with the delightful white crisps, that were a novelty to me. When I saw them a few years later, as Chinese food gained in popularity, I saw them as Prawn Crackers. With the holds empty and no cargo , we were awaiting orders , depression set in .we were getting scared of the doubleheader , Soon we were told that the TSS Clan Mactaggart was off to Shangai to breakers , all non essential personnel to come off , and the ship to be stripped and made ready for sale .

Stan was not overjoyed at the "little yellow buggers "having their hands on the once proud, but twenty year old Clyde built Steamer, but make ready he did. I was hoping that he would insult Chairman Mao and languish in a Shangai jail for at least a hundred years.

I now confirmed as Junior Engineer and joined the King Arthur .It arrived in Mombasa as we got the breaking news of "Clan McTaggart's " fate. I was not a great admirer of these

Bullard King boats since my old college acquaintance Ian Atkinson electrocuted on one the previous year by an ignorant third engineer .He had misunderstood the new wiring colours and thinking that brown was an earthy colour. The third engineer ignored the bright green and yellow stripes of earth, and the label on the cord, wired mains to earth, bringing Ian's death in a bilge the moment he pressed the drill's trigger.

The King Arthur was the biggest collection of misfits imaginable; the Chief Engineer was Archie McLean, "The White Haired Animal" a highlander on his final voyage. Archie never made it home, dying in Glasgow as he waited for his train back to Fort William. The second Engineer, Eddie Senervaratne, a Ceylonese, or Sri Lankan as they are now known, I was on watch with the fourth Engineer Sandy McCloud, another Highlander, who would spend the evenings practicing the Bagpipes. The ship was old and decrepit, the crew the roughest UK crew I had ever seen, and they were serious drunkards, prone to wild nights ashore. We were loading for home, although at twelve knots, as the little Doxford engine, it was a powerful main engine at sea. On deck, we had seven young Elephants and seven Water Buffalo destined for an English wildlife park, and a Kenyan handler to clean up after them. The hatch combing was covered in their fodder, mainly sugar cane .The below deck cargo was stinking hides and crates of copper bars.

We set off with water rationed to eight gallons per man per day, which meant showers turned on from six AM until seven , and water was only for the galley until six to seven in the evening. The cabin temperatures were unbearable, and most of the engineer officers slept in makeshift hammocks slung under the deck awning, so at least the night air would breeze by. The crew in the engine room were Londoners, Glaswegians on deck .We chugged past the cape, headed North, missing all the potential water stops, until we reached London Docks.

I had a note, on your way to the Station call in to see Charlie Banks, Personnel Officer. Charlie was good at sending men in directions that they did not want to go, so I was on my guard as he offered coffee and biscuits, and seeking my opinion of the excellent bigot Stanley Steel. I was shown Stan's report on Tony Hickman and me. Dina sends any more of these English buggers, one was a Catholic, and the other bugger did not like football. Send the replacements for my next ship, I want an Inside right and a left back for my team. Mr Banks asked my opinion, and the words rambling idiot came to mind.

What ship do you want asked Charlie , I was still mindful of the catch ,many a clever engineer had ended in a hell hole for an eternity on this man's words of friendship . The Elbe Ore, I suggested, tentatively, as the new Bulk Carrier was just out of its commissioning trials and on its first voyage as a Bulk Carrier. No! Cannot do, staffed for the next twelve months, was the definite answer. RMS Pendennis Castle then ,I suggested , The Pendennis was the Commodore Engineers flagship and the last of the passenger vessels designed for Union Castle , the later editions of Windsor and Transvaal Castles were not Harland and Wolf , Belfast ships , and were designed for the amalgamated company rather than Union Castle . Southampton bound within a week resplendent with a whole bag of new uniforms freshly purchased I headed for The Pendennis Castle , I arrived on my Birthday , went for a drink with Andy Braidwood , who was about to join the renamed SA Vaal , as the Transvaal Castle had been renamed when she was sold to Safmarine , although still Union Castle manned . That Birthday I got the best present I could ever have wished for, my Barbara.

The Pendennis was ten years old and had rivets at deck level to enable her to be converted to an aircraft carrier in the event of war. This made her sleek and exceptionally fast, twenty-six knots was easily achievable, and there were extra nozzles on the turbine to make her even faster. This was not the fast eighteen knots that had helped many of the Clan Liners evade the torpedoes from Germany's U Boats but a cruising speed of twenty-three knots, with some in reserve so the timetable could be held, and the mail delivered on time. The Royal Mail Pennant flew from the masthead as we took a priority in the harbour and these were not the old "SS " of the Steamers tramping around the capes, these were RMS ships, Royal Mail Ships. The lavender hull sitting on the red boot topping, giving rise to the name the "Lavender Hull Mob "paraphrased from an old black and white film of a similar name.

The uniforms were the usual Number one Black doeskin jacket and trousers with white shirt, stiff collar, black tie, black socks and shoes, shined to a reflection. Shirts were plain , the popular later fashion for pilot shirts was not in existence here This uniform reigned six AM to six PM all North of Las Palmas, and was worn by on duty officers on the bridge or in pursers and catering offices. After six and throughout the night until past midnight the choice was Blue Mess Dress, or White Mess Undress. The blue mess, known as the jacket with all the buttonholes, this was similar to a Victorian officer's uniform and was an elaborate expensive affair, normally purchased from the Southampton Office uniform second Hand store, regularly replenished from officers, barred from the passenger fleet for life. This banishment was normally connected with the old maritime rules against broaching the cargo, as liaising with passengers was more legally known. There were some well-known Lotharios as many were senior officers as the younger social climbers; some of the passengers were just as bad. A young lady from a well known North Eastern chain of men's outfitters always joined her family on a winter cruise to South Africa, outward bound on the Pendennis Castle. Homeward six weeks later, after they had visited friends and family in South Africa, they always took the same first class cabins. The lady in question in her late teens was always in cabin A7, and her fan club of uniformed studs spanned all ranks, they were collectively known as the "A7" club. I believe that at least one Captain had joined, several Deck, Engineer, and Radio officers, and a large force from the minority heterosexual Petty Officers and ratings .For the record, no! too promiscuous for my liking , and the fear of disease always overwhelmed me besides , if you have read chapter two , then my dream was home in Southampton , and that is where I wanted to be .

Number tens with a tight neck collar in starched white, were worn from Las Palmas with stiff white trousers white socks and shoes. Shorts and shirts for daytime only, or duty officers in the afternoon whilst to scurry around decks or eat lunch, this pain of an outfit was required, the disadvantage were swapping shoulder boards every few hours across uniforms. Red Sea Rig, where the short tropical shirt was worn with the heavier number one black trousers was frowned upon even on colder days .

Tropical evenings demanded White Mess – Dress, and White Mess- Undress, as well as the rarely used Blue Mess Dress worn from evening dinner at eight o'clock until midnight had passed. The Blue was until the night before Las Palmas. The white mess was a "bum freezer, "short jacket, over dress trousers, which normally meant the Doeskins of the number 1 uniform. The Black silk cummerbund held your waist firmly in place and the Black bow tie completed it, most had clip on ties, because of the painful difficulties trying to tie a proper one.

The on watch navigation officer rarely leaving the Bridge ignored this and stuck to the traditional shirt and shorts, as did the on duty Radio Officers. If you could avoid going on deck the completely engineering department lounged in the cleanest boiler suit available. This could be problematic, as meals were supposed to be eaten in the first class salon not grouped together in cabins .Where there is a will there is always a bribable steward .We had the will and bottles of scotch whiskey were a convertible currency... We ate in the first class dining salon, and as junior officers were allowed on deck in all areas except the First Class Cocktail Bar, which was the reserve of senior officers only.

The food, well where do I begin , there was enough to feed the fifteen hundred people on board and daily about the same amount jettisoned over board , in an early morning ritual .Breakfast , was a vast affair , juice , cereal , fish ,always a smoked selection , Salmon, haddock , Herring , Kedgeree followed then a ,Full English , with every addition imaginable . There appeared some unique items such as Dropped egg. This, a lightly boiled egg dropped in a vast ball of butter and blended by hand to a creamy scramble. In order to find out what it was I ordered it one day, much to the annoyance of the officers' steward. The preparation was fiddly but the problem was getting the commis chef on breakfasts to soft boil an egg. , Eggs, how many? How do you want them was the question. Full English Breakfast was full indeed , Eggs bacon sausage , fried bread , bubble and squeak , tomatoes , kidney , black pudding , fresh baked rolls from the night bakers , toast , everything that could feed a man for a week if he so desired .

Luncheon was vast a soup of the day , often freshly prepared Consommé , Fish , Entree , Main Course , Salad Course and a sweet course , followed by cheese . We normally dodged this in warmer weather and settled for the deck buffet in the First Class Lido bar, where you could tuck in to a South African Crayfish, all manner of seafood, and meats and salads unbelievable. The 12 – four watch ate in the salon at eleven thirty, as they had invariably slept through breakfast, the 8-12 by the time they emerged from the engine room dived for the deck buffet. The only watch-keepers who enjoyed three meals a day in splendour were the 4 – 8 watch, headed by the second engineer. The Second Engineer had his own dining table and hosted eight passengers .He also got an eight pounds a week wine allowance. That allowance was signed for on his wine card, we all signed for our bar bills and the company reduced them by 30% to encourage our presence amongst the walking cargo .Afternoon led to using the first class pool, or beers in the lido bar, by the first class pool.

Dinner was unbelievable. Hor D'Ouvres, followed by more soup, a choice of Consommé or a thickened potage, Fish would have several options, smoked, fresh and a seafood, the omelette course, of plain, mushroom, cheese, or Spanish followed chased this, then the Entree, a choice of ragouts, highly flavoured meats, served in a smaller portion, The main course was a Relevee or roast course. Cold meat course followed, pudding, and Scotch woodcock to finish after a sumptuous cheese board, coffee, and petit fours were there for those still hungry. These huge dinners were a multiple choice from twelve courses, most omitted, although one first class winger (steward) on the South African costal voyage, where South African whites cruised up and down the coast was heard to remark that he was to see the Chief Steward, and change his tray for a wheelbarrow if he served another table of South Africans. The food was fine dining at its best, Foie Gras Beluga Caviar, seafood galore, smoked capon, Dover sole, all freshly prepared and ladled with sauces .Steak was to order, unlike Clan Line where it was to wish for. Desserts piled high with cream rounded the meal, coffee, cheeses, biscuits, petit four served to help you linger at the table .Wine cost us less than sixty pence a bottle and we took turns amongst the watch to pay. KWV Kold Duk and Gran Mousec Vin Doux was the choice for very special occasions. The dinner started promptly at eight PM, and lasted until somewhere after nine thirty. A steak sandwich in the cabin was always a favourite, but dine we must, so dine we did. Supper served two and a half hour later at midnight and was spaghetti Bolognese, savoury mince hot pot of a similar one-plate evening warmer. Still Hungary the night bakery gang always had stew, scouse, or a one-pot dish ready about 3:00. Twenty four hours a day hot food catering at your finger tips .The wine waiters were sommeliers not just reassigned wingers, and part of the bar staff rather than stewards. The old trick at passenger parties was to place French champagne empty bottles in a sink of water and slide the label across to a denuded South African, substitute, at a tenth of the price .Oh, and pocket the difference.

Once a wine waiter showed me the differences between a dry vintage champagne from France and the Cape alternative the South African sweeter wine , I preferred , and so did most people , snobbery prevented critical derision , and once again all marvelled at the tale of the emperor's new clothes . What a great playground to learn about snobbery and the false atmosphere engendered by wealth. Money certainly did not maketh the man. Back in Southampton, it was the Chief barman with the new Jaguar XJ6, and the house in Bassett, the Captain had an older Ford Cortina.

The machinery was well looked after the job ran well and I have times to see my newfound love for one whole week in six. The Cape Mail Boat ran to a tighter timetable on the six thousand and nine mile sea to Cape Town than the railway, through Southampton. The engineering was the pinnacle of nineteen fifties marine engineering. It was surprisingly well kept. The lay alongside was well organised and ran well, each turn around became a mini service and the ship herself returned to a high state of readiness. The engines were the standard Triple expansion Parsons Turbine fed from seven hundred and fifty pound Babcock's and Wilcox D type Boilers, which at sea drove the vessel forwards at her regular twenty four knots .

Each day covered a five hundred and twenty sea miles as a minimum .There was an elaborate and expensive sweepstake that sold a ticket today for the Captain's best distance guess and the ten tickets either side. These twenty-one tickets were numbered and put with blanks to pad out the interest, You bought a ticket and drew a paper from the box, it may be blank, or it may be one of the prized numbered tokens. You then watched the auction, and if you had a ticket with mileage in the auction you paid half price for it, the proceeds were divided between seafarers' charities and the prize pot on a 50/50 basis, the winner took 50% of the pot and 10 miles either side took 25% each. The first prize could be over a £1000, first class playing for fun, tourist for a lottery-sized win. The Captains best guess, ticket at auction could cost over £600, which was six months wages to a junior engineer. Tourist gamblers would ask about weather, engine revs, all kinds of questions, but the stuffed wallets in first always seemed to be the buyers and thus the winners.

 The class divide was at its most obvious here ,the first class and tourist designations was reminiscent of the Titanic's story , the dividing lines were gated decks of which the tourist class passenger read the reminder " First Class Only " . The food was vastly different too. A tour down into the tourist-dining salon was compulsory, but you got the wine paid for as recompense. You dutifully filled in the report card, on the service and quality, and returned it to the Chief Purser/Catering Officer. Mark the openly camp head waiter , picked you a table of reasonable people so dinner wasn't too dull and supplied a couple of bottles of Neederburg Stein , gratis to entertain , there was never a poor report returned , despite the ample , well presented but dull menu , that was akin to Cargo Ship food , rather than the opulence that was the normality . The other Liners on the seas , P & O , Cunard , Chandris , United States Line , Holland – America , British India Steam Navigation , the junior officers ate in a mess in their accommodation , and Union Castle were unique in feeding the officers so well . The Chefs, Commis, Bakers, and Butchers were amongst the best in the world, and if you showed an interest they enthused about their job. Eating Steak Tartar one evening , and sitting at the officers table , the one nearest the kitchen door , you overheard the gossip as the wingers passed each other , they poured scorn down on their passengers who were out of their depths , as one commented in that effeminate tone of the hurt steward , "God she has just asked for it well done ",. His mincing compatriot said, "well what are you going to do "? The reply, and action, was to get the unsuspecting woman a Burger from the tourist menu, as opposed to the raw beef and raw egg delicacy that was listed.

My job was generator watch-keeping officer and my eight hours a day was spent watching the huge W H Allen turbo generators; these produced seven thousand amps each. In port, the duty taken by three eight-cylinder Harland and Wolf diesels, of which one was always in maintenance, whilst the other two produced their four and a half thousand amps each. These diesels were our sea time job, we stripped and rebuilt them on a cycle keeping them in the best condition, but always making sure that all three were available as stand by rang on the Telegraph at each port. After a year here, you may get a job on the platform as Intermediate fourth engineer, then after a further two years, maybe the boiler room as intermediate third engineer, rising to the Junior second engineer's job when your sea time equated to a Certificate of Competency. After that a return to a senior watch keeper's job on the platform and a long wait for a senior position. The close definition of the junior rolls meant that it took many years to get the required sea time in to sit your qualifying exam. The lap of luxury, had to be reviewed, the two weeks with Barbara in every seven would be fine if we didn't want to buy houses and lift ourselves. Big decisions, but those decisions were minded to let me move on, qualify, and grow together.

There were four electrical officers and four Refrigeration Engineer officers to back up the marine engineers .There was a Mechanic too, but he was a Chief Petty-Officer, in the same status as the carpenters. These men wore uniforms with silver braid, one, or two stripes dependant on rate. The mechanic was effectively the ships plumber, and roved the passenger decks fixing taps and sinks. The Chief electrician was a rare sight, venturing into the labyrinth of darkness that constituted the engine rooms, only for stand by and rare inspections. His second electrician was next to the huge switchboard in the generator room for standby, but rarely moved from a perch he made of wiper rags, by the door of his small workshop. The third electrician was young and a Welshman who had been traumatised by the Abervan disaster, where he had helped dig for the poor bodies of the unfortunate schoolchildren. He spent much time changing passenger light bulbs, but after accepting a "tip" for repairing a cabin heater as we steamed down the Solent, he never returned to the ship again. The fridge engineers were a whole new world , a rare scattering of refrigeration experts , the Chief Refrigeration Engineer being Mr John " Jack" Frost , the second one an odd character named Trevor , and the third fridge , the delightful Ian McKrill , as Mackerel was officially known . Ian was an ex W H Allen service engineer , with a disastrously failed marriage behind him , and a rare war record .He had worked for one of the special operations units , and was a commissioned Army Captain , positioned on some obscure list that meant for a small pension he was recallable for life , it seemed . Our Captain took exception to receiving an official letter for the Mackerel one day , and stuffily reminded Ian that there was only one Captain here , Ian accepted the reproach , and gently pointed out that Ian's captaincy was warranted by the late King George .As engineers we were a little parochial , rarely mixing with non engineers . The Doctor was a regular drinking companion in the bar, despite him drinking little. He drifted into tourist because his nursing sister and the physiotherapist were not allowed in First Class off duty. Our grumpy second engineer and Doctor John didn't get on, and when Dr John compared medicine and the physiology of the human body with marine engineering, it was quickly pointed out that we rarely buried our mistakes.

he evenings normally meant a few pints in the Tourist class Cocktail Bar , Here the non uniformed personnel were allowed to imbibe , the pianist , the photographer , the dancers , the hairdressers and the junior officers unique to these ships , the Children's Hostess, the Pursurette and the others that didn't belong in the standard Merchant Navy structure . The Shopkeepers and telephonists, launderer and variety of other "trades" were all rated as PO's. What always, for many years, struck me as odd, was the level of homosexuality? The very attractive telephonists, not only shared duties and a cabin, but also were romantically attached to each other. From the four hundred ratings a fair estimate was that two thirds were what is now known as "Gay." The other third being Deck and Engine room hands.

The beer was in tanks in the holds, built into the hull, this was to stop the fiddle where six casks in a line were coupled and the sixth cask was water. Barmen had venturi's and water introduced into the nylon pipes somewhere because the flatness and lack of lustre , belied the additional volume , the low temperature disguised , and apologised for the weakness of the mix .There was a selection , a small one , of officers invited to be honoury members of the CPO's bar . This bar had its own tank , and five or six pints here could render you legless , despite double that having no effect on the passenger decks .This bar had the atmosphere of a small local pub and even in those far off days had "Quiz Nights " . PO's were barred from here, there being a blanket ban on ordinary ratings and PO's having spirits as a beverage, the "Pig and Whistle "being beer and soft drink only. The beer there had an even higher water content than that served to passengers. There was a compulsion to attend the "Crew Dance" held the night before Las Palmas , on the homeward leg , but after the Captain had danced with an attractive previously unseen young lady , and asked her where she worked , he was somewhat taken aback to realise that he had been attracted to a Transsexual second class waiter . After that Officer representation at the crew dance became less ordered.

A quiet drink in the Tourist or first class lido bars was the alternative to the loud music from the tourist cocktail bar. Women were the attraction, and my attraction sat in Southampton. Time came that told me leave this; go for the qualifications build a life.

Marriage dawned like a bright star, in an effort to save

something towards it I moved again to the Clan MacIndoe, and here I took my last African Voyage, A trip from Birkenhead, finished loading in Avonmouth then the South African Coast. The ship was a bit of a collection of Oddments. The second mate had his wife on board, and she was prima donna, notice me material. The electrician was the South African known as Old 97 , which he thought belied his love of trains , but came from an expression made one night ,that for any twenty five year old to have done what he claims , he must be an old 97 year old , and the name stuck . The Chief Engineer had a tremendous stammer, and it was a motley bunch in general. I was here for the trip, and to return home where Barbara was arranging our day. In Durban at the Indian Gold market, I selected her wedding ring a 9-carat gold bark ring with crosses through the bark finish. She still has that ring today though the bark wore away over the years exposing the crosses like an unbroken band of kisses .In Cape Town I visited an old acquaintance Alex the Chief Butcher at OK bazaar and collected some T-Bone steaks for freezing and my arrival home . I collected a case of Gran Mousec Vin Doux, for our wedding and sailed North. There was no threat of a Mediterranean experience. The white cliffs were a welcome sight as we rounded the South East Coast heading to Hull .In Hull I hired a one way Hertz Ford Cortina, and drove home, returning to Barbara.

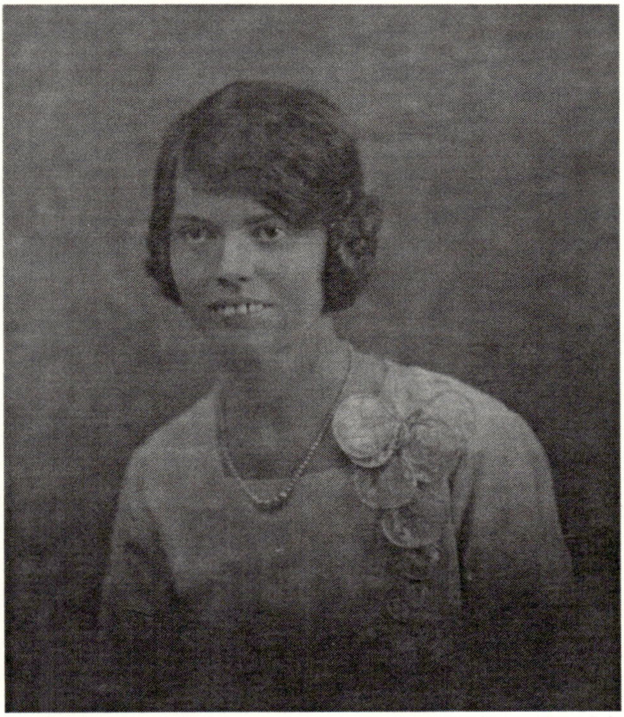

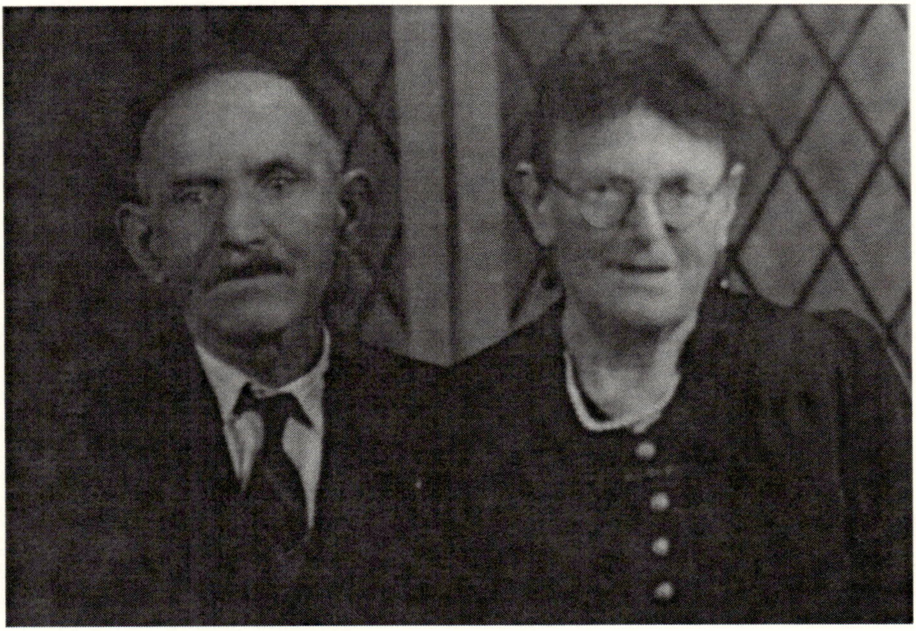

Chapter 17 the Rogers

The whole history of Barbara's side is a little distant from me, as we had the rest of our lives to put together the Genealogy of that part of our inheritance. We were deprived of that time, the time we had expected to be our dotage, when we enjoyed each other, interspaced with our family. Sadly our plans did not meet the eventuality and all was lost. Barbara was the youngest daughter of the five children of John Norman Cecil Rogers and Alice, nee Othen. She had one younger Brother Brian Roy Rogers, one elder brother, David, and Betty Nora and Margaret Alice as elder sisters. They lived at 93 Oxford Avenue for their childhood, although I believe they had moved there from Northam previously. David was evacuated; the others lived there throughout the war.

Barbara seemed to be a very quiet child, and her reputation was to shy away from aunties and visiting grandparents. She carried that shyness into her adulthood. It was always difficult to get Barbara to come forward and stand proud. She was principled though and given a just cause would fight it with all her might, popular or not she stuck firmly to truth .Always giving the impression that the shy little redhead hid in the corner of the room, and stayed away from the frontline, as Barbara quietly strolled through life she never enjoyed the spotlights, or the applause. All Barbara ever seemed to desire was the love that I and the children gave her , and her response to that love was boundless .When in her later years challenged to say something " I'm always Quiet " was the answer . It is true as sometimes we managed that interchange of ideas that hold thought transference. Knowing what the other one has in mind. I was once asked what love is, and my answer, I would have willingly had that cancer for her to see her spared. We discussed this one night as we cried our tears together, and got a severe rocket, she had this to bear and for whatever reason accepted it. Each birthday I place roses on her moss covered grave , and wish on the world that we will reunite one day , I still accept what has happened , but feel as cheated as the man who has had his world stolen , and is then mugged.

I loved that Ginger hair and was the only person who she willingly let call her Ginger, as she knew how much I loved it, anyone else referring to the Titian tones received sharp rebuke. We were growing closer together like conjoined twins, and when we were ripped apart by the cancer, we both lost, her life, and me mine. The future hopes dashed at a blow, by mutating cells that medicine could not control. We were to an extent blessed with private medical insurance that was paid for at some £600 a year for Barbara although mine was a benefit, taxed, as everything is. We travelled to BUPA in Barton's Road at Havant weekly for more x-rays and more of the debilitating chemicals. The Taxol on which we based so much hope as the results from the USA had been phenomenal was privately funded too, my Barbara had over £110,000 in treatment, none funded from the NHS. It shows that money cannot buy health or happiness, we looked at the famous victims, like Linda McCartney, and realised that you cannot but the antidote, or the cure, God's will was not for sale.

. Barbara's mum was a prolific caterer, and each day bought roast and curry, as well as cakes, and puddings, there was as Barbara remembered prolific amounts of food. I well remember the Bread Puddings that we returned home with, on many a Saturday. They were spicy as the cinnamon gave a pungency and flavour , there was a pride in the manufacture, always with old bread , so the body was firm and the fruit moistened , never with the modern bread that was mass produced by the on line process , that overburdens the recipe with yeast to save time. The modern brown bread being a stable mate of the white with colouring added, the raw ingredient was that old-fashioned staple. There on a Saturday too Fairy cakes and Rock cakes for the children to enjoy as each brood passed through the Oxford Avenue home. Barbara loved those family gatherings on a Saturday, when all her family passed through the home of their childhood, Saturday was earmarked as the day you visited Mum!

The house was a large terraced building, originally rented, the property owner, never committing to improvements. The front yard was small and the property bordered by a brick wall and an entrance gate. The black front door stood to the left, and as you entered, a long hallway led the length of the front section. There were two downstairs rooms in this part of the house, a front room that formed the living room, and a room with a rear aspect that would have formed the dining room. Behind this lay a huge kitchen, with what would have been a chimney at the far end, a door from here leading to a scullery area, and a single story bathroom, and the rear door. Beyond the bathroom was a solidly built coalbunker, which Jack had constructed as a concrete exercise to permanence .The hall had a long stairway on the joining wall, which led to a landing. There were two bedrooms at the front, one over the dining room at the rear and another pair over the Kitchen .making the whole house spacious. The three girls not only shared a room but also slept in a large bed competing regularly over the available space. . That I believe was a useful device, as on the rare occasions when they all got a smack, beating the bed cover, covered them all

   The principle illumination in Barbara's youth was gas, the yellow flickering light issued from wall brackets as they flared and hissed. The flimsy mantles glowing with a pulsing flame as they turned the old town coal gas into illumination. The landlord wouldn't pay for the conversion and Jack certainly wasn't going to either. This meant that there was an inordinate delay before the electric light came into Barbara's life. On one occasion when a teacher was asking questions , as teachers do , about how people's houses were lit , Barbara offered sufferance to her class mate if she uttered a word about gas , they all dutifully admitted to the incandescent glow of electricity . Barbara schools were in nearby Mount Pleasant Road, the secondary school geared to single sex education, and to secretarial subjects. When introduced to Friends Reunited one winters night as we entered the Millenium there was a description of one of the teachers , "Friends Reunited " having taken away this forum , probably due to giving vocal opportunity to the idiot minority to slanderise , we found a description , verified by various sources , of a heavily built teacher, in brogue shoes and tweeds that created a formidable force , she was well remembered by many of her class mates , which had more than a fair share of twins . The teachers asked stupid questions, they pried beyond their brief; another embarrassing one that Barbara managed to deflect was on the custom of recycling the "Daily Mirror "as toilet paper. In the days when the tabloids and red-bannered papers had a great secondary use, not aligned to the outer insulation of the fish and chips. The problem with the softer alternative to San Izal was it left its mark, in the layer of newsprint ink transferred to the user.

   The back garden had a huge plum tree as a central feature. The rear abutted the next street's rear gardens. It always seemed to me in those early days of our courtship , that this house sat permanently with the kettle boiling every Saturday , and the individual families bustled through , shopping in hand , eager to exchange the weeks news with each other . The shopping came largely from the St. Mary's Street market, as we bustled for bargains with the stallholders that had pitched the same places. From what was time immemorial? Barbara knew the Butcher and the Greengrocers from her youth .Barbara's mum had used the local shops , the local butcher and grocers having served out the rationed meat to the family for the last thirty years . These shops now losing their way to supermarkets and mini markets serving the eclectic tastes of the migrants filling the area as the families fleeing poor conditions in their homelands arrived they bought the shops , and the cheaper housing everywhere they could . The odour of West Indian spices and eastern exotic flavours permeating the atmosphere as the garlic fumes and the pungency of chillies blend and waft around the whole area. The local stores on Derby Road stocked all manner of Chapattis, pompadoms, homemade samosas with strong flavoured meat or, fiery vegetable. The rice came in twenty varieties instead of just long or short grain, an s the demand for carrots fell away, Moolie, and coriander replaced their more mundane British equivalents

Derby Road was also getting a poor reputation as the area not to live in, so Barbara's dad decided, as this huge house housed only the two of them, to downsize. Despite offers from the Asian family next door , he choose the council route , selling the house to the council for re-development as two flats , and being re-housed in a quiet corner of North East Close , of North East Road in the suburb of Sholing . Memory reminds me that they took a short holiday and Barbara's two elder sisters masterminded a move and reduction the smaller flat had demanded. The disappearance of the de-cluttered positions did not endear Jack to the move.

Nine North east close , was nearer to Betty and Margaret and a quiet area , the two , double story blocks , were purpose built as pensioners accommodation some years previously .

There was a small entrance hall, and a small kitchen leading from it. This did not have the palatial spaciousness of the previous kitchen, but housed fridge and cooker adequately. The lounge had picture windows and glass door to the front and was light and airy. The one bedroom was at the front next to the lounge and the Bathroom opposite the kitchen. The dominant dark oak dresser had gone from the lounge, and purchased as a period piece by an acquaintance of Brian's. It was at that address that Barbara's mum was to enjoy for the next twenty-five years. It was here that Jack thought it a great sport to mercilessly tease people , Barbara Ann falling foul many a day to his taunts , he fell foul though when provoking the small Kerry , I'll punch your eyes out was her response ,as she attempted to lift the chair leg and topple him from his seat . Jack seemed to respond to the defence mechanism of the toddler who wasn't going to be intimidated by his taunts were acts of silliness like giving a chid a spoon of jam from the jar , them condemning them for licking jam off his spoon .

The Saturday clan gatherings still carried on, just the venue was changed, and to some extent the order of visiting, as shopping had to be now separate .Dave and Greta, with their two girls arrived, later in the afternoons, we seemed to get there just after lunch. These Saturday family gatherings were so important to Barbara, as was tending to her mum. It kept the family up to speed on all the individual happenings of each household... I used to gather Jack up and head for the Robin Hood, public House off South East Road. The Landlord there was not only a steward of Newbury racecourse, but owned shares in several horses, this multiple horse owning gave him Saturday access to the stables and the trainer's staff, this to a professional gambler, with a hobby pub was the lifeline that helped him win in the battle against the bookmakers. I had began to notice a pattern in his tips , a regular would come in , "got a good tip mate " would be hailed , and they were given a good chance horse as a free gift . One Saturday Jack and I worked this out, the landlords bet was the "Gimcrack "tipsters choice or nap tip straight from the pages of "The Sun." I happened by total accident one Saturday hear him on the phone and he put four hundred pounds straight to win on three horses. He had identified the horses by time course and allocated number, after collecting Jack's beloved Marston's from the bar, I circled the three on Jack's newspaper. He phoned the Bookie he knew well at Northam Club and placed a series of five pence best known as a " Round Robin " three bets to win , three doubles and an accumulator , a total of thirty five pence . The bet romped home and returned Jack over thirty five pounds. It was from here with a small fund from the house sale in the bank that Barbara has organised his "Summer Bus Trips. " He charted a Bus and took the whole family to the Seaside , the first outing to Weston-super-Mare , resulted in a burst front tyre in Bristol , and a family effort to change it , as the Driver watched without a clue as to what to do next . The year after it was Brighton on the agenda .He would enlist some of his cronies from the Northam to accompany us and off we set picnic bag overflowing on Jacks Trip .This small degree of affluence gave them freedom to take holidays with ever-popular bus tours being high on the list. The ever certain Jack related how he had suspected throat cancer, which he self cured by Garlic Liquifruita sitting in the same seat, with a huge water jug by his side. He ended in the Countess Mountbatten Hospice at West End, and is buried in the Butts Road Cemetery, in Sholing. Jack's grave shows no markers, but when Alice died, it seemed appropriate to take the floral arrangement to place on his grave, we were clueless, but a trip to the superintendant's office soon led us to the correct plot. Here we laid the wreath on the earth.

Barbara's mum carried on with holidays , trips , flights to Scotland , coach tours , and took off with her sisters for summer excursions . She became a weekend visitor with us many times, and had a party trick of sleeping through all of Saturday evening and wakening around eleven to gain interest in a late night movie, so ensuring we all stayed awake beyond one AM. She became a regular visitor, and took on a Christmas roster, so she shared her time amongst us all. If I had to describe Barbara in a single sentence it would be "loves her family. " Barbara adored her family. children, parents, all of us. She endeared herself to her dad on afternoons when she bussed over to see them by taking a Rum and Blackcurrant, always stronger than she wanted, but one of those small things that remains imbedded in memory as a bright star in the firmament of imagination. There on the pelmets of North East close were some plastic ornaments, disliked by Alice, but a press of a button and the small plastic doors of the toy flew open to reveal a urinating boy who turned and watered the unsuspecting audience. A piece of seaside tat, which amused Jack, and all the grandchildren but drew, frosted glances from Alice. Those toys disappeared soon after Jack's internment, never to see the light of day again.

Barbara's dad died on Kerry's birthday in nineteen eighty five, after pancreatic cancer, and her Mum lived until her ninety seventh year dying on Alison's birthday in two thousand and two . She had been well until a fall caused a broken hip. She was taken into Southampton General Hospital, who took several days to arrange an operation, to correct the fracture. There seemed to be a general lack of care, and the wards were filthy. One patient in an adjacent bed , had been a suicide attempt , but after jumping from a window , had survived , with a broken spine , he had his food left by the side of his bed , as did an Alzheimer's patient .The nursing care was abysmal , and there was an overall air of neglect . The hospital foyer was resplendent, with the Burger King, and the Prêt á Mange, W H Smith, the clothes store and the solicitors office, this was a poor example of how to maximise the NHS Trust's income without consideration of the patient. We contacted Betty and Dennis in Thessaloniki, and they were soon on the plane heading home .This catastrophe was six weeks after I had had the spinal surgery. I was not passed to drive, but we needed to get Barbara to her Mum's bedside. We set out from home and at the first roundabout there was a rearward impact as a car ran into us, Barbara leapt out of her seat, and although the impact was slight and the damage non-existent, she lost no time in letting the offending driver know that I was fragile and, the woman should take more care. I felt Southampton General Hospital were not at their best with the care given. Barbara's mum was enjoying life and aiming towards a 100th Birthday telegram, she was always non-complaining and cheerful and to watch, what was tantamount to negligence was a sad episode.

One of Barbara's plans for her own retirement revolved around a once weekly bus trip to see her mum, and then she would take a second car trip later in the week. So many times have our plans been thwarted. Barbara used to point out that planning our future was a painful waste of time, hers, and mine. How I wish that predictability was not true, but when the 27-bus service was under threat, the Southsea to Southampton service, which Barbara joined in Commercial Road, we were amongst the writers of protest letters that forced a reconsideration of the services existence.

Barbara's dad had one Brother Norman, and two Sisters. They were Gertrude and Dorothy 1 lived in Totton, the other in Shaftsbury Avenue at Portswood. Norman was just off the Avenue, his wife was a Tartar of a woman, who by all reports was a harsh person, certainly on the occasions that we took Jack she was scarce of endearing ways. They had a son Alan who once lived near us in Lordshill and was the father of twins. When his father was ill Barbara had a strong overwhelming feeling that she must go to take Alan to see his poorly parent, so we set off to find him at the Hotel at Lyndhurst where he worked in the kitchens to get him to the Hospital. The sisters weren't high on Jack's list of favourite people, but we took him once to Totton to visit Dorothy Stride, she had a son Roger who lives in Marchwood. The atmosphere was slightly abrasive, and Jack gave a general feeling that his sisters weren't his best of friends. We have little information about his parents. They lived in the old streets of Northam, long gone, his father worked for a baker and his mother, we have no details of. She certainly knows she was disliked by Alice, as a mother in law; she had not been welcoming when as newlyweds they had lived there.

Barbara's mum was from Shirley at the Western fringes of Southampton .In 1901 the family lived at 46 Endle Street , just adjacent to the Chain Ferry from Southampton to Woolston. Shortly after this, the family moved to Pound Street in Shirley, It was here that Alice was born. She was part of a huge family. The eldest Brother, William Bertram Othen, a Stoker First Class, was lost when HMS Queen Mary was sunk in the First World War,

OTHEN, WILLIAM BERTRAM

Initials: W B

Nationality: United Kingdom

Rank: Stoker 1st Class

Regiment/Service: Royal Navy

Unit Text: H.M.S. "Queen Mary."

Age: 21

Date of Death: 31/05/1916

Service No: SS/112770

Additional information: Son of Mr. and Mrs. William Thomas Othen, of 86; Pound St., Shirley, Southampton.

Casualty Type: Commonwealth War Dead

Grave/Memorial Reference: 19.

Memorial: **PORTSMOUTH NAVAL MEMORIAL**

, who was sank in World War I at the battle of Jutland with

the loss of HMS Queen Mary. Dora kept the back door unlocked in case William was to miraculously return home. There was a Arthur , Edward & George and probably a William before William am Bertram , the renaming after an infant has died seemed a very common practice .I don't ever recall meeting any of the male line , and the sisters , The Sisters were Lillian Dora , Nellie Florence , Jennifer , Cissie , Alice , Emily , and last of all Doris . There were twelve children in all. The eldest surviving one Jennifer, bore three children, and lived at Totton. Her youngest daughter lived in the Tendering Rest Home at Totton, until a stroke in late 2008, meant her domicile at Sherfield English in a care home there. The other sisters alive in the later years were Emily and Dolly. Aunty Dolly was at Barbara's funeral despite having many heart problems over the year, and gave us a sudden realistic reminder off Barbara's dear mother. She is the last survivor and in 2008 lives in a pensioners block in Tremona Road in Southampton. Emily lived in Bitterne. /

Barbara's mum was born Alice Othen in 1905 in Shirley at the Pound Street house. Her parents' families are well documented and the family tree for the Othens and the Hatch families go back many years .Her mother's side goes back even further, Dora Hatch could have traced her family back several hundred years to their new forest roots.

Chapter 18 Barbara & I

Where do you start explaining what constituted the happiest days of my life, it is so easy to ignore what you have then realise the pain when you lose it. I know these chapters keep returning to those days, they are significant. Two years after her untimely death I wander the house hoping to smell her perfume, or to feel her warmth, what a sad old man! comes to mind , but the loss is something that there is no understanding of until it happens .

I had been going with Barb for some months and took to "working by," the staying working on Southampton Cape Mail Ships between voyages, instead of going home. This meant living in digs, the infamous Mr Channer, where the TV had a huge slot box, but whatever monies were in there it ran out at the six o'clock news, that is until some engineering expert (Not Me!) built a long thin blade that registered the ten pence additions, just by sliding it in the slot and bouncing it up and down. These "Digs" were always the recommended ones, if you happened to call in the office, Dave Redding would arrange them for you, a nice service. for which Mr Redding received a nice backhander! This kept me in Southampton between the six-week voyages. The mail run followed a pattern , the SA Oranje followed the Windsor , the Pendennis Castle followed her , the Good Hope behind , the SA Vaal then the Edinburgh Castle and the Southampton Castle every Friday at 10 o'clock another one left , and returned to leave again in seven weeks time .

Barbara decided that it was time I met mum and dad, and we set off on a Saturday morning to 97 Oxford Avenue greeted at the door by Margaret, Barbara's eldest sister. It is all right I have told dad you have a boyfriend! Was our greeting a warning, was I to meet an overprotective father, my mind was working out the impending threat as we entered. I did not need to carry a warning to my arrival, and was too old to have fear of any girlfriend's dad. We ushered in to the front room were face to face , all seemed friendly so far .There was an imposing dark oak dresser , and a table , her dad exchanged the usual pleasantries , and we sat around drinking tea . Those Saturdays tripping home were always important to Barbara it seemed to be almost a ritual reunification of her family as they all passed through the house in a few short hours every week .

I have already confessed my infatuation and love, so soon afterwards, I proposed. Barbara was living at 328 Hinkler Road in Thornhill, and one evening I suggested that we became a couple forever. I did say that if she didn't accept I would have to give in as the love I had for her was already tearing into me. I must stop giving ultimatums without choice, but to be part of Barbara's life, and now eternity was my only goal.

I arranged my transferred from the mail service to the Clan MacIndoe to help save some money towards our wedding, Junior Engineers wages not being huge at £88 per month. I rang Charlie Banks and explained my need to transfer back to the cargo fleet, packed away all the surplus uniforms required of a Mail Boat Officer, repacked my suitcases, and headed for the train. Barbara started organising our wedding. She arranged the Bugle Street Registry Office for a time after my due return date in the following February, booked St Christopher's Church Hall, for a reception, and paid the fifty pence to have the Banns posted at Belper Registry. So there I was bought and paid for!

The trip was to be a four month round cape voyage as far as Beira and straight back. This was Promised!!! by personnel at the two & four St Mary Axe, office block. This citadel of untruths, with the huge world map in the foyer showing the position of the hundred plus ships on a day-by-day basis m, as tiny models were moved across the map, affixed by magnets as far as one could tell. The office knew where we were by this huge artistic sculptured wall. I took Charlie Banks at his word, but secured a promise that if the Mediterranean became a turning point then I would fly home from Genoa. I took the sleeper from Euston to Liverpool, The only time I enjoyed the experience. When getting off at Lime Street Station , I couldn't find my ticket , the only time in my life this has happened , but , saved by the Guard from the train , who reminded the ticket collector that Sleeper Passengers had their tickets taken by the Sleeping Car attendant . It was time to search the docks for the two red bands of the funnel, and settle into my new home for the next three months. The taxi along the dock road led through the dock gates at Bootle to the waiting ship. This was my last voyage as a single man and the homecoming was to be magnificent. On my way to happiness, I repeated, as I knew what a great future laid before me.

The Clan MacIndoe was one of the pre "control room "ships with a five cylinder Doxford engine, and relatively modern cabins and bar facilities, although it was still a treck to the showers. The second mate had his wife on board and she was acting like a prima donna, this had already dropped the atmosphere to a low , before we unleashed ourselves from the dock to start what seemed along voyage .We left Liverpool, crossed the welsh coast and finished loading at Avonmouth. The trip was uneventful although we though, blessed with a South African electrician known throughout the company as old 97, because of his exploits would have taken ninety-seven years to complete

The coastal Chief Steward was the infamous Jimmy "mother" Harper, who was so camp he made Butlins look straight. He was though a good friend of Bernard Cayzer, the chairman's equally dubious brother. We were looking for extra beer and spirits one night and Jimmy had the Chief of Customs in his cabin entertaining him. James set off opened the bond adjusted the books, and resealed it. The costal catering was above the normal, Jimmy inspiring the catering crew. For one departing engineer whose daughter was due her ninth birthday James created a cake covered in pink marzipan roses, as though they were appearing from a woven garden trug. This was a masterpiece of confectionary for which Mother Harper was famous. As we left Avonmouth I looked back at England thinking of my return to be united with Barbara.

Las Palmas for Bunkers , then Cape Town ,Port Elizabeth , and Durban , where I bought the bark formed crossed ring , from the Indian Gold Market , I never saw another ring like that one that Barbara keeps even today . The return trip was by the Island of St Helena with a deck cargo of petrol in 50-gallon drums as they were out of fuel. this was our skippers last foreign port before his retirement , and we entered St Helena's harbour at Jamestown with stand by , full astern , finished with engines , and a phone call from the skipper , anchors firmly down ,, asking if we were complaining about the amount of movements again . We soon arrived back in Hull and a hire car at the ready I headed south towards the wedding that Barbara had arranged for us .The third of March approached

We were married at the Bugle Street Registry Office in Southampton on the Saturday morning. The whole Minibus load from Derbyshire due a couple of hours before our eleven o'clock allotted time was to schedule. Barbara had paid the required fifty pence to Belper Registry office, and reassured me that has she had paid, I was hers.

We had a buffet in St Christopher's church hall, which we had prepared with help from Barbara's old friend Jean, and we slipped away for a quiet couple of days in a hotel to enjoy ourselves. We had our first Chinese meal, and Barbara was less than impressed with the weak green China tea

I looked at the finances and decided time on tankers would be more lucrative so joined the UK shipping division of Gulf oil for just over £2300 per year, which was £800 than Clan Line paid.ter 19 the Gulf Oil experience

I didn't want to go, but knew no other job, so a tearful farewell as April arrived and I was off to London, where in those days check in for Heathrow was at Victoria, and you joined a coach for the terminal. I took a KLM flight on an old McDonald Douglas DC9 to Schipol Airport and Taxi to Sheepdam where the Gulf Finn lay under repair at the NDSM yard. What a leap from the devil you know to this. The main turbines were Brown Boveri, converted at the design stage from power station turbines, by, the addition of an astern nozzle and blades .The boilers were 750 psi Foster Wheeler's, and steam generators BTH. The food was atrocious. The first meal aboard was turkey soup as a main course, not the lavish meals of Clan Ships. Breakfast was still one egg though. The cabin and en suite shower were however huge and spacious, I sat at the desk and started my first daily letter to Barbara. We read those letters in recent years and decided the thoughts there were private and ours, so we shredded the evidence. The crew were mainly Scottish Islanders from Stornaway. The officers, the Chief engineer was piggy eyed Miller, whose round face stuck portrait like into the porthole overlooking the flying bridge. The second Engineer Ben was high as a kite on pot most days, and had a dumpy little American wife Betty, He was saving hard to return to his native Queensland

and buy a boat. I was on watch with Tommy Mowat from Paisley, and the rest I forget. Asked to fly out urgently, was somewhat surprised to find the ship locked into a Dutch dry dock strike .My howl of protest got me a return flight home for an unexpected weekend break. As Barbara did not have the telegram, it was a surprise for both of us.

Back to sea though and off to do the Bantry Bay to Emden run repeatedly, until on one trip a telegram diverted us in ballast to collect oil in Angola and deliver it to Port Arthur in Texas. This went quickly and we were soon backing in Angola, the evening entertainment was watching tracer shells interchange between the government forces and the rebels. I was taking to one of the Pontoon roustabouts, an American, and I deplored the fighting, he explained how the US Government backed the anti-communist rebels, and how the CIA backed the government. This was beyond my belief but the price of oil was such that gasoline was $0.50 a US gallon, and if the blend was mixed with African blood then so be it .I started to judge the morals of the industry, and didn't; like what I saw. It was many years later , breakfasting at the Ivy Farm House bed & Breakfast , at Swarkeston in South Derbyshire , in conversation with an ex patriot Rhodesian (Zimbabwean) that he explained ,having been there as a mercenary soldier , that the balance of power was actually oil and Diamonds . One of each side having to sell more of their commodity to buy more arms to kill more of the other side so they had to sell more of their commodity to buy more arms. How much blood is there in American gasoline? I had been convinced for , years , after a night in a bar in Walvis Bay_talking to the crew of the seismology ship , tied alongside us_that_the next great oil find was underneath the Falklands Islands . I was also convinced in 1982 that the unenthusiastic responses from the USA to come to our support to remove the Argentinean forces , who had invaded was due to the US desire to obtain the oil rights to the Falklands deposit . The biggest clue to me was that Dennis Thatcher the much-maligned husband of the Prime Minister, was chairman of Burma – Castrol, one of the largest European oil companies. He would have had the insider knowledge about those deposits. The technology of the steerable drill not being available made then un economical to extract at the time.

After several very boring runs at that, my sea time to enable my certification was totting up fast. I left the ship in September for three months leave and knew that one more trip would hold me enough time for my long desired Second Engineers certificate. The August weather was atrocious and we entangled ourselves with a hurricane. Bearing in mind that a loaded oil tanker is fully buoyant did nothing to ease the worry. So many latent Christians were asking the lords help as we tossed violently in the huge seas. The eight hundred foot by one hundred foot ship was jumping forty feet in the air and crashing down. The cook tied himself to the fiddle rails of the stove and offered anything that would stick to the stove's hot plate. Steak or chop and a lump of bread were the best option. Sad though we had in the ships stern accommodation no beer it being stored amidships in the centre castle we organised a ballot of six of us who wanted beer, and the unlucky looser was the Bosun. We tied a rope coil to him and as a lull came, he ran to the bus shelter on the flying bridge, another lull got him to the centre castle where he loaded twelve crates onto a two wheeled sack truck. We have no food here whined the skipper, Shame said the bosun, organise a run as we did. With a huge pull, he streamed along the flying bridge beer intact... The storm lasted five days and if you were not in the ballot, you got no beer. The Second engineer thought he would , get some of Tommy's and mine but was sorely disappointed and fell into a deep sulk .The skipper and Deck officers managed to find a case of corned beef and enjoyed that for the five days , before the waters subsided .

I flew from Port Arthur to New York, crossed New York,

and joined the newly formed BA flight home. The BOAC emblem was still on the tail of the ancient VC10, Heathrow, beckoned, and the shuttle bus bought Woking Station in sight, Soon Southampton and Home.

The second trip was started on New Year's Day 1974 and I flew again to Huston but this time we were bussed to Port Arthur, arriving at the hotel in the dead of night, with Gilbert Wood a third engineer from Edinburgh. The ship we were to, urgently, join arrived three days later.

This time we sailed to Portland in Maine with refined oil from Port Arthur. Then headed to Venezuela, we were to take the Armoy Bay run but turned to Angola again, and a stormy South Atlantic, after discharge this time we took to the Panama Canal. Through the canal we turned south to Esmeraldas in Ecuador, to load, an uninteresting port mainly loading banana boats, we arrived as the water festival held, to hail the first rains of spring. The welcome for strangers in this celebration was a free cold shower as you entered the bar for good luck after the landlord bought the first round the anger subsided over a free beer. We enjoyed that free bucket of cold pond water showering everyone else.

Gilbert was an ex Brown Brothers, steering gear apprentice and whilst showing a first tripper, in the steering flat, showed him that aligning holes in hydraulic gear can lose you an index finger. Gilbert was on his way home and I was not relishing the rest of the trip with the Solitary, teetotal, reformed alcoholic I suspect, Edward "Molly" Weir, but Woody's replacement arrived, Peter Skinley ex RFA, who was a bitter sad looser, that had become psychotic after finding his New Zealand wife sharing the marital bed with his friend s. He was a total utter creep in all sense of the word. No wonder his wife found him lacking. I was struggling on a difficult job one afternoon, after our normal watch and he waltzed off for his afternoon debrief with Ben and Mrs Hardy by the pool. I explained that he carried out his self-inspection any deeper he would perform the same trick as the fabulous Ozzelum bird. He threw a punch at me that resulted in a black eye , I didn't retaliate , because the dislike I had for the slime ball would have caused me to go too far , so I left it with ,if that's the best you have , then walk quickly ashore on pay off day . The R.O. had his wife aboard, as did the skipper. In the afternoon, they succeeded in getting the pool and that deck-designated for ladies only from 2.00 to 4.00. The hottest part of the day when everyone wanted to swim .The bosun complained about Betty sunbathing topless, and the captain failed to understand why a young lady baring all offended the bosun. The bosun retorted, cause she is fat ugly 'vet got at home, he emphasised, and obnoxious, and her appendages hang to her waist, just like the old trout at home. "That is why I ran away to sea Skipper "was his final reply. Then two sailors streaked the length of the decks, whilst an astonished pilot and the two ladies of the centre castle looked on. The captain gave way ordered Mrs. Hardy to cover up and took the restrictive hours off the pool. I got ashore in Hartington beach and landed at San Pedro on the Los Angeles Harbour front. We had a telephone at home now and I intended to use it. Barbara was distraught, my wages had failed to reach the bank, my bond bill had the decimal point in the wrong place, and there was no pay. Ever resourceful a tearful Barbara had a job at Fergusons Television factory and despite an error with the busses got home okay. I rang the office that spotted the mistake and corrected it. I rang Barbara back and to my surprise, she told of at least three telegrams sent. The Irish RO was always with a glass of Coke in his hand, I had not realised it was a disguise for his daily litre of Bacardi. I had had enough of this and asked the skipper for an immediate transfer off. The transfer coincided with my year in the company to qualify for study leave, and the full quota of watch time for the exams.

An overnight stay at a downtown Los Angeles Hotel and the three PM Jumbo Jet home awaited me as I climbed down the rope pilot ladder. Luggage lowered on a rope, into the waiting fast boat. . Flying fifteen hours over the pole , with a complement of staff and seven passengers in total , each moment was bringing me closer to my Barbara , and I resolved to get out of this being apart , I miss her so much , money was no substitute for being home . Hi, Barbie I am home rang throughout the house that Monday Morning. I signed on at the college and put in for one of the new build houses at Lords hill that we quickly got. There Barbara's plan to extend our family was unfolded and the new Baby, named Kerry Ann from the point of conception was announced within four weeks. Greta said she had known for weeks, which was somewhat a surprise, as we had only known a day. I was due to leave soon with the ink drying on my new certificate of competency. Remembering how lies and damn lies had happened the last trip , I rang Gulf and was asked if I would sail as Third Engineer to the same Mr Edward Weir that I had previously disliked as the company didn't want to upset him by demoting him mid voyage , all the excuse I wanted , stuff the job I'm off .

Chapter 20 the Sealink years

A pregnant wife and no wages was never a problem to a marine Engineer with a Second Engineers certificate. A trip to the Shipping Federation and I was employed by British Rail, Sealink Ferries, Weymouth, Second Engineer, Maid of Kent, Week on Week off, leave accumulated at normal rated home every night on the week on, and more money than Gulf. Start Monday. Reporting to the Personnel man Bill Newman acquiring a first class rail pass, then boarded the Clyde built SS Maid of Kent e Clyde built SS Maid of Kent. The triple expansion Parson engine, and the three generators pushing out 220 volts DC, was like a step back in time. This was a home from home to any Clan Line Steam Engineer .Harry Dean a Sunderland man known as Dixie was Chief Engineer , the rest a mixture of Weymouth and Southampton men , I was spending a week learning the ship . The engine room crew were all locals with the exception of Ken Rigney a coloured South African who was Southampton based. Barbara, I was home every night. The ship left Weymouth at 10:30 Daily for Cherbourg and returned before 7:00 p.m. so Captain Escudier could get home before Coronation Street started. That meant the 7:40 fast train home, and by 10:00 each night, I was indoors.

The 6:30 out of Southampton got me back to Weymouth a day later after my day off. At last, we were getting time together as a family. We bought an old Austin A60 Farina registration 66 MPH, and had a good summer. I transferred to the Normannia that was a night away as it travelled to Jersey stayed overnight and returned the next day. Every time we anchored we got four hours pay, and every shifting on the quay was two. Leave Weymouth, Arrive Guernsey, no entrance because the mail Boat was in Anchor, Discharge, out for the other mail boat, anchor, and back in. Into Jersey Shift Ship, clear the car ramp, and then shift back again. The AM to Guernsey had a similar ritual, and then, the days off came. For the three days, a week the top line was in 1983 over £700 per week. The Normannia was a tub and you could see light through the wooden upper deck planks that formed the cabin deck head. Barbara did a trip with me but the ever-growing presence of Kerry laid her low with a bout of seasickness .Barbara kept the ever-growing hump in her front oiled to keep her skin supple. November soon arrived, and so did the Baby. That was no easy birth, but Barbara wanted a fourth to complete her set and was annoyed when I did not. I couldn't watch that amount of pain in one go , willingly again .I stuck to the steamships , but suffered a pay drop in the winter standing by the Mail Boats , the Caesarea and Sarnia , keeping the generators ticking over and checking all was in running order . There was a drop back in winter to third engineer too as less crews were needed. The sea time soon in I was back at college within two years for Chief Engineer's Part A , then a year later for part B and my ticket , I transferred to the motor ships at this stage . There had been an uproar when the Weymouth old stagers who did not want car ferries at any price, found out what the wages were. The howl of the Dorset meanie rattled the chalk hills of Hardy's County , money was involved , no matter that, the locals didn't want the car ferry , they wanted a fair share of the money . We became consolidated salary wise and some of the old hands left their mail boat homes, kicking and screaming into the much harder work of the diesel ferries .I had succeeded in stopping smoking but after the first hour of the Earl Godwin the Ex Svea Drott I sent the steward for 200 urgently. The Engines were Deutz, two six and two V- twelve engines. The injection fuel pipes crossed the exhaust manifold and they were prone for the odd fire amongst a raft of other problems. The Swede's at the end of its life had sold the bloody thing and it was dropping to bits. We spearheaded a new route though, out of Portsmouth, soon to be joined by my new home the Earl William, an ex Viking ship from Thorosens. This was a much better cared for ship than the Godwin, and entered the Portsmouth service well. The travelling time was reduced, and the crewing one on two off, with full leave. My motor Endorsement issued so my combined certificate came through the post .Home and dry. There was applications requested for establishment jobs and I became an established Second Engineer.

Barbara and the three children now enjoyed first class rail passes, and one first class continental annual pass .So we took off to Spain a small resort just beyond Sitges. We travelled across on the Maid of Kent, caught the Cherbourg to Paris Gare de Nord train. We tried to get a taxi at the Gare but faced a problem, Only four persons to a taxi and we were five ,despite the five year old being quite small .A twenty franc note fixed all that and we boarded the Spain bound train , which was crowded and huge . A word with the guard produced us a Couchette cabin. There was though no buffet and Barbara left guarding the door at the next long stop whilst I raced to the station Buffet. Fed and watered we slept through the night, and the border changing trains at Narbonne to the Spanish RENFE, this took us to Barcelona, where a further change took us on to the apartment. We had fourteen nights there Wednesday to Wednesday. With the travelling, this became a sixteen-night stay. The stories here belong to my children really, and I was laid up for three days with severe tonsillitis. Kerry though developed a fear of old ladies with keys when a nice old lady lead her away to give her a cake , but the freezers and that huge bunch of Keys panicked Kerry , who seemed to get the idea that we had sold her to this old lady . So after 1981 we never returned to Spain.

The Austin replaced with Uncle Sam's Riley 1.5 replaced with the Hillman Avenger GT. We moved to a new home in Waterlooville. The prefabricated Lordshill house was going to become difficult to mortgage so we got rid at our earliest chance. We put it on the market around Alison's birthday in 1982, and sold it to a young couple that November. There were many reasons to move but the main one was the predicted un-mortgageable aspects of the REEMA pre-fabricated house. If we hadn't sold when we did the obscure fact that there was future resale problems in raising a mortgage would have dried up our potential market. We had about six months grace before the REEMA mortgages dried up, so the move was by the skin of our teeth. Our house search intensified and we lost 44 Sutherland Road to a new home at 28 Chaplains Avenue, in Cowplain.

We moved in January 1983, and saw the furniture van depart, as we arrived, car stuffed with kids and Dog, We saw no sign on route and were there before them. Panic set in but they had stopped on the way for lunch, so the panic was soon over. We now had to collect Kerry, farmed out for the day. The other two had themselves included as volunteers helpers, but that did not work quite to plan. We had still stuff to collect, and there was no room in the car for Barbara's black collie / sheepdog cross, Sam. We left him secured in the garden, but his constant howling had the police on the doorstep after our return with all children in tow. The Tuesday bought the cheque for the surplus on the house sale so we bought a Video Recorder, the height of fashion in those distant days and with it a new television, and a dishwasher. That video recorder remained a firm favourite of Barbara's because of its basic functions and ease of use.

We bought a Trailer Tent .We fitted the Avenger GT, with a hook and electrics and headed to Ashford in the water in Derbyshire. Alison having moved in with Dave Hinton by this time we set off as a family of four .Seven days at Ashford gave the proofing a failure , it had soaked us, but the next week on the Cliff-tops of Hastings at the Haven Camp soon bought a drying wind.

Sealink taken over the following year and now we were running five crews on the Earl Granville and the new owners Sea Containers had decided on a luxury service at a premium that was the craziest idea yet, the bookings and profitability were down. We took maximum advantage of the help us bed the service in, free offers, and both Dad and Barbara took regular trips that year when my parents were visiting.

The inevitable came and I took the redundancy package, changed cars to an Opel that we wrote off in a crash. That rouge car replaced with the first Audi a 100 model with a "W" registration plate denoting 1980. We fitted this with a towing hook, and bought our first caravan Ace Airstream .We joined the camping club so in 1986 with two children now flown the nest we set off weekends to caravan.

As the redundancy set in the bank, we bought a Peugeot diesel van and hawking and market stalls became a daily grind selling fish. We never could make enough so I returned to engineering and Barbara resumed work.

Chapter 21 the Dairy

The Portsmouth Co-op Dairy was looking for an engineer the job was with two Agencies; both said I would not be suitable, so I wrote direct. As there was no engineering function, on site, the invitation to go to Manchester to the CWS Engineers office adjacent to Lancashire Dairies and the Prison arrived. Interviewed by Frank Rammel whom, thinking this was wasting his time started to showing a drawing of an Alfa Laval self-cleaning separator that was new to the Co-op movement, their first installed shortly at Portsmouth, a gift to any marine engineer. It was new to Frank too. Gift, what a Gift, I had been working on these for twenty years purifying oil. Frank was struggling with h the sliding bowl operation as he began his explanation. I asked for the drawing and took him through it in detail. His attitude changed and he offered coffee. I had my guide and mentor in the Audi , dad was parked facing the walls of Strangeway's Jail .The interview over , dad home , Barbara and by that stage solitary child in the car , we drove South .

Job started with the useless two weeks amongst the snow in Blaydon. I left Barbara a Farmhouse cookbook as recognition that I had been doing most of the catering and caught the Newcastle train from Kings Cross. I was ensconced in a scruffy Indian owned hotel in Jesmond, and whiled away the days with Dave Lackenby, and his assistant, amongst the fitters, there Kevin Scott became the engineer after Dave transferred to distribution, and John Smith there in those days is Chief Engineer as I write this. I took the opportunity to see how Kath Lavrick was fairing , and despite it being twenty years before that I was in there in Digs she looked no different , Sandra didn't either and she now had two very lively boys . She is married the man who was her driving instructor , After a career in Nursing Sandra and her now long term best friend Susan had done paediatric Oncology , which I think must be one of the hardest tasks in Nursing's whole spectrum .

Back in Portsmouth new job started, Barbara began working at Hampshire Aerosols, but on seeing the archaic and dangerous practices moved to Wessex Advanced Switching Products, as WASP it is better known. It was around this time she acquired an abscess on her bottom and spent three days in a private room at the Queen Alexandra Hospital, having it drained. I do not think Barbara ever understood my hatred and Phobia of Hospitals, but the broken leg all those years before, as a twelve year old in an adult ward .left me scarred.

Whilst she was here I changed the Caravan for an ACE Globetrotter, that had the fridge and toilet so needed in the Airstream, it had a full awning, and off we trotted, Weekends and summer holidays,

We headed to Torquay in the first year with Solent DA of the caravanning and Camping Club and stayed the first week with them, .We camped the second week at a place between Honiton and the Chiddeok hill, a farm with a pool. This was with Coventry DA and we were next to a Coventry Family , whose Youngest was Ruby ,because when she was delivered

, there was so much blood on the floor , they just had to call her Ruby

We had great fun with the van and engineered long weekends, our lone child left at home used to vanish on arrival, and return to for feeding times , and just before departure. She camped with the youth section, in her own tent.

We went to the 1990 Caravan Show; this had become an annual event with Barbara's brother Brian and his wife Barbara. The Audi was a later model 100 on an "A" plate this was a 100 CD- A 451 TVW a 1984 car. We drove and parked opposite Earls Court on the rough car park, which lay expensively awaiting Earls Courts visitors .We all went our separate ways and I took Barbara to the Adria Stand where we purchased a new van. That van was with us for several years until sitting on the New Milton Cliffs in our usual September Holiday we looked and said sunshine next year. Therefore, in 1993 began the Grecian Holidays. The van energetically used for Bashley weekends. We now towed with a white Audi 90 H921BOT that was a wonderfully powerful small car .The caravan used less and less and in nineteen, ninety-five we sold it on using the money for another Grecian Holiday the tow bar made redundant.

The job took up far more time than it deserved and the home time was increasingly lost. After one particularly long run of 56 days without a day off Clive suggested a paid for weekend away. We chose the Albrighton Hotel near Shrewsbury, I ordered flowers in the room, and the four-poster was part of the deluxe experience. Barbara refused to move from the meltingly warm Jacuzzi , and fell into huge fresh fluffy towels each time she emerged. We had a fantastic weekend and to help, transported Andrew in each direction so he could caravan in North Wales with Barbara and Brian's friends. The false starts returning Andrew for forgotten items put us in the Newbury traffic queue, and we lost an hour in traffic, but to be together was great. The return meant further delays as we had to collect Andrew's trophies from his friends to transport home

The Dairy now after twenty years renewing it has ended for me, and my future is an open book.

Chapter 22 Greece

1992 Laganas Borcelino
This was our first experience as a couple , and my first experience with night flight and charter airlines and Gatwick , Joanne's dad Rod drove us to the airport We deliberately arrived early and ate at the airport . As check in opened joining a throng as we found our way to the Air 2000 plane, with its very restricted legroom. We landed at Zakynthos airport as the first plane at Six o'clock and scrambled aboard the bus that dropped us and other new arrivals off hotel-by-hotel. The room was basic and steamy hot, so we thought to catch up with our sleep. The patio door flung open, as we tried to settle. The Cicadas' were in full chorus, but tolerable, then the Cockerel woke the dog who barked and woke a peacock, I thought we transported to a zoo. Sleep impossible we walked into town and found breakfast at the Pythari Pool bar, the reps meeting was across the road, and we listened intently as they told of the available tours. The Rep also told us if we pay by credit card, it takes months to go out of your account. I have found in Greece if money is, involved transactions are instantaneous.

We chose a single trip Kampi sunset and resolved to source our own round Island bus tour and boat tour. The Rep suggested that her tour was the only one not in a converted Caravi as the big blue fishing boats were called. Her bus tour was also the only one with a licensed bus. The lies got bigger, and as they did, reliance on reps got smaller. I then knew how their meagre salaries became a liveable income only by selling tours hard .Barbara was about five days into the holiday and fell on the bed wanting to go home, she just missed her children. We got over that but it made me realise just how important her brood was to her. We walked the town and, Bisto Gravy served with Chips here! Was this amongst the signs that encouraged us to use the Pythari restaurant It was here we met Dennis Fournougerakis who was supplementing starting his sign-writer's business with a summer waiting tables , for Nikos and Christos the Pythari's owners . We in those days took a daily paper delivered at three o'clock in the afternoon on the day after publication. We bought our paper and the rest of our needs from Dennis and Margarita at the paper shop and general dealers ,"Victoria Stores " on the road into Laganas, Your go the son-in-law and their daughter (Your go's sister-in-law) Katarina ran the shop with them. Yougos was an actor in his home town of Athens.

1993 Laganas "Apartment Tony's"

This was opposite the Pythari and again a night flight, as we walked in the flooded toilet with the seat on the floor should have been a warning, but after a long flight, we flopped on the bed. Not for long, the bites started almost as soon as we lay there. Barbara stripped the bed and it was lousy with Bed Bugs. A trip to the store was on the cards at nine o'clock and we scrubbed the apartment and be loused the bed. We had snoozed on the plastic chairs on the balcony. The lady next door was an Irish lady who had sat in the outer of the three seats on the plane. She insisted during the flight that she enjoyed flying and was alone as her husband was so scared of flying he would forgo a holiday rather than fly anywhere. As the plane approached the island, she ran her rosary beads frantically through her fingers and crossed herself fervently. She did not mind flying. Though certainly sure scarred of landings .The next night the young Anglo Spanish girls on an end of exam spree arrived into the apartment at the rear of us and started a loud party at three thirty in the morning. A second night of this and no rep visible we ran our hire car, hired from Fox autos, the friendly but unreliable Andreas, to the agency in Argassi. No one else has complained was the attitude. Your rep has not called I suggested, so the manager called the rep. No, there was no one waiting to see her so she cycled past her allotted four - five PM slot on her way to nobody knows, but far more important than doing her job. That evening she had the desired queue and issued warning notices to the Rodriguez sisters that one more complaint would result in cancellation of their air ticket. At last, the rep was awake, and Cosmos Tours delisted from our book of tour operators. We walked and dined at the ever-decreasing authentic Greek Tavernas. We decided to upgrade our holiday to apartments with warm water on tap and not reliant on solar heating

   1994 Laganas Pythari - 1995 Laganas Pythari

   Well we ate there and drank there so we might as well book with Air tours and stay there, still the night flights out of Gatwick. Katarina Kosti invited us on the First year here to the uncle's wedding, as every tourist should see a Greek wedding. It was however, in Athens and a seven-hour drive across the Peloponnese began. We were to stop at her apartment that we were to treat as our own. Barbara newly christened Varvara or Vara the Greek version of Barbara. We toured the sights of Athens, the Parthenon .Likkabettis, watched the changing of the guard, and took a day trip to Poseidon's temple at Sounio. The wedding was at St Barbara's Church. We took a Taxi there and were unfamiliar with the Greek Taxi sharing system, as we were in the two occupiers looked in their leather coats, like low life hoodlums, and I sensed Barbara's apprehension. Never have I been so glad to get out of a taxi in my life .We found the church. This had the appearance of a Nissan hut with a tree growing through the roof. The inside though was in total contrast, and the shabby exterior hid a fabulous internal decoration to rival the finest churches. Barbara pulled to the front so she could see better, and soon realised that the rice pelted at the bride, groom, priest, and the front rows. The five sugared almonds so delicately wrapped is also symbolic , the five signifies the odd number cannot be easily divided as a husband and wife's possessions cannot be easily divided , the almonds for longevity and the sugar coating for sweetness in marriage . The reception was at the groom's house but by 5 AM, we were a loss, and returned to Katie's apartment. Around nine AM we woke and after a discussion with Margareta decided that, as Sunday was a busy day on the single bus back to the island, we should quickly find the Ktel bus station and book in. A long hot trip back , on the Killini to Zakynthos ferry Barbara watched as an armed immigration gave a handcuffed captive prisoner very harsh treatment , and, was ever Barbara like annoyed when I refused to chastise the policeman .

The year after again the Pythari , although we no longer ate there , not just because the food was no longer served by Dennis , but because it was unpalatable ,cooked by the Brothers Nikko and Christo , not the greatest Greek chefs . We started to dislike Laganas because of the element of tourism that if had now attracted. We were ending our love affair with Zante, but decided on Alikanas, next year as a last fling.

1996 Alikanas Zakynthos

- The last time to Zakynthos , our night flying also over after Barbara having a once only panic attack on the way home , having been dehydrated in the Airport queue , the one AM pick up , on the bus ,waiting in the steaming evening heat outside the old air terminal , had , all taken their toll , the airplane was stuffy and unbearable too . We were now daytime flyers .The apartment was OK but the carnival atmosphere of Laganas had reached here too, we were not good party animals, so, decided to kiss a last goodbye to Zakynthos, its beautiful verdant land, and the great people we met. We called at the Victoria stores one last time and found Margarita had been to London for oncology. Sakis bought us five litres of his mother's delicious fresh olive oil. We had grown away from the party time as time together became precious .The plane was late yet again and we queued in the blazing sunshine outside the airport. This was the last Zakynthos for us.

1999 Argostoli Kefalonia 1998 Argostoli Kefalonia 1997 Argostoli Kefalonia
- We were to pastures new, and Kosmar flew us into the airport in daylight to a nice apartment on a hill slope with a small pool .We hired a car and toured the island. On the second visit, we took a trip to Ithaca, the magical island of Odysseus. That peace there was unbelievable, and we had fun watching the yacht charterers make docking an impossible task. There was a party of Scousers who created about green mould in their Tyropita , Parsley was obvious but with great fuss they stormed off refusing to pay the bill for all the food and drinks they had eaten .The food was more " Greek " to in Kefalonia , like Zakynthos in the early days . We ate in town after a walk or at the nearby Jimmy's tavern, named after the owner's son who had died in a motorbike accident some time before. The early evening watering hole was the Thallasomilo, where the water wheel rotated in the bar as the sea ran past turning it. The bar was machined from the roots of Olive trees, and had a character all of its own. We knew that interest in the coming film Captain Corelli is Mandolin, would make this a busy island next year, so we after three years changed to Greek options and Stoupa in the Mani.

2000 Stoupa   2001 Stoupa   2002 Stoupa 2003 Stoupa

The Mani was to be a new experience for us, the place was certainly more off the beaten track than anywhere else we had visited, and the first year we took the Monemvassia trip to that fantastic little isthmus of preserved Byzantine paradise, and decided that one day we would return there and take a second honeymoon. The second year we started our explorations of Mystras and visited the Pirgos Diros caves in the south of the Mani; we hired our car from the airport and drove ourselves to Stoupa as we have done each holiday since. The apartments were the same ones each year and we travelled with Greek options, we started to fall into habits of either Mystras or Monemvassia, always a day to Gythion and Aeropolis, and Always local sausage and chips at the Lemon tree tavern at St Nicolas, the Loukanika has orange zest threaded into the meat imparting a wonderful tangy flavour. The "Butchers" restaurant and his delicious roast pork on the Stoupa seafront was a regular feature too. The lady who cleaned the apartments presented us with Tsipero as a gift one year, her home made fiery spirit from the same formula as Createn Raki .Stoupa became an idyll to us, and it typified the Greek things we both loved so much.

2004 No Holiday the planned and booked trip to Agio Nicolas in Kefalonia cancelled

2005 Lassi in Kefalonia

The 2004 holiday, cancelled and the earmarked money, used to pay for the second, mastectomy that our insurers would not pay for, as it was cosmetic and not medical. The ongoing treatments also meant that Barbara would not be well enough to travel, so we planned a couple of weekends and prayed that this was the last time we would cancel. In 2005 Barbara fell and we set off with her arm in plaster despite the awkwardness she was determined that the holiday go ahead. It went to a bad start that is a blot on my landscape, Simon had already angered me, when I was at the hospital with Barbara by pushing that a management meeting was more important than being at Barbara's side whilst she had her arm reset. The eve of the Holiday, when I was to go home and pack to await the taxi in the early hours he insisted on paperwork being finished that meant I did not leave until past eight o'clock. the holiday was good, and Barbara bought a gold bracelet at Veronicas Jewellery store ,, Veronicas had a goldsmith exclusive to them and could do designed pieces, so I set at out working on a "B " with a Bar in it, or a "B" in a bar form so it was exclusive as my Bar B . I never finished the design, and she never got the exclusive piece.

2006. No holiday, long weekends at Melborne and Preston

2007 Dimitsana, Zakynthos, Galaxidi, Corinth

Momemvassia Gythion Kardamili
   2008 Zakynthos for Greek Easter
   2008, Methoni, Dimitsana Naplion Corinth   Gythion Kardimili
   2009 Azores
   2009 Patmos & Samos & Ephasus

Chapter 22 the New Millenium

The New Millenium started badly , we were scalded on our first footing , surprisingly two doors away our return being an hour past midnight , we had asked dad to come with us , but he had selected to go to bed , which he changed to awaiting our return , in our absence , so thought he had been abandoned . He was still complaining of the Heartburn and stabbing pains that had bedevilled for his of widowhood. I had a premonition that these pains were more than he was revealing, but rested assured in the thought that the doctor had him in sight. He told us he was expecting us in February. We had a week off booked and my intention was to spend it with Barbara. We took him back to the station the following week and he was sure we would be on our way to Derbyshire on my early February holiday I was not! We intended to spend time together as a precious together break and I intended to stick to it. It was to be a post Millenium catch up for us. .That weekend that started our break in early February , we called Dad on the Sunday and all seemed well , until Uncle Frank indicated that he had the Paramedics with Dad and there was little hope .Dad had his Sunday lunch and slumped in his chair and died the afternoon ,a quiet week at home was beckoning us. We drove North on the Sunday and were phoned as we drove towards Sutton Scotney by uncle Frank with the news , and the suggestion that we return home .I pulled over and was sick , guilt at not going must have beaten me . We carried on North though as he had requested as he thought that we needed to take inventory , feeling his nearby in laws may take stock before we stock-took . We nailed the locations down. We did locate all we needed and on the Monday made all the arrangements with the undertaker. My mother had harsh memories of a neighbour losing the necessities of life so she had dictated many years before that we would leave the essentials for Uncle Frank. Little did we know that those weekends would be our last chance to see those little touches , like the button tin so prized as a junk tin as a child , the cast iron plates that dad valued , all lost to us .

We arranged a funeral, with his old friend at Archway Funeral services, who he had arranged Mum's funeral with. with the exception of the pink linings, which we changed to blue, we instructed Terry Daniels to follow the exact pattern of the previous ceremony. We avoided the 16th as being Mums Birthday, and chose the 17th that had been Uncle Ceph's Birthday. The snow fell as we turned into the back lane to Markeaton, and we weaved through the virgin snow to the Crematorium. The chapel had been filled to capacity and Nether Heage Chapel and the Ambergate British Legion Benefitted from the donations.

I then later in the year started feeling more than a little uncomfortable walking, and after some badgering from Barbara went and arranged a knee operation in early 2002 and in an effort to bring Mr Magnus McLaren into the 21st Century arranged a Buy one get one free and had a carpel tunnel carried out at the same time. Some weeks later the limp had not disappeared. After being asked for a rebate due to lack of progress, despite removing a small knee abscess "That is spine or Brain," Mr McLaren declared and I spent a weekend in shock. The dislocated spine operation performed at a cost of twelve thousand pounds to the insurer and titanium plates and screws secured three vertebras together, we engaged Mr Nicolas Brooke and had the operation in the Chalybeate Hospital opposite the general Hospital in Southampton. Barbara was at my side as I came round from the six-hour operation, which delayed because a nurse put an unsterilized cloth on the specialist instruments required. I awoke in recovery in the next bed to Lord Montague of Beaulieu, who had had a night in intensive care due to a heart problem. Barbara's mum was not impressed; she did not particularly like his lordship and mumbled under her breath... The accident was a result of a car crash earlier that a poor choice of solicitor had given me £800 in compensation for what seemed to be pretend Whiplash, The junior Solicitor appointed by the Basingstoke partnership not helpful to me at all. Amery Parkes though, felt they had done a great job and the matter stopped there.

As my recovery took, hold the love and devotion of my Barbara who was working now for City Technology, as a popular member of their team showed through, the worry and care she showed was the best. Soon all will be Okay she said and rubbed my hair with that special way that she solved all our problems. When she soothed you knew the world would be right.

As my illness subsided, we looked at car replacement and despite not being in a position to drive looked at a red Audi A4 in Slough. It does not have cup holders I cried, but there are leather seats Barbara commented. In the year, they say it is it should have Cup Holders and it has none. I asked for the paperwork and found this to be an import and three years older that its "T" plate indicated , but it was most probably clocked on the mileage , it was average for a 1999 car but not for a 1996 one. We drove through Drayton on the way home and saw our new Red Audi A4 put on the forecourt at the old BP Garage and bought it there and then. T 457 XNP was home in our garage waiting for the weeks before I could drive to begin.

Barbara's dear mum fell and Broke her hip which necessitated me driving against better judgement and Barbara's pleas to be careful to the general Hospital We spent a few days there finally losing Barbara's Mum on Alison's Birthday.

Then as 2003 arrived Barbara suggested we book an early bank holiday weekend at Sandown in the Isle of Wight, the Balmoral was to be out get away weekend for the rest Barbara thought I needed, and booked it before the lump she had self discovered revealed that it was potentially more threatening. It was the weekend before her Mastectomy, and we spent the weekend in a state of shock. With my silly wife apologising for ruining my weekend.

I stop my introduction there as the detailed medical records are still with me and stored for anyone to see and I still feel distraught, our future when I made good all the lost days was gone.

Chapter 24 the Genealogy

There is not space in a small volume to do the whole "who begat who" business. Much of the research now will require visits to the sources of the information. The internet resource "Ancestry.com "has been a major source contributor to this document and its membership infinitely useful without it much time would have had been spend trawling through dusty records . To prove the Blantons links much more research is required. In eighteen sixty-one George Blanton born in Newport Shropshire (1814), His wife Jane from Pattingham in Staffordshire were living with their six-year-old son George at "The Wheel Inn" 36 Blilbrook Lane in Codshall. Ten years before that George, an Agricultural labourer, from Albrighton was living nearby, was he the same George that was at Orgrieve in at Alrewas in Shropshire. These are the problems to solve along the way. Much guesswork fails the fact test, and much lays un-proven .The Wheel inn has disappeared but the site is five doors from a Tesco express. To trawl county records will require much time and travel. The records will not disappear so the search can wait .There seems to be some basic building blocks time needs to be spent on verifying the family tree created so far. The aim is to put the whole tree and its background in similar form to this in the future it is a strong desire to know who we are. What powers this dream of genealogy, the relentless need to find answers to the gaps in the tree there is no way of telling . The dream of knowing what is our make –up still drives forward. Never realising the scale of our descent the calculation on numbers doubles each step in the ladder. Two parents give four grandparents, eight great grandparents, but that leads quickly to tell me that the tenth generation shows one thousand and twenty four, and the fifteenth generation thirty two thousand four hundred grandparents. That generation relates me to the year fifteen hundred, and the four million populations was miniscule in comparison to todays. In relative terms my tree base at that time would have been over half the population of London .To relate back to the times of the conqueror I need a billion grandparents to reach the thirtieth generation

Parents	Year	Generation	Parents	Year	Generation	Parents	Year	Generation
2	1950	1	2,048	1650	11	2,097,152	1350	21
4	1920	2	4,096	1620	12	4,194,304	1320	22
8	1890	3	8,192	1590	13	8,388,608	1290	23
16	1860	4	16,384	1560	14	16,777,216	1260	24
32	1830	5	32,768	1530	15	33,554,432	1230	25
64	1800	6	65,536	1500	16	67,108,864	1200	26
128	1770	7	131,072	1470	17	134,217,728	1170	27
256	1740	8	262,144	1440	18	268,435,456	1140	28
512	1710	9	524,288	1410	19	536,870,912	1110	29
1,024	1680	10	1,048,576	1380	20	1,073,741,824	1080	30

How we manage to account related to the entire known world's population is breathtaking, and I offer no explanation. Those who take this Genealogy study on a more serious level than I do these statistics must be mind blowing. If I manage to get past the sixty five thousand Grandparents of Fifteen Hundred AD, I will be looking toward one in a million within a hundred years.

Chapter 25 the future

Is yours!

Printed in the United Kingdom by
Lightning Source UK Ltd., Milton Keynes
138855UK00001B/216/P